MEDIEVALIA ET HUMANISTICA

S. Harrison Thomson

MEDIEVALIA ET HUMANISTICA

STUDIES IN MEDIEVAL & RENAISSANCE CULTURE

Founded in 1943 by S. Harrison Thomson

NEW SERIES
NUMBER 1

IN HONOR OF
S. HARRISON THOMSON

Edited by Paul Maurice Clogan
CASE WESTERN RESERVE UNIVERSITY

The Press of
Case Western Reserve University
Cleveland & London
1970

Editorial Note

Founded in 1943 by S. Harrison Thomson and now under new editorship and management, *Medievalia et Humanistica* will continue to publish, in a series of annual volumes, significant scholarship, criticism, and reviews in all areas of medieval and Renaissance culture: literature, art, archaeology, history, law, music, philosophy, science, and social and economic institutions. *Medievalia et Humanistica* will encourage the individual scholar to examine the relationship of his discipline to other disciplines and to relate his study in a theoretical or practical way to its cultural and historical context. Review articles will examine significant recent publications, and contributing editors will report on the progress of medieval and Renaissance studies in the United States and Canada.

Medievalia et Humanistica is not the organ of any association, center, or institution, and publication in the series is open to contributions from all sources. The editorial board welcomes interdisciplinary, historical and critical studies by senior or junior scholars. Texts, maps, illustrations, and diagrams will be published when they are essential to the documentation of the article.

Books for review and manuscripts (which should be prepared in conformity with *The MLA Style Sheet* and accompanied by a stamped, self-addressed envelope) should be addressed to the Editor, *Medievalia et Humanistica*, P.O. Box 2567, Cleveland, Ohio 44112. Inquiries regarding single or standing orders and fasciculi 1–17 should be addressed to The Press of Case Western Reserve University, Frank Adgate Quail Building, Cleveland, Ohio 44106.

Preface

MEDIEVALIA ET HUMANISTICA publishes the first volume in the new series in honor of its founder and former editor, S. Harrison Thomson. During his judicious editorship, from 1943 to 1968, *Medievalia et Humanistica* achieved national and international recognition and distinction as the first American scholarly publication devoted exclusively to the study of the Middle Ages and Renaissance, with special attention to Latin civilization from A.D. 300 to 1600.

Unlike those of a *festschrift*, all the articles in this honorary volume were written by specialists who in one way or another share Professor Thomson's wide scholarly interests in the intellectual and cultural traditions of the Middle Ages and Renaissance. Each article makes a new, original, and significant contribution to knowledge or understanding of a text or subject of particular interest to the former editor. The texts and subjects examined range in time from the date of Bede's death to the German Peasants' War of 1525 and include the fields of art, archaeology, history, law, literature, music, philosophy, and social and economic institutions. In this way, the volume finds unity and coherence and at the same time mirrors and reflects the intellectual world of S. Harrison Thomson. A recent bibliography of his more than 400 publications is available in Lubomyr R. Wynar's *S. Harrison Thomson: Bio-Bibliography*.

In compiling and editing the articles in this first volume, the editor is most grateful to the members of the editorial board for their expert criticism; to Ruth J. Dean, John H. Fisher, William Nelson, R. M. Lumiansky, and Van Courtlandt Elliott for their advice and counsel; to John S. Diekhoff, Vice Provost of Case Western Reserve University, Lester G. Crocker, Dean of Humanities, and The Press of Case Western Reserve University for their encouragement and support of humanistic studies. Forthcoming volumes in the series will include reviews of medieval and Renaissance studies and discussions of artistic styles and literary themes in their cultural and historical contexts.

MEDIEVALIA ET HUMANISTICA

Paul Maurice Clogan, Editor
CASE WESTERN RESERVE UNIVERSITY

EDITORIAL BOARD

Contents

MEDIEVALIA ET HUMANISTICA

Katherine Zell

Roland H. Bainton

KATHERINE ZELL described herself as "a splinter from the rib of that blessed man Matthew Zell."[1] He would have called her at least two ribs. He referred to her as "Mein Helfer."[2] The first help she gave him was when he was under excommunication by the bishop for having married her. Opponents of the Reformation circulated the tale that she had caught him with the maid and that, when she protested, he had thrashed her. Katherine published a refutation in which she said: "I have never had a maid. I have had the help only of a little girl, too young for that sort of thing, and as for thrashing me, my husband and I have never had an unpleasant fifteen minutes. We could have no greater honor than to die rejected of men and from two crosses to speak to each other words of comfort." She not only refutes this particular slander but also makes a vigorous defense of clerical marriage and denounces the "celibate" priest who gets seven women pregnant at the same time. "You remind me," she says, "that the Apostle Paul told women to be silent in church. I would remind you of the word of this same apostle that in Christ there is no longer male nor female and of the prophecy of Joel: 'I will pour forth my spirit upon all flesh and your sons and your *daughters* will prophesy.' I do not pretend to be John the Baptist rebuking the Pharisees. I do not claim to be Nathan upbraiding David. I aspire only to be Balaam's ass, castigating his master."[3]

A defense of clerical marriage was very much in order in Strasbourg in the year 1523. Seven priests including Katherine's husband were under excommunication for having married. The man who had taken the lead in this matter was Martin Butzer. He was not the first evangelical minister at Strasbourg. That honor falls to Zell; Butzer came already married. An ex-Dominican, he had taken to wife an ex-nun, Elizabeth Silberstein. Cast out in every quarter, Butzer and his wife had taken refuge in his native Strasbourg. Zell set him up in his own house to give lectures on the Epistle to the Romans and later succeeded in placing him in a parish. Butzer began urging marriage upon his colleagues and even endeavored to find a partner for his fellow priest Wolfgang Capito. To that end Butzer addressed "the noble, honorable, Christian Lady, Ottilie von Hohenheim" of Basel. He informed her that marriage, to be sure, was not a necessity for many priests as a remedy for sin, since they were capable of continence, but for the sake of those not so gifted, those under no necessity were in duty bound to render the marriage of the clergy reputable. This they could not do without partners. All of the eligibles for Capito had been reviewed, and none was deemed more suitable than Ottilie. "Your deportment hitherto has been exemplary. You will crown your witness by assuming a reviled and crucified marriage. I beseech you in the name of Christ, crucified and accursed." Ottilie did not feel that this was her cross. Capito did succeed in marrying a daughter of one of the chief magistrates of Strasbourg.[4] That her father should have consented to such a union shows the degree to which the members of the government supported the reform. Without this aid the reformers would never have been able to withstand the bishop.

Another priest married. Anthony Firn took to wife his concubine. The officiating priest was Matthew Zell, who took advantage of the occasion to deliver a homily on the validity of clerical marriage. "Hitherto it has been the custom," said he, "for the minister at a wedding to say, 'If any know just cause why these two may not lawfully be joined together let him now speak. . . .' This is a wholesome practice, but there are those who come forward with very unjust causes, claiming that priests should not marry. Such a union is not an innovation but simply a return to the word of God who instituted marriage at the creation, and now, because we have not heeded God's ordinance we are worse than Sodom and Gomorrah. Wherefore, dear brother Anthony, fear not. Blessed are you because this day you are breaking the power of Antichrist. If you are banished or put to death this cannot hurt you, because you are doing what God has commanded, and many more brothers, God willing, will follow your example, who until now have been intimidated. Antichrist has established his kingdom by lies. Let us establish the truth that Christ may reign forever and ever."[5]

The next priest to follow the example of Anthony Firn, after only three weeks (December 3, 1523), was this same Matthew Zell. The vows were administered by Martin Butzer.[6] The bride was no previous concubine, but the intrepid Katherine Schütz, who had been delivered from dire anguish of spirit by reading the tracts of Martin Luther.[7] On the occasion of her marriage, Luther sent her a letter of congratulation.[8] She was in her twenty-fifth or twenty-sixth year and her husband twenty years older. This union brought the number of married priests up to four. Three more followed, making the total of seven. The bishop then excommunicated them all. As a group they defended their action to their superior.[9] Katherine sent him a letter which admittedly "smoked"[10] and, in addition, brought out a tract of which the bishop complained to the council as abusive.[11] The council forbad like fulminations but at the same time upheld the married priests. In consequence, until 1529 Catholic and Evangelical services took place side by side in the cathedral of Strasbourg. The bishop's appointee preached from the high pulpit, Zell from a pulpit improvised by his parishioners and trundled on wheels to the center of the nave where he addressed auditors to the number of three thousand.[12]

Since Katherine and her husband were so completely a team, we must first glance at the stand taken by the husband. One cannot say, as some insinuated, that he was led by apron strings, since he had been a vigorous reformer before ever he married. He had come to Strasbourg three years earlier in 1520, when he was forty-two or forty-three, and was assigned to the staff of the cathedral with the special office of *poenitentiarius*, authorized to levy fines and grant or withhold absolution for sins. In the discharge of this office he was deemed by the bishop and his treasurer to be egregiously lax. Zell would absolve peasants without a fine for eating butter on fast days and would not levy a fee on a woman who came for purification after a miscarriage. What need had she to be purified or absolved?[13] While the bishop grumbled, the cathedral chapter often gave Zell support.

Worse was to come. In the 1520's the tracts of Luther were circulating, and Zell's sermons betrayed their influence. He was taxed with a long list of heresies to which he made a lengthy reply, the first manifesto of the reform in Strasbourg. "We are told," he began, "to make no innovations but to wait for the decisions of a general council. If the apostles had waited for a general council of the Jews to endorse Christ, they would have waited a very long time. I am accused of having read Luther. To be sure I have. How is a shepherd to know where to pasture his sheep if he has not tried out the pastures? If Luther is guilty of some errors, that does not make him a heretic. Which of the church Fathers was ever free from all error? Men say that Luther's language is too rough. I agree, but the question is not whether he is rough or gentle but whether he is right. He is being read all over Germany and am I alone to be forbidden to read him? I follow Luther in so far as he follows the Scripture. . . . What a shame to be ashamed of the eternal Word of God! A noble work it would be if the bishop himself were to preach in his own cathedral city instead of spending his time with falcons and hounds. . . . Scripture, Scripture, my Lords, I say, not the iron sword. Send out preachers. If you do not, they will come anyway. And though you issue a thousand bulls against them, though you use up the whole Schwarzwald to burn them, though you scatter them over the earth, it will do you no good. If you root them out, from their roots will grow others."[14]

This was the man to whom Katherine Zell was a "Helfer." Throughout his lifetime she was able to devote herself almost exclusively to this role because having early lost two children in infancy, there were, to her grief, no more. She was prone to think of her childlessness as a mark of the divine displeasure because of her sins.[15] Her spirit was frequently overcast by a sense of guilt, though one who did not know the secrets of her heart might well have numbered her among the saints. The doctrine of justification by faith no more brought to her an unbroken assurance than to Luther. Both were subject to depressions and recurrent wrestlings with the angel. Perhaps she was thereby all the more impelled to engage so unfailingly in works of mercy.

Her days and nights were abundantly filled with such ministries. Strasbourg became a city of refuge, being a "free city," not immediately under the control of the imperial house of Austria, so bent upon enforcing the Edict of Worms against Luther and his followers. Neighboring towns did not enjoy such immunity. At Kensingen in Breisgau the minister was forced to leave. One hundred and fifty men of the parish accompanied him for several miles. When they returned, the gates were closed and guarded by the troops of Austria. One man was caught and executed. The rest fled to the river and secured passage to Strasbourg.[16] Katherine bedded eighty in the parsonage and fed sixty for three weeks, while finding provision elsewhere for the remainder. At the same time she wrote a letter, published as a tract, to the wives left behind in Kensingen. "To my fellow sisters in Christ, day and night I pray God that he may increase your faith that you forget not his invincible Word. 'My thoughts are not your thoughts,' saith the Lord [Is. 55:8]. 'Whom I make alive I kill' [Dt. 32:39]. The Lord would wean you from the world that you may rely only on him. Has he not told us that we must forsake father and mother, wife and

Katherine Zell's message of consolation to the women of Kensingen.
Copies at the Crozer Theological Seminary and the library of the Foundation for Reformation Research at St. Louis.

child [Lk. 14:26]? 'He who denies me him will I deny in the presence of my father' [Mk. 10:33]. 'Those who would reign with me must also suffer with me' [2 Tim. 2:12]. Had I been chosen," said Katherine, "to suffer as you women I would account myself happier than all the magistrates of Strasbourg at the fair with their necklaces and golden chains. Remember the word of the Lord in the prophet Isaiah [54:8], 'In overflowing wrath for a moment I hid my face from you, but with everlasting love I will have compassion on you.' 'Can a woman forget her sucking child? Even these may forget, but I will not forget you' [Is. 49:15]. Are not these golden words? Faith is not faith which is not tried. . . . 'Blessed are those that mourn.' Pray, then, for those who persecute you that you 'may be perfect as your Father in heaven is perfect' [Mt. 5:4,44,48]. Anno Domini MDxxiiij, Katherine Schütz, wife of Matthew Zell, proclaimer of the Word of God in the Christian congregation of Strasbourg." [17]

A calamity more dire befell the city not long thereafter. Fifteen twenty-five was the year of the Peasants' War. Contingents from different parts of Germany were clustered around Strasbourg. The ministers Capito and Zell, accompanied by Katherine, visited their encampments and pleaded for the avoidance of violence. [18] The pleas went unheeded, and the peasants were massacred. Survivors, together with the wives and children of the slaughtered, flocked into Strasbourg to the number of three thousand. This influx put a tremendous strain on the economy of a city of only twenty-five thousand. Strasbourg, at the moment, was in the throes of revamping the whole system of poor relief. Luther taught that almsgiving did not facilitate entry into heaven. In consequence, he proposed to suppress begging. Those able to work should work, and those unable should be supported by the community. Strasbourg was introducing this practice but extended the relief only to citizens. Here now were three thousand who were not citizens. The problem was tackled by two persons. The first was Lucas Hackfurt, an ardent member of the municipal directors of relief and, incidentally, at the time an Anabaptist. The second was Katherine Zell. Presumably, since Hackfurt was involved, the city must have relaxed in some measure the rule of citizens only. The bulk of the refugees were lodged en masse in the Franciscan church; but much of the feeding and housing must have been handled privately, and here the lead would fall to Katherine. The emergency lasted for half a year until the war subsided and the families were able to return to their farms. Out of this experience came two lessons: that Strasbourg, in times of persecution abroad and famine nearby, must enlarge her bounty and that, because congestion of refugees in one lodging was a hazard to health, distribution in homes was to be preferred.[19] The role played by Katherine throws light on the remark of Butzer, "She is a trifle imperious."[20]

The Reformation in Strasbourg was assuming a form midway between the Lutheran in Germany and the Zwinglian in Switzerland. The big difference was as to the interpretation of the Lord's Supper. Luther understood the words "This is my body" to mean that the physical body of Christ is present on the altar. Zwingli declared that in this sentence the word *is* means *signifies*. The rite is a memorial of Christ's death. Butzer and the Strasbourgers believed in a spiritual presence. The matter assumed political proportions in 1529 when Philip of Hesse sought to unite the Germans and the Swiss in a league of mutual defense. To that end he invited theologians from the three areas to assemble at his capital city of Marburg. Zwingli of Zürich and Oecolampadius of Basel passed on their way through Strasbourg and were entertained by the Zells. "For fourteen days I was their cook and maid," said Katherine.[21]

Butzer went with the group to Marburg. The theologians failed to reach agreement. Philip of Hesse suggested that they practice inter-communion nevertheless. Luther was so inclined until Melanchthon pointed out to him that to come to terms with the Swiss would close the door to the Catholics.[22] When the news reached Strasbourg that Luther had declined, Katherine sent him a remonstrance pleading that love is above all else. "Yes," replied Luther, "except where God's Word is at stake."[23]

The entertainment of distinguished personages fell more than once to Katherine. In 1538 Calvin was in Strasbourg, having been expelled from Geneva. He was frightfully upset when the Strasbourg ministers gave a letter of confidence to Pierre Caroli, a very vacillating person of whose unreliability Calvin had had painful experience. Unwilling to sign the letter and loath to dissent from his ministerial hosts, he took his distress to the magistrate Jacob Sturm, who brought him to Butzer, by whom he was taken to the home of the ever-reconciling Zells. There, as he later confessed, Calvin blew up disgracefully until he was mollified. How much Katherine had to do with the cooling we do not know. She was the hostess.[24]

While the Protestants were seeking to close their ranks, negotiations were also in progress in the hope of reunion with the Catholics.

A preliminary interchange among the theologians of both confessions took place in 1540 at Hagenau near Strasbourg. At one time or another Katherine entertained thirty of the delegates coming from Wittenberg, Saxony, Hesse, Nürnberg, Swabia and other areas.[25] Katherine and her husband were at other times the guests. Together they travelled six hundred miles in 1538 to visit Luther and Melanchthon at Witten-

The printer's mark of Jacob Frölich on Katherine Zell's hymn booklets.
Paul Heitz and August Barack, *Elsässische Buchmarken* (Strasbourg, 1892), taf. xxv.

berg. Other trips were made together to Switzerland, Constance, Swabia, Nürnberg and the Palatinate.[26]

The years 1529 to 1533 were very trying to the reformers of Strasbourg because of the great influx of a veritable swarm of sectaries.[27] The reformers did indeed object to their views, but even more to their behavior. They were secessionists who threatened to split the reformed community. Grave consequences might well ensue, because even the free city of Strasbourg might be attacked by the imperial forces if the reformers were too drastic or anarchic. Most of the outstanding leaders — Carlstadt, Denck, Haetzer, Marbeck, Hofmann, Servetus, Schwenckfeld, Sebastian Franck — of what is sometimes called the left wing of the Reformation, or the radical Reformation, were in Strasbourg at this time. The ministers were in favor of persuasion rather than coercion, but when persuasion failed, they had recourse to banishment and imprisonment and condoned even death, though there were only two executions and these for reasons other than belief. Zell, among the reformers, was the most liberal. "Any one," said he, "who acknowledges Christ as the true Son of God and the sole Savior of mankind is welcome at my board."[28] Behind Matthew Zell was Katherine, who was suspected of giving the pitch.[29]

She secured permission from the council to visit Melchior Hofmann in prison.[30] He was one of the most troublesome of the sectaries, who had betaken himself to Strasbourg in pursuance of a prophecy that he would there be imprisoned for six months and then at the coming of the Lord would lead the one hundred and forty-four saints in the slaughter of the ungodly. Only the first part of the prophecy was fulfilled and that not exactly. He languished in prison not for six months but for ten years until his death. Katherine's visit implied no approval of his views. She visited anyone in prison. An entry in the record of the council grants her permission "to visit a poor prisoner under sentence of death."[31] Neither did she endorse the theology of Michael Servetus, but when he was executed in Geneva, she spoke of him with great compassion.

There was, however, one dissident to whom she was genuinely attracted, the Silesian nobleman Caspar Schwenckfeld of gracious demeanor and courteous manner, who taught that Christ's body on the altar is his celestial body and a moratorium should be declared on the Lord's Supper until it could be observed without contention. Butzer said that Katherine, without endorsing his errors, regarded them leniently, since he imposed on her by his courtly manners and to all appearance saintly deportment.[32] She later testified to the edification derived from his lectures,[33] corresponded with him over the years and defended his orthodoxy.[34]

The Zells were at times somewhat at odds on matters of church unity with Butzer and the other ministers, who wanted organic unity through theological agreement. The Zells were concerned rather for brotherliness despite theological disagreement. Butzer felt that Matthew lagged because Katherine dragged.[35] Matthew devoted himself to resolving squabbles. For example, the congregation at Schaffhausen was wrangling over whether the chalice should be of silver or gold, and whether the bread in the sacrament should be a wafer or a chunk broken each time from the loaf.[36] A dispute arose at Strasbourg over whether to continue the custom of having godparents at baptisms. Among the Catholics the sponsors contracted spiritual relations so that their children could not marry the godchildren without dispensations. The new marriage ordinance at Strasbourg had abolished the whole system of spiritual consanguinity. The Zells feared nevertheless that superstition would linger. Butzer argued that the assumption by friends of responsibility for the religious upbringing of children was in itself wholesome and should be continued. The Zells did not disrupt the unity of Strasbourg over a matter of no great consequence.[37]

Matthew Zell, his wife's senior by twenty years, died in January of 1548. After the eulogy by Butzer, Katherine delivered an address,[38] thereby feeding the allegation that she aspired to be "Doctor Katrina." "I am not usurping the office of preacher or apostle," said she. "I am like the dear Mary Magdalene, who with no thought of being an apostle, came to tell the disciples that she had encountered the risen Lord." After having braced herself for this ordeal Katherine collapsed. She was persuaded to go to Basel to stay for a while with Pastor Myconius. Butzer, who had on occasion spoken somewhat slightingly of Katherine, now wrote to her host, "The widow of our Zell, a godly and saintly woman, comes to you that perchance she may find some solace for her grief. She is human. How does the heavenly Father humble those endowed with great gifts. Her zeal is incredible for Christ's lowliest and afflicted. She knows and searches the mysteries of Christ. Because she is resentful of this dispensation she heaps upon herself frightful reproaches. She is all too human. Truly this is a trial from the Lord and it is astounding. Comfort her patiently for the love

Matthew Zell.
Woodcut reproduced in Johannes Ficker, "Bildnisse der Strassburger Reformation," in *Quellen und Forschungen zur Kirchen- und Kulturgeschichte von Elsass und Lothringen*, IV (Strasbourg, 1914), p. 15.

of her husband, a sincere and faithful servant of Christ, even if, like the rest of us, he did not perfectly fulfill all that he might." [39]

From Basel Katherine went to Zürich for a visit in the home of the distinguished Hebraist Conrad Pellikan. Back in Strasbourg on January 4, 1549, she sent him a letter of thanks which speedily broke into a lament because of the introduction of the *Interim*. This term was applied to a compromise adjustment of the dispute between Catholics and Protestants to be imposed by the emperor during the interim pending a definitive solution by the Council of Trent. The compromise granted to the Protestants only that the Mass might be celebrated in both ways and that clerical marriages already contracted would be recognized. Katherine informed Pellikan that the Mass had been reinstated in the whole land of Württemberg, in Ulm, Augsburg and other places. In some cases Spanish priests had been installed. "We do not know what is in store for Strasbourg. Jacob Sturm [the magistrate] came to see me so choked that he could not speak. . . . I am sending your wife and your daughter-in-law each a pound of flax for spinning shawls. I would have sent more if I had had a carrier. I have been allowed to keep the parsonage which belongs to the parish. I take any one who comes. It is always full. I don't know how long I can keep it. [She was permitted for nearly three years.] 'One thing have I asked of the Lord. That will I seek after, that I may dwell in the house of the Lord' to behold my noble husband with all the saints in the vision of God." [40]

She was not long in finding out what the *Interim* would mean for Strasbourg. The Mass was to be restored in the cathedral and in all the churches save three, where evangelical preaching would be allowed provided it was not controversial. The two leading ministers, Butzer and Fagius, were exiled. They prepared to go to England whither they had been invited by Cranmer, the Archbishop of Canterbury. But they overstayed the stipulated time for departure by three weeks. During that period they were hidden by Katherine Zell.[41] They left behind them two gold pieces for Katherine and from England sent a letter of thanks. She responded that whereas in England evidently the harvest was plentiful, the laborers few, in Strasbourg the laborers were plentiful but the harvest scant. As for the gold pieces: "You put me to shame to think that you would leave money for me, as if I would take a heller from you poor pilgrims and my revered ministers. I wish I could have done better for you but my Matthew has taken all my gaiety with him.

I intended to return the two gold pieces with this letter, as Joseph put the money in the sack of his brother, but a refugee minister has just come in with five children, and the wife of another who saw her husband beheaded before her eyes. I divided the one gold piece between them as a present from you. The other I enclose. You will need it."[42]

Katherine's health began to fail. She suffered from dropsy and several letters are written from the baths.[43] But her incredible zeal did not flag. In 1558 one of the chief magistrates of Strasbourg, Felix Ambrosiaster, was stricken with leprosy, or whatever was thus diagnosed. He was required to leave his family and live beyond the walls in a quarantined institution. He petitioned that instead he might be allowed to live in a little hut with a garden. Permission was granted, but his daughter should not be given leave to attend him.[44] There was one who visited frequently, however, and that was Katherine Zell. For him she wrote a little treatise of consolation which was published.[45] Here is an abridgement.

> My dear Lord Felix, since we have known each other for a full thirty years I am moved to visit you in your long and frightful illness. I have not been able to come as often as I would like, because of the load here for the poor and the sick, but you have been ever in my thoughts. We have often talked of how you have been stricken, cut off from rank, office, from your wife and friends, from all dealings with the world which recoils from your loathsome disease and leaves you in utter loneliness. At first you were bitter and utterly cast down till God gave you strength and patience and now you are able to thank him that out of love he has taught you to bear the cross. Because I know that your illness weighs upon you daily and may easily cause you again to fall into despair and rebelliousness I have gathered some passages which may make your yoke light in the spirit, though not in the flesh. I have written meditations on the fifty-first Psalm: "Have mercy upon me, O God, according to thy lovingkindness," and the one hundred and thirtieth, "Out of the depths have I cried unto thee, O Lord." And then on the Lord's Prayer and the Creed.

Here in brief is her meditation on the Lord's Prayer.

> "Our Father, who art in heaven." He is called not Lord or Judge, but Father. And since through his Son we are born again we may call him grandfather, too. He may be likened also to a mother, who has known the pangs of birth and the joy of giving suck.

"Hallowed be thy name." May we hold it in reverence, nor by our behavior cause others to hold it in irreverence.

"Thy kingdom come." Reign thou in our hearts, soul, body and conscience.

"Thy will be done." Save us from murmuring against any cross laid upon us.

"Give us this day our daily bread." Bless the labor of our hands that we may have food for ourselves and others. Give us of the bread and the water of life, of which if a man eat and drink he shall never more hunger or thirst. As the grains of wheat become in the loaf one bread, so may we be united in Christ, ready with him to endure want, pain and shame.

"Forgive us our debts." Save us from resentment when we are maligned and scorned, like Christ who as a sheep before the shearers was dumb and opened not his mouth.

"Lead us not into the temptation" of believing that we have truly forgiven, while rancor lingers, and the temptation of despairing of thy mercy, forgetting that Peter and Mary Magdalene were forgiven.

"Deliver us from the evils" of hunger, war, famine and pestilence, though only if it be thy will.

"For thine is the kingdom." May Christ reign in heaven and on earth.

"And the power." As thou didst deliver Israel, so deliver us.

"And the glory." Thou givest breath to every living thing. Wherefore of thy glory there is no end.

Katherine visited Felix Ambrosiaster as a friend. She felt a more direct responsibility for a nephew stricken with syphilis. The disease was in that day a frightful scourge, partly because of the inadequacy of the cure, partly because of ignorance as to the transmission, which can be by any open cut or even by a kiss. When the nephew could not be cared for at home, he was placed in the hospital for syphilitics. Katherine went to live with him. She was appalled by the mismanagement of the institution and sent the town council a devastating critique. The manager and his wife live in luxury, she said, and neglect the patients. Beds rot. Water is not heated for baths. Tough and sometimes wormy meat is served indiscriminately, whereas some require a soft diet. There is no religious instruction, and some patients do not know the Lord's Prayer. The manager mumbles a grace so that one cannot tell whether he may not be swearing. The mercury cure martyrs the patients. There should be a dedicated couple in charge. The number of maids should be reduced. The fewer, the less quarrelling. Get rid of the savage dog which mangles all the cats. Give up swine and goats in favor of a hundred hens. Have religious instruction every morning while the heart is fresh. For medication use only guyac. Her recommendations were adopted almost in toto but were hard to implement. She appears to have discontinued her residence, but not her contribution.[46]

Both Katherine and her husband were interested in popular education. He put out two simple catechisms for children.[47] She issued in 1534 a collection of hymns in the form of four little penny-a-piece separate pamphlets. They were translations already made from Czech into German. In her preface Katherine said, "When I read these hymns I felt that the writer had the whole Bible in his heart. This is not just a hymn book but a lesson book of prayer and praise. When so many filthy songs are on the lips of men and women and even children I think it well that folk should with lusty zeal and clear voice sing the songs of their salvation. God is glad when the craftsman at his bench, the maid at the sink, the farmer at the plough, the dresser at the vines, the mother at the cradle break forth in hymns of prayer, praise and instruction." A singing swan above a viola and a sheet of music, the device of the printer Frölich of Strasbourg, was fortuitously highly appropriate. In this instance the swan might also easily be identified with the goose, the symbol of the Czech John Hus, whose name in that language means goose.[48]

Katherine's last days were plagued by strife. The *Interim* ended with the defeat of the emperor. The Peace of Augsburg in 1555 granted toleration to the Lutherans in designated areas. Strasbourg committed herself, to Lutheranism. Some of the ministers vented the invective formerly bestowed upon the Catholics now upon the sectaries. One of the chief offenders was Ludwig Rabus, a former resident in the Zell's home and confessedly indebted to Katherine for spiritual counsel. Now in a Christmas sermon he digressed from the text to rail against Schwenckfeld, "Stenckfeld [Stinkfield], that emissary of Satan." Katherine remonstrated with him in private. Rabus called her a "disturber of the peace of the church." "A disturber of the peace am I? Yes indeed, of my own peace. Do you call this disturbing the peace that instead of spending my time in frivolous amusements I have visited the plague-infested and carried out the dead? I have visited those in prison and under sentence of death. Often for three days and three nights I have neither eaten nor slept. I have never mounted the pulpit, but I have done more than any minister in visiting those in misery. Is this disturbing the peace of the church?[49]

"Why do you rail at Schwenckfeld? You talk as if you would have him burned like the poor Servetus at Geneva. You say that you have left Strasbourg and gone to Ulm because the ministers here are too lenient toward Schwenckfelders, Zwinglians and Anabaptists. You behave as if you had been brought up by savages in a jungle. The Anabaptists are pursued as by a hunter with dogs chasing wild boars. Yet the Anabaptists accept Christ in all essentials as we do. They have borne witness to their faith in misery, prison, fire and water. You young fellows tread on the graves of the first fathers of this church in Strasbourg and punish all who disagree with you, but faith cannot be forced. You should read that man Bellius who collected statements from the early reformers on religious liberty from which alas some have since receded. [She is referring to the pseudonymous work of Castellio *Concerning Heretics*.][50] You say that Strasbourg by her laxity is a shame and scorn to all Germany. Not yet, my dear fellow. She is rather an example of mercy and compassion. My Matthew testified in private and from the pulpit that he would not be guilty of the crucifixion of these poor folk. The Good Samaritan, when he came upon the man, who had fallen among thieves, did not ask him to what denomination he belonged, but put him on his ass and took him to an inn. Remember the words of the Lord Jesus, 'I am meek and lowly of heart.' "

Katherine's last service was in the year 1562 to a disciple of Schwenckfeld, the wife of the distinguished physician Günther of Andernach. On her death the husband asked one of the pastors to conduct the funeral. He replied that the superintendent would suffer him to do so only on condition that after lauding her virtues, he should then declare her to have fallen away from the true faith. The husband declined and arranged to have the interment at six in the morning when none would notice. Katherine Zell, now too weak to walk, was taken at that hour in a carriage to the cemetery and herself conducted the service. The town council decreed that if Katherine got well she should receive a reprimand.[51]

It was never delivered, for in that same year Katherine, like Moses, "died of the kiss of God and no man knows the place of her burial."

BIBLIOGRAPHY

The fullest autobiographical source for Katherine Zell is No. 5 of her works listed below, referred to in the notes as Füsslin. The best study to date is that of William Klaustermeyer, "The Role of Matthew and

Catherine Zell in the Strassburg Reformation" (unpublished doctoral dissertation, Stanford University, 1965). His account is fuller for Matthew than for Katherine, and in her case he has not utilized quite all of the material available. The works to which reference is made in the notes are the following:

Adam, Johann, *Evangelische Kirchengeschichte der Stadt Strassburg* (Strasbourg, 1922).

Baum, Johann Wilhelm, *Capito und Butzer* (Elberfeld, 1860).

Röhrich, Timotheus Wilhelm. *Geschichte der Reformation im Elsass und besonders in Strassburg*, 3 vols. (Strasbourg, 1830–32).

————, "Matthaeus Zell," *Beiträge zu der theol. Wissenschaften*, II (1851), 144–92.

————, *Kathrina Zell* (Strasbourg, 1853), less detailed than the above.

Wendel, François, *L'Église de Strasbourg . . . 1532–1535* (Paris, 1942).

————, *Le Marriage à Strasbourg . . . 1520–1692* (Strasbourg, 1928).

Winkelmann, Otto, "Das Fürsorgewesen der Stadt Strassburg," *Quellen und Forschungen zur Reformationsgeschichte*, V (1922).

ABBREVIATIONS. The letter X signifies that a document is available in Xerox in the Yale library.

BSC Bulletin de la Société pour la Conservation des Monuments Historiques d'Alsace, II, Ser. XIX (1899, Strasbourg).

CR Corpus Reformatorum, Calvini Opera.

CS Corpus Schwenckfeldianorum.

Oek. "Briefe und Akten zum Leben Oekolampads," ed. Ernst Staehelin, *Quellen und Forschungen zur Reformationsgeschichte*, XIX (1934).

Schiess *Ambrosius und Thomas Blaurer Briefwechsel*, 3 vols., ed. Traugott Schiess (Freiburg i.Br., 1908–12).

Täuferakten *Quellen zur Geschichte der Täufer*, VIII *Elsass*, Teil II (Strasbourg, 1523–35), ed. Manfred Krebs and Hans Georg Rott.

Thesaurus Baumianus, manuscript letters of the reformers, some originals as of Katherine Zell, but mostly transcriptions by J. W. Baum. There is a published index by Johannes Ficker, *Thesaurus Baumianus* (Strasbourg, 1905).

Works of Matthew Zell.

1. Christeliche Verantwortung M. Matthes Zell von Keysberssberg Pfarrhers und predigers im Münster zu Strassburg / vber Artickel

im vom Bischöfflichem Fiscal daselbs entgegen gesetzt/ vnnd im rechten vbergeben. . . . (Colophon) Getruckt in der löblichen Satt Strassburg/ durch Wolffgangum Köpffel. . . . M.D. xxiij. *X* from the Stadtbibliothek, Zürich.

2. Ein Collation auff die einfuerung M. Anthonij Pfarrhens zu S. Thomans zu Strassburg/ vnnd Katharina seines eelichen gemahls/ von Matthes Zeell. . . . (Colophon) Durch Wolff Köpffel. . . . M.D. xxiij vj Kalen. Decem. *X* from the Stadtbibliothek, Zürich.

The following two works were issued under the name of Matthew Zell and others. Baum lists No. 3 with a German title and says that it was the work of Capito. P. 252, note, and p. 580, no. 14.

3. Appelatio Sacerdotvm Maritorvm, Vrbis Argentinae, adversus insanam excommunicationem Episcopi/ 1524. *X* from the Stadtbibliothek, Zürich.

4. Doctor Capito Mathis Zellen/ vnnd ander Predicanten zu Strassburg wahrhaftige Verantwortung. . . . *X* from the Stadtbibliothek, Munich.

Works of Katherine Zell.
1. Entschuldigung Katharina Schützinn/ für M. Matthes Zellen/ jren Ehegemahel . . . (Strasbourg ?, 1524). *X* from the Stadtbibliothek, Zürich.

2. Den leydenden Christglaubigen weybern der gemain zu Kentzingen meinen mitschwestern in Christo Jesu zu handen. Katharina Schützin. M.D. xxiiij. Contoura copy from the Crozer Theol. Sem. Another copy at the Foundation for Reformation Research, St. Louis, Mo.

3. Von Christo Jesu. . . . Lobgsäng. Hymns in four small separate parts (Strasbourg, 1534).

4. Klagrede und Ermahnung Katharina Zellin zum Volk bei dem Grab M. Matheus Zellen. Printed from manuscript in W. Horning, *Beiträge zur Kirchengeschichte des Elsasses*, VII (1887), 49–79 and 113–21. *X*.

5. Ein Brief an die genze Bürgerschaft der Stadt Strassburg, betreffend Hern Ludwig Rabus. . . . 1557 (Schottenloher, 17593). Reprinted in J. C. Füsslin, *Beyträge zur Erläuterung der Kirchen-Reformationsgeschichten des Schweitzerlandes*, V (1753), 191–354. The fullest autobiographical source for Katherine. Copies Yale, Cornell.

6. Den Psalmen Misere/ mit dem Khünig David bedacht/ gebettet/ vnd paraphrasirt von Katharina Zellin M. Matthei Zellen seligen nachgelassne Ehefraw. . . . Augstmonat, 1558. *X* from the Stadtbibliothek, Zürich.

NOTES

1. Füsslin, p. 200.
2. *Ibid.*, 302.
3. K. Zell, No. 1, aij and verso, bvij–ciij.
4. Baum, pp. 263–64.
5. M. Zell, No. 2.
6. Adam, p. 62, and Röhrich, *Beiträge*, pp. 173–74. Firn was married November 9, Zell on December 3.
7. Füsslin, p. 197.
8. *Weimarer Ausgabe, Briefwechsel*, No. 808.
9. M. Zell, No. 3.
10. Füsslin, p. 238.
11. *BSC*, No. 4540.

   Als mster. Mathisen frauw ein schmachbüchlein üss sol haben gon lassen, sollen Jac. Sturm und Jac. Meiger in befragen, und im ernstlich sagen, dass er denk, und dass solchs nim geschee, auch dass die gedruckten bücher nit von handen kommen bis dass sie besehen worden, auch ir sagen, dass sie denk und nichts mehr lass üssgon oder drucken. Seind porro die bücher in die cantzley genommen worden. Eins titulirt: Entschuldigung Katharinae Schützin für Meister Mathisen.
   Und ward daruff ein mandat wider die schandbücher und gemalt (gemählde) publicirt.
12. Baum, p. 196; Adam, p. 31; Röhrich, *Beiträge*, p. 160; M. Zell, No. 1b.
13. M. Zell, No. 1, Vij.
14. *Ibid.*, Ciij, diij, qii verso, qiii, yii, yiv.
15. To Ambrosius Blaurer, Sept. 30, 1534. The letter is reproduced in Schiess, Vol. I, No. 465, but the opening portion is so condensed that the point of her lament is lost. The full text is here given from the copy in the *Thesaurus Baumianus* (VII, 247 D). Ehrhard Schnepf of Heilbronn (1493–1558) was a professor at Marburg (Schiess I, p. 511, note). The rumor of Blaurer's lapse was false (see Klaustermeyer).
   Der Geist des Raths, der Stärke und der Weisheit wonn allezeit in Euch, damit Jr jetz und allezeit klug, weisseigen in alle händlen des diensts Jesu Christi, mein ehrsamer sehr lieber Ich sag Euch grossen dank umb Euw. freuntlich Schreÿben, ja des selbigen Wunsches, so Jr mir mit thun. Beger von Gott durch Christum den Herrn, das er Euch einen heiligen, wahrhafften Propheten seÿn lasse in disen zweijen Stücken, das ich gewaschen werde inwendig von allen Sünden durch das Blut des Lämblins und mir ein frucht verlyhen werde zur merung des reichs Christi und zum Zeichen der gnade und Fridens zwischen Gott und mir. Solches aber wünsch ich Euch ebenzugleich wie mir

selbs, denn wie ich Kinder achte, dass sÿ sÿen sichtbarliche und auf-
gesteckte Zeichen des Gunsts Gottes, herwiderumb, wo die nit sind,
was anfechtung ich da hab, wolt ich gern gnug einmal mit mein herz
erleichtern und mein gewüssen stärken. Jetz wil ichs aber dem Herrn
befehlen, der erbarm sich mein mit der traurigen Anna deren gleich
gelübt ich Gott gethan habe: der erfreue mich mit Sara und Rebecca.
Ich will auch gern mein Tagwerk willig thun. Mein hauswirth ist eben
die Nacht auch kommen zu mir, da mir Euer brief waren. Sagt mir
Ir wären auch in Hofnung mit Euerer lieben Hausfruen siner Frucht,
göne ichs euch von Herzen und wünsche dass es mit Freuden wahr
werde und mit glück herfür bräche. Amen. M. L. Herr, mein Hauswirt
ist wieder von mir und Strassburg zu. Es ist Zeit. Hat Euren Brief an
Butzer mit jhm. Ich wird bis Sonntag zu mittag auch hinweg. Haben
Jr etwas auf Strassburg zu senden mögen mirs hie zwischen lassen zu-
kommen. Wils auch fleissig ausrichten. Der Fürst hat ein Prediger hie.
Ich kan seiner Predigen nit satt, vil minder müde werden, so herrlich
spricht er die Epistel zu den Galatern aus. Gott seÿs dank durch Jesum
Christum der solche Erkentnus in unser herz gelegt hat. Das Volk von
Memmingen ist hinweg. Hab Inen hüt aber Eurn gruss gschriben,
nützlich wäre es wenn Ir Zeit hättet dem alten auch selbsten zuschrei-
ben. Man bekümmert sich heftig, Jr haben widerruft des Sakraments
halben, der Fürst hab Euch nit wollen predigen lassen. Jr haben dann
H. Erhárd Schnepfen underschriben. Ich hab vil kampf umb Euch
im Bad. Der Herr wende es alles zu seinem Lob. Amen. Jetz nichts
mehr. Gott stärke Euch in aller Schwachheiten Geist Seel und Leib.
So Jr bottschaft haben, bitt Euch grüssen mir von hertzen Euere liebe
nächste Gesellin und die Euere liebe Schwester. andernächst Gott
liess Euch mit Freuden widerum einander sehen. Amen. Datum in
Wildbad September 1534.

Kathrin Mattheus Zellen Frau
Euwern dienerin in Herrn allzütt.

16. Füsslin, p. 300; Baum, p. 267; Röhrich, *Geschichte*, I, 267–68, 405–7; Winkelmann, p. 100.
17. See the title page on p. 7. Copies at Crozer Theol. Sem. and Foundation
for Reformation Research, St. Louis, Mo.
18. M. Zell, No. 4, analyzed in Röhrich, *Beiträge*. On Katherine's visitation,
Füsslin, p. 264.
19. Füsslin, pp. 303–4; Winkelmann, p. 102.
20. Butzer several times in his correspondence voiced the conviction that
Matthew would have been more tractable had it not been for Katherine.
Witness the following entries.

July 9, 1533, to Margareta Blaurer (Täuferakten, No. 406, and Schiess, II,
Anhang II, No. 19):

Meister Matthisen frau ist, wie ich gesagt, eyn gotsforchtig fromm
mensch, alleyn das sy sich self, wie wyr alle, eyn wenig zu liebe hat. Daher
etwan die vbrige weyssheyt vnd der regierpräest [Herrschsucht] desto meer
herfur brichet. Nun jetz kumet meyn Adam auch wider. Nov. 18, 1553, to
Ambrose Blaurer (Schiess, I, No. 377):

22

Mattheus pius quidem, sed prorsus ingenio incocto et γυναικοκρατουμένῳ et ab ea, quae furit sese amando.

21. Füsslin, p. 313. Cf. Oek., No. 691.
22. See my article "Luther and the Via Media at the Marburg Colloquy," *Collected Papers*, Vol. II (Boston, 1963). Katherine herself makes the same comment, Füsslin, p. 270.
23. *Weimarer Ausgabe, Briefwechsel*, No. 1777.
24. *CR*, X, No. 188, p. 398. Calvin to Farel, Oct. 5, 1539.
25. Füsslin, p. 316.
26. *Ibid.*, 312.
27. The most recent work on the Strasbourg sectaries is the microfilmed Yale dissertation of Charles B. Mitchell, "Martin Bucer and Sectarian Dissent" (1960).
28. Füsslin, p. 270.
29. Schiess, I, No. 377 (given in note 20 above), and Füsslin, p. 270.
30. Täuferakten, No. 451. Montag 10. November [1533] Erkannt: Mathis [Zell] zu Melchior Hofmann lassen, der ganz schwach seyn soll, dass man besorge, dass er nicht aufkomme. Auch andere predicanten zu ihm lassen und meister Mathisen frau (hat den rothen fluss gehabt, darum er auch öl und ein licht begehrt, sich damit zu schmieren; ist ihm alles vergönnet).
31. *BSC*, No. 4924.
    Catharina, mster. Mathis Zellen frau, ist zu den armen sündern, die zum tod verurtheilt, gangen sie zu trösten.
32. Feb. 3, 1534, to Margareta Blaurer. Täuferakten, No. 502 in Latin; Schiess, II, Anhang II, No. 26 in German translation.

    . . . Schwenkfeldium certo deprehendisti. Dominus eum illuminet. Uxor Cellii pia est et non probat in Schvenckfeldio, quae nos damnamus, tantum mitius accipit quaedam et sperat melius. Mores enim isti blandissimi et in speciem sanctissimi, tum quo eam numen facit, conciliant viro huius animum. Sed salua res est. Ostendit mihi tuo et Schvenckfeldii omnia suaque ad vos. Amamus nos paulo indulgentius et docemus libenter. . . .

33. Light on this point is given in a letter written on Schwenckfeld's behalf in 1533 and not addressed to him in the second person as implied in the description accompanying the facsimile and transcription of the last paragraph in Johannes Ficker und Otto Winkelman, "Handschriftproben des 16. Jahrhunderts nach Strassburger Originalen," II (Strassburg, 1905). The treatise, otherwise unpublished, of which I have a Xerox, does not merit reproduction in full because much of the content reappears in the reply to Rabus (in Füsslin). But a few details deserve attention. The manuscript makes obvious an error in Füsslin (p. 209) where *Buler* should read *Butzer*. Katherine points out that the first preachers at Strasbourg did not rail at Schwenckfeld as did the next generation. Capito and Hedio did not: auch Butzer selbst, der doch sonst gantz hart und streng widder jn gewesen, hat jn jhe also uff offner Kantzel vor dem volck, so grüwlich anzogen, jn nÿe keiner so offentlich und pressel fur jm unehren gedacht, und auch euch noch zur zeit jren lebens nit gestattet.

One section supplies details as to the relations of Schwenckfeld with Capito and Zell during the period of the Strasbourg residence from 1529–34, and of the edification received by Katherine from his lectures:

mynen ehemann, von jnen geachtet sein, das ich Schwenckfeldts bücher lise und zum theil press [i.e., drucken ?] vnd den ehren Christi möchen achte, den die ihren sage ich sÿ jutzen [i.e., justificare ?] ich hab sÿ doch 24 jaren gelesen, vnd mer haben in die auch der fromm Doctor Capito selig, schöne vorreden gemacht, darynnen sinem geist vnd gaben guths zügknuss geben habe; Ich habe noch nie nichts heling oder heÿmlich von mynem lieben Man gehapt, besonder Inn geistlichen sache dan mir alle zit das mehrentheil ein glehrter Verstandt vnd Vrtheil, Inn heiliger Schrifft gehapt habe jm anfang, mittel vnd ennde, so lang wir by einander gewesen sint, hat sy auch zu Zitt selbst gelesen, mich sy gern hören lesen, vnd Ihn Jnn seinem Hüss nie lassen vbel redden, jn geliep vnd mich syne lectiones lassen hören, dies angethan habe, yber die zwo Episteln des heiligen Petri vnd ander mehr, Jnn des lieben D. Capitons selig huss ders auch sein weib liesse hören, da er sein Dischgenoss vnd inn auch lieb war, vnd ich habe auch H. Caspar Schwenckfeld nit viel geschrieben (welches ich dan nie on wissen mynes manns gethan habe), das er mich zu. nit auch ein grüss von seinen Wegen hat heissen dörfen setzen, ob ers schon nit alles verstanden noch angenommen hat, wass Schwenck-feldt geschrieben, hat ers aber auch nit gelestert noch also verdampt angesehen. . . .

34. *CS*, IV, 846, 848; VIII, 400 f.; IX, 86–92, 95–98; XII, 688 ff., 691; XIII, 318; Füsslin, p. 271.

35. Jan. 8, 1534, to Ambrose Blaurer (Schiess, I, No. 390. Cf. No. 394). Si nos rite urgeremus et maxime si Mattheus, qui solus adhuc populum habet, in vindicando ministerio et ecclesiae unitate acrior esset fidemque plenius praedicaret, vere nihil queri deberemus. Ad opera uxor eum detrudit. . . .

36. *Ibid.*, No. 391.

37. On the *Patenschaft*, Schiess, I, Nos. 396, 402, and II, Anhang II; Täuferak-ten, Nos. 455, 622; Wendel, *Église*, pp. 80–81 and 213; *Mariage*, p. 82.

38. K. Zell, No. 4. We learn here that the Zells had had two children.

39. Butzer to Myconius, July 16, 1549 (*Thesaurus Baumianus*, XIX, 84). X.

S. D. Zelli nostri uidua et pia et sancta mulier, venit ad nos, si forsan inde doloris sui remissionem aliquam inveniat. Hac enim in parte multum homo est. Sic enim ingenia magnis donis praedita humiliat Clementissimus pater. Incredibile studium huius est in minimos et afflic-tos Christi. Et mysteria Christi praeclaro novit et sectatur. In eo quod impatienter fert suorum desiderium et quod in eo suas mirabiles culpas sibi fingit, nimis agit humaniter. Verum haec Domini est tentatio, et admiranda. Tu in ea parte patienter illam et solere, amore viri eius, certe synceri et fidelis Christi servi, utcunque non omnia, sicut nec quisquam nostrum, praestiterit officii sui, Musculus noster, si et istic, saluta eum officiosissime meo nomine et roga ut mihi scribat, quam primum. Nostri videntur in dies plus spei dare. Utinam utinam Christi servi servis unanimonne [*sic*] pluris fiant, et plus valeant. Opto te optime valere uxorem et collegas.

40. Hooper to Butzer, June 19, 1548 (*CR*, XII, No. 1037). [Pellicanus] recipit hospitio viduam D. Matthiae, piam ac probem mulierem. Ex quo intellexi te per illam ad me dedisse literas.

Katherine Zell to Pellikan, Jan. 4, 1549 (*Thesaurus Baumianus*, XX, 4-5D). *X*.

dem Ehrwüdigen und Gottseligen Herrn Conradt Pellicano, zy Zürÿch meinem günstigen lieben Herrn und Freund zu handen. der Herr Christus der allein ein König der Ehren ist, von dem sich auch die hellischen portten müssen uffthun, der wolle sich unser aller erbarmen. Amen. Ehrwürdiger lieber Herr Pellican, die wÿl diser unser lieber Mann neüer Mitbürger zu Zürich zu uns kummen ist, so hab ich üch unseren mitt disen briffli ansprächen, denn ich nitt vergässen der liebe, treue und vil Trosts, so ich von üch empfangen hab, lass uch aber wissen, dass ich noch ein betrübt and angefochten mensch bin und weine je länger je mehr um meinen frommen, trüwen und uffrichtigen Mann. O Gott wie dörfften wir ihn jetzt so wohl, und haben alle nit gewist, was wir gehabt haben. Wie hat uns Gott so vil in ihm gezeiget, aber mein und aller augen sind blind gewesen. Wie viel frommer lüt vom gemeinen mann weÿnen und süfzen mit mir umb ihn, denen er auch in sin Leben ein grosser Trost und sehr lieb ist gesÿn. Ach Herr Gott wir gehen jetzt Trost und meisterlos wie die schaaf ohn ein hirten. Wiewol mich das etwan tröst wan ich gedenk sinen nutz und gewinn, und bevor in diser gantzen bösen Zeÿt, und dankc Gott dem Herrn das er ihn mit sinem lieben Sun Christo verborgen hat vor den zänkischen Zungen und yedermanns Hochmuth, den wir armen jetzt sehen und noch mehr sehen werden. O lieber Herr, wie stehe es so übel allenthalben, kcin Predig noch handlung des Evangelii ist mehr im gantzen Land Wirtemberg, Ulm, Auspurg und andern Orten, dessglÿchen das Bapsts Sakrament ist wider in dem Hüysslin. Man zankt um bäpstl. Pfaffen, böt ihnen vil gelds an, kann dennocht nit genug überkommen. An etlichen Orten spanische Pfaffen. O grosser Jammer. Der Knecht [?] von Ulm selb sechs liegt noch gfangen, ander mehr dazu, aller tÿranny sind wir by uns wartend. unser Bischoff Thumstifft und Statt habend jetzt etlich wuchen mit einander gehandlet, ist aber alles still und verborgen. Wir achten aber nach dem Schwörtag (der dann uff den nächsten Zinstag wirdt) werdt es mit unser aller leidt ussbrächen. Gestern hat H. Jacob Sturm mit mir geredt und geweÿnet nÿmmer reden hat können, also weist er die sachen stehen. Aber über alles sind vil bereit in tod zu gehen, wann die lehr einhellig gieng, mit einer hie, der ander dort hinuss. O Gott, wären wir alle in der ersten hitz und ÿfer hingangen, wo hat uns unseren Trennung hinpracht? Wie ist das gebet Christi so gar bÿ uns uss der acht gelassen. Vater ich bitt dass sÿ eins seÿen, wie ich und du eins sind &c ach da wir diese einigkeit den Tüffel haben lassen zerÿs-sen, so haben wir auch kein beständigen Geyst mehr und das ist mir gar schwehr, dass die nödt jetz uns auch noch nit wider zusammen gibt, dass ich sihe, dass sich doch Gott gar von uns gethan hat. Ich glaube auch, dass Gott sinn Gnad beweÿsen werde, wir verzÿhen dann alle einandern, und fallen sammenthafft mit einandern für ihn und bekennen under aller unrecht und Gottlos wesen: O Herr Jesu, wie ist und wird die Kirch, die dir so sür ist worden, jetzt gen Babel gefürt. Wie hat min lieber Mann so oft gesagt: wir gleerten werden schuldig an dem armen Volk, und bekert sich aber noch niemand. O wee des grossen Jammers und nimpsts niemand zu hertzen. Was grossen Todskampf lid ich umb meiner sünd willen, wie will erst die gemein straf und Kampf in der anfechtung sÿn. Doch beten, beten und lassend uns alle mit einandern beten und für den herren Christum niderfallen, da wir allein gnad finden werden.

Mein lieber Herr ich hab vor langen von Joachim von Schaffhusen empfangen eüwer schrifft, des Herren Bullingers Predigten, darum ich üch sehr dank, wiewohl ich auch begert hat und daruff gehofft die predig des lieben herrn Gwalterij uss dem VI Cap. Johan. von denen ich ungern schiede. Wolan ich bit üch Gott flÿssig für mich arme beküm-merte frow zu betten und von minen wegen flÿssig zu grüssen eẅer lieb hussfrau, und Sun, sin hussfrow und ir schwester. Der Herr erhalt üch alle bÿ syner Warheit ewiglich Amen. Ich schicke eẅer hussfrauen und Sonsfrowen jeder ein Pfundt Flachs zu einem Gedenkzeichen, schleÿher daraus zu spinnen. Ich wollt gern vil haben geschickt, wenn ich ein Botten hett gehabt, der es tragen oder füren hät wollen. Ich bin noch vil ir schuldner leb ich, wil ich ein andermal aber etwas daran geben. Ich bin

---

Ach Gott, ich hab die frow versümpt, und hat sich dieser Mann beschert zu tragen. vils Gott so will ich ihn ein andermal schiken oder meer dazu. gibt es uns Gott dass wir meer spinnen sollend [in margin.]

---

noch in meinem huss, welches doch zum Pfarr gehörig und dem Stift ist, und nimt sich niemandt an. Ich nimm uff wer zu mir kumpt, hab immer das huss voll lüth, und redt mir kein Mensch darin, als ob es min wäre. nitt weÿss ich wie lang es währen und also blÿben wirt, wolan wenn Gott wil, so mach ers nach seinem Gefallen er geb mir herberg und platz. Ich sag mit David: Ein ding habe ich vom Herren gebeten, das will ich von inim fordern, dass wohnen mög in sinem Huss und ich minen frummen Mann bÿ im finde und mit allen Heiligen, in Gott Anschoud mög anschaun. Amen. Der Herr verwahr üch sampt eẅeren ganzen hussgesind under sinem schirm. Ich sörg der Tüffel werde üch aber nie andern anfëchten und riteren. Derr Herr geb aber das eẅer und unser glaub in den Herren Christum nit abgehe, vil minder zus-chanden werde. Amen.

Katherine had in her possession a collection of eleven tracts against the *Interim* (X), with her marginal annotations. When they were bound in one the margins were clipped and some notes bifurcated. But there is no great loss because the ones intact are simply indications of the content with an added note of approval in one instance.

41. Füsslin, p. 263.
42. From England Butzer sent Katherine a letter of thanks published by J. V. Pollet, *Martin Bucer, Études sur la Correspondance*, I (Paris, 1958), 251–56. Katherine Zell to Butzer and Fagius, March 25, 1549 (*Thesaurus Baumianus*, XX, 71). X.

Den erwürdigen und gottsförchtigen herren Martinus Butzerus und Paulus Fagius mein lieben Herrn und sondern fründen jezt in England zu iren eigenen Handen. [She begins with a lament that since the death of her husband she is no longer herself.] sunst bin ich also blöd und zerstört im Haupt und gantzer natur. . . . Der Herr hat mich geschlagen. das sint schwere streith. Die hant Gottes füret mich. den biten für mich armen einigen betrüpten Menschen. [She says that whereas she understands the harvest in England is plentiful, the laborers few, in Strasbourg the laborers are plentiful but the harvest scant. Then after some greetings she continues.] Ich hab üch anfangs nach euerem hinscheiden geschriben, wie Jr mich betrübt und zu mynner schmach mit gelt (mir doch gar üng [erecht] gewesen) inn einen brieff gelassen, domit eüre Wordt recht standen, crützischn mÿntz, ihr haben mir ein Crütz am hertzen gmacht, da ich nÿe gedacht hab ein heller zu begeren vil mÿnder zu nemen, ich üch auch wie arme Pilgern und mynen geachteten Predikanten gehalten habe, ich weiss es und Ihr wüssens auch wol, das ich im etwa anders hätte gethan. Matthaus hat all mÿn kunst und froüdt hin weg mit ihm. Uff das aber mÿne schramröte eines theils hingelegt wurde, hab ich euch diese zwei stück goldts widerumb in disen brief gewolt legen wie Joseph sinen brüdern. Do ist ein verjagten Predikant mit fünff Kindern zu mir kummen und eine Predikanten frouv deren hat iren man den Kopff abgeschlagen, vor ihren augen, die hab ich zween tag bÿ mir behabt und diess eine stück goldt diesen beiden zur Zerung von üeyeren wegen geschenkt, und den anderen uch widerumb inn diesen brieff gethon, denn Jr selber sollen bruchen und ein andermal nit so gnädig sein. Ir werden noch viel bedörffen, auch eüer volk, sollen sÿ hinnach kummen und sint also Gott befolen in sinen schutz. . . . [Greetings.]

43. Compare, for example, note 15 above.
44. Johann Adam, "Eine unbeachtete Schrift der Katharina Zell aus Strassburg," *Zeitschrift für die Geschichte des Oberrheins*, N.F., XXXI (1916), 451–55.
45. K. Zell, No. 6.
46. Winkelmann, pp. 172–77, and Urkunden, Nos. 33 and 34.
47. Matthew Zell's catechisms are reproduced in Johann Michael Reu, *Quellen zur Geschichte des kirchlichen Unterrichts.* . . . , 2 vols. in 8 (Gütersloh, 1904–35).
48. K. Zell, No. 3. There is a full description in Philipp Wackernagel, *Bibliographie zur Geschichte des deutschen Kirchenliedes im XVI. Jahrhundert*, No. MLXXXII (Hildersheim reprint, 1961), 469–70. A further description and an account of the printer Jacob Frölich is given by Johannes Ficker, "Die

grösste Prachtwerk des Strassburger Buchdrucker," *Archiv für Reformationsgeschichte*, XXXVIII (1941), 198–230. Frölich's printer's mark, a singing swan above a viola and a sheet of music, is reproduced in Paul Heitz and Karl August Barack, *Elsässische Buchmarken*, Taf. xxv (Strasbourg, 1892). A comparison of this collection with other contemporary hymnbooks is given by Alfred Erichson, "Wolfgang Musculus-Kathrina Zell," *Monatschrift für Gottesdienst und kirchliche Kunst*, II (1898), 236–42.

49. K. Zell, No. 5.

50. See my *Castellio Concerning Heretics* (reprint New York, Octagon Press, 1965).

51. On Katherine's last illness, Conrad Hubert from Strasbourg to Ludwig Lavater at Zürich, March 2, 1562 (*Thesaurus Baumianus*, MS. S103, No. 142). *X*: Zellia semimortua ac diuturno morbo atque nova calamitate tusisse.

An account of how she conducted the funeral in a letter of Gerwig Blaurer to Thomas Blaurer from Strasbourg on April 1, 1562 (Schiess, III, No. 2443):

Dr. Andernachs Gattin ist gestorben, und Katharina Zell, die inforge Wassersucht in einem Wagen zum Grab geführt werden musste, hat die Grabrede gehalten. Du weisst, dass die ganze Familie Schär Schwenckfeld anhängt. Deshalb rief die Verstorbene während ihrer mehrtägigen Krankheit keinen Prediger; als dann die Erben den Pfarrer am jungen St. Peter, neben dem Andernach wohnt, die Grabrede zu halten baten, sagte er zu unter der Bedingung, dass er zuert die Wohltätigkeit der Toten und ihre sonstigen Tugenden preisen, dann aber ihren Abfall von der Kirche Christi darlegen werde; so habe der Superintendent Marbach ihm geboten. Andernach, Schär und die Schwester Elisabeth weigerten sich dagegen und nahmen das Begräbnis zu ungewohnter Stunde, morgens um 6 Uhr, vor, und da niemand zugegen war, um das Leichengefolge zu ermahnen und trösten, übernahm die Zellin mit Glück diese Aufgabe. Solche Prediger haben wir.

Fuller details are given by J. Bernays, "Zur Biographie Johann Winters von Andernach," *Zeitschrift för die Geschichte des Oberrheins*, N.F., XVI (1901), 28–57. *X*. He records a decision of the town council that Katherine should receive a reprimand if she recovered: "sturbt sie dann, so thut sies one daz nimer."

Katherine died on September 5, 1562. Details of her funeral are given by Klaustermeyer.

My hearty thanks to Dr. Jean Rott at Strasbourg, to the *Bibliotheque Nationale et Universitaire*, and to the *Archives et Bibliotheque de la Ville de Strasbourg* for identifying and supplying materials; to Professor Robert Walton for checking at Zürich; to the *Zentralbibliothek* and *Stadt Bibliothek* at Zürich and to the *Bayerische Staats Bibliothek* at München for Xeroxes; to Professor Miriam Chrisman for the loan of her copy of Röhrich's *Geschichte*; and to Mrs. Dejon of the Yale library for checking my readings.

Wyclif and the Augustinian Tradition

with Special Reference to His *De Trinitate*

Gordon Leff

JOHN WYCLIF'S OUTLOOK can be regarded as one in a long series
of reinterpretations of the Augustinian tradition. That it led to something very different from traditional Augustinianism should not blind
us to his Augustinian inspiration. It informed every aspect of his
thought — on being, the Bible, the Church, dominion, grace, predesti-
nation, even the Eucharist. All recent work on Wyclif[1] points to the
same conclusion, that he saw himself as the upholder of Christian truth
in a world where it was being undermined or betrayed. He took his stand
as the disciple of St. Augustine, last in a line reaching back through Anselm, Hugh of St. Victor, Grosseteste, Bradwardine and FitzRalph. For
Wyclif, they all had in common a loyalty to the Bible and the *sensus
catholicus*. Wyclif's natural evangelism was accentuated by his isola-
tion from the main intellectual currents of his time. In an age when
terminism, with its stress upon signs rather than things, was dominant,
Wyclif's metaphysical realism was a bizarre extravagance. It is a feature of Wyclif's thinking that it became increasingly extreme as the
direct outcome of his opposition first to the terminists and later to
the church hierarchy. Both his metaphysics and his ecclesiology in
their developed forms are so far removed from Augustinianism that
their connexion tends to be obscured. It is to be seen perhaps most
clearly in his *De Trinitate*,[2] written probably between 1365 and 1372
when Wyclif was studying in the theological faculty at Oxford. Whether
or not it formed part of Wyclif's lost *Commentary on the Sentences*,
as has been conjectured,[3] its exclusively academic, noncontroversial
nature enables us to catch many of the elements of Wyclif's thought
in their original state before they became distended by subsequent conflict. In particular, the treatise throws valuable light on Wyclif's view
of human cognition and of the relation of faith to natural knowledge.
It is these which I wish to consider in the following pages.

Wyclif's *De Trinitate* is modelled on that of St. Augustine, who, as in all Wyclif's works, constitutes his main authority. But it also draws upon subsequent Augustinian tradition, most notably that represented by Richard FitzRalph. Although Wyclif does not cite FitzRalph's *Commentary on the Sentences*, his own notion of the mind's powers, especially its mode of illumination, has close affinities with that enunciated by FitzRalph. At the same time, however, Wyclif had a distinctive conception of the place of knowledge in elucidating the tenets of faith which belongs more to the thirteenth century than to the fourteenth and illustrates, even at this comparatively early stage, the strongly apologetic vein in Wyclif's outlook.

So far as Wyclif's doctrine of the soul and its faculties are concerned, he began from Augustine's position that the human mind is formed in the image of the trinity. Its three components of memory, reason, and will constitute a single essence, as the three persons of the Godhead subsist in a single divine essence. Wyclif's grounds for making the connexion is exemplarism, one of the hallmarks of pre-Scotist Augustinianism: namely, the doctrine that the forms in creatures have their archetype in God, and hence that the soul's nature must reflect the divine nature.[4] Both the concept and the summary way in which Wyclif deploys it are characteristic. The notion of an eternal chain of being from the archetype (*esse intelligibile*) eternally present in God as part of his being to its created manifestations in this world is central to Wyclif's metaphysical realism; it led him to treat all being as necessary, sempiternal and indestructible.[5] He takes this so much for granted that it is enough for him to state it for the connexion between the divine and the created trinities to be established. This is in turn bound up with Wyclif's conception of the relation of faith to reason, which we shall consider more closely later. Here it is enough to point to his unfashionable acceptance of the complementarity between faith and reason, so that while faith was the prerequisite for the deductions made by reason, the articles of belief could still be known naturally.[6] Their harmony lay in the harmony between the divine and the created.

God manifests himself not only in the soul's triune nature but throughout creation. It is this that enables us to draw analogies between them. Thus there is a proportion between the divine persons and natural beings, which, to be complete, have a parallel threefold order of being — of matter, form and their union, making them at once triune and of a single essence.[7] The same applies to every aspect of creation; indeed the whole of philosophy and logic is founded in knowledge of the trinity, as can be seen from each of the seven liberal arts: logic, for example, has a third term between its major and minor premises; rhetoric posits a triple mode of eloquence; in geometry there is the equilateral triangle; music has a threefold proportion of sound, and so on.[8]

In the case of the soul, Wyclif, while not treating its faculties systematically, regards it in a light very similar to that of FitzRalph. Although his object is to consider it in its different trinitarian aspects, Wyclif, in much more summary form, reaches substantially the same positions.[9] To begin with he accepts that the soul has habitual knowledge (*notitia adepta*) of itself which comes from the memory and upon which the will is able to act. Like FitzRalph he also translates these concepts into Aristotelian terms of the active and possible intellects. By their conjunction the soul can understand itself, because it is present to itself through these faculties which are an inseparable part of its substance.[10] The highest part of the rational soul is *mens* or *memoria*, which contains all first principles; it is there that the spirit strives towards God, and the soul is able to know its own substance naturally. From it derives actual knowledge, which is called the word in the soul; this in turn engenders either quietude or will. They owe nothing to any external stimulus but are sempiternal with the soul.[11] In the second place, however, the soul knows what is external to it. Here Wyclif, like FitzRalph and before him the pre-Scotist Augustinians, followed the Aristotelian order of the active and possible intellects to explain the process of knowing. Under the impulsion of the active intellect the species, derived from the senses, is impressed into the mind to produce the possible intellect. It is then rendered into actual knowledge by the active intellect, constituting the word in the soul. As such it is threefold — either of things in their natural state independently of any species or sign, or by means of natural signs or a natural species, which are prior to any language, or by means of signs which are spoken or written. Such knowledge in turn engenders love of knowledge and disposes a man to love God.[12] Despite Wyclif's use of Aristotelian terminology, his emphasis is essentially Augustinian, being placed on the state of the soul both in its cognitive power through the word and in its moral inclinations, which he treats as inseparable.[13] Similarly he posits a parallel order for knowledge of sensory objects to that for the soul's knowledge of itself. In the case of the former their material images in the imagination are stored in the memory as intelligible species from which the mind can recognize them by an act of memory and know what exists outside it.[14] The soul's faculties therefore operate as a paradigm of the uncreated trinity.[15] To demonstrate this has been the object of all Wyclif's discussion. Perfunctory though it is, it leaves no doubt about its directly Augustinian antecedents.

When we turn to the wider consideration of the place of knowledge in matters of faith, there is a similar sense of unity between the natural and the supernatural. From it, however, Wyclif draws conclusions which go beyond St. Augustine or most Augustinians. They are characterized by a confidence in the certainty of natural knowledge which springs principally from his realism. In *De Trinitate* it does not take the extreme form to be found in other parts of the *Summa de Ente*. Instead he employs the notion of being to explain the relation of the divine persons to the divine essence and to define the status of the signs or terms which apply to the trinity. This in turn bears directly upon how Wyclif regards the role of reason, and finally what can be said about God. Let us examine each of these aspects.

As is well known, Wyclif believed that all signs to be true must correspond to what is. In taking up this position Wyclif was putting himself in a minority of little more than one against the prevailing terminist orthodoxy. As he expressed it in his treatise, "Therefore they are foolishly deceived who think that the philosophers understand universals as verbal expressions or merely conventions of human signs. . . . every subject denotes itself because some accident inheres in any subject, and every accident denotes its subject, as has been said. Therefore a subject is denoted by its accident. . . . And in the same way anything denotes anything."[16] From this standpoint Wyclif rejected any distinction between a signification and what was signified. On the contrary, whatever existed in the world was a sign in appropriate degree.[17] A sign was designed to denote a certain thing according to human convention, whether by words or writing. The supreme sign was God, and after him the genera or essences of things described naturally. Here as elsewhere Wyclif posited a threefold gradation of created being: the lowest was that of accidents, which existed in virtue of their subject and not in their own right; next came the universal, as genus or species, by means of which individuals were defined; finally, highest of all, was the form making things intrinsically good, which means the inherence in them of the word as first principle. The latter seems here to have the same role as the *esse intelligibile*,[18] the uncreated archetype from which all being derives and which is eternally present in God's being. It establishes God's participation in creation and the direct analogy between created and uncreated signs, which we have earlier considered. The same conception of being led Wyclif to explain the distinction between the divine essence and the divine persons as that between the universal and the individual.[19] For the same reason syllogisms about the trinity, such as "All the divine nature is the son; every father is the divine nature; therefore every father is the son," can be resolved as soon as they are seen to refer to universals; they are thus true and necessary.[20] It is upon this basis of universals that Wyclif saw the harmony between faith and reason.

As we have mentioned earlier, Wyclif accepted faith as the prerequisite of all theological understanding and the foundation of all the virtues. He defined faith in traditional terms as firm adherence to any truth to which God inclines a creature's assent. Accordingly such understanding of anything, whether by intuition or reason, presupposes God's authority as its cause. As St. Paul said, without faith it is impossible to be pleasing to God.[21] Its disposition resides primarily in the will since it must be voluntary. Although faith is concerned with what is not seen, that did not mean that what was believed could not also be apparent. Indeed, Wyclif asserted that insofar as something was believed it constituted knowledge in the light of faith, albeit *in enigmate*.[22] He therefore saw them as complementary. The thing believed stood at once in the light of natural reason and in the light of faith, since the means by which it was known as true was also the light in which it was seen. Each was proportional to the other.[23] Otherwise Wyclif could not see how any rational creature could know at all.[24]

Now Wyclif had two reasons for putting such trust in natural reason. The first was that of Aristotle, that first truths were demonstrable *a posteriori*, that is syllogistically. By that means Wyclif clearly believed that God's own existence could be proved from the argument of a first unmoved mover. Indeed Wyclif first puts forward this proof near the opening of his treatise, quoting the authority of Augustine, Anselm, Grosseteste, Richard, and Hugh of St. Victor for treating syllogistically the articles of faith as naturally demonstrable; he later repeats the same argument of an unmoved mover.[25] At this level Wyclif was basing himself upon the Aristotelian theory of demonstration which Grosseteste had elaborated in his Commentary on the *Posterior Analytics* and which had become one of the hallmarks of the Oxford school during the thirteenth and fourteenth centuries.[26] Wyclif only cites Grosseteste's Commentary once, for he was not concerned with his predecessor's elaboration of demonstrative method as both deductive and inductive. But he attaches comparable importance to formal demonstration to establish the truth.

Where he does show an even greater affinity with Grosseteste and the entire Augustinian tradition is in his second ground for the validity of natural knowledge: namely, that the created mind knows in the supernatural light which is from God. By that means every truth is knowable demonstratively.[27] Their conjunction moreover once more forms a trinity, giving rise to faith or the disposition to assent to universal truths, for which the natural light of reason would not alone suffice. Like so many thinkers before him Wyclif took the same analogies of the sun and the moon and the stars to describe the different kinds of light belonging to the divine, the natural and infused faith.[28] Since, also, faith is the foundation of all knowledge, it follows that when a second cause — i.e., a creature — gives assent to a truth, God must move it to do so; and this act of belief, which takes place through an internal movement from God, is meritorious. For Wyclif it is evidence that here as everywhere else there is one principle to which everything is reducible as the measure of all things.[29]

Not surprisingly, then, he regards reason as a positive aid to faith. That is the main theme of the *De Trinitate*, and of Wyclif's outlook as a whole. At this stage, however, he still conceived their relation in exclusively speculative terms as they bore upon the truths of theology.

Within the present context its purpose is to give evidence of the uncreated trinity through its created signs, united as they are by the essences which derive from the archetypes in God. Even the pure philosopher by an examination of the evidence can elicit which part of an alternative is the more probable. In the case of the trinity Wyclif held that the reasons in support of its truth were more evident and plausible than their contrary to anyone who philosophised correctly, whether believer or infidel.[30] This can be seen both from the kinds of evidence that can be had for the articles of faith and from the terms which are used to describe God. So far as the first are concerned, there is not just one kind of evidence or one way in which we recognize it. At one extreme there was the natural knowledge which we have of natural things as well as the valid deductions by a syllogism to which man had to assent in a purely natural light. This held as much for the infidel, nurtured in logic, as for the believer, so that in Wyclif's view the unbeliever was no less bound than the believer to accept the arguments for the soul as a trinity.[31] In the same way there are numerous other conclusions which hold independently of their treatment as articles of faith; therefore these too do not require more than natural assent. Conversely there are propositions which depend on neither natural reason nor faith, and hence lack evidence altogether, such as the statement that God does not exist, or that something can be and not be. Accordingly, something can only be accepted in proportion to its evidence.[32]

The evidence for faith was not therefore exclusively of one kind. If we only saw it as through a glass darkly in this world, we nevertheless saw it in the mind's eye. Every kind of light was germane to faith. Accordingly, it was wrong to reject what was not evident exclusively in one light as inevident. There was the evidence from testimony of miraculous signs and from authority which made the unseen become seen.[33] Miracles indeed led naturally to adherence to faith. Even should grace or faith be afterwards infused, this did not alter the fact that the initial movement had taken place naturally.[34]

By the same token much that we hold on faith is known in the light of natural reason; for example, the proposition that "every statement of which God is the author must be believed; therefore every article of faith is to be believed." We accept the major premise as deduced by natural reason from the truth that it is necessary for God to know everything infallibly and that he cannot lie. The minor draws on natural evidence derived from facts such as that miracles are beyond the ordinary course of nature. It is this very power of natural reason which enables the mind to know universals and so reach universal truth.[35] For Wyclif man was naturally ordained to know such truths, for man's end was the felicity which consisted in contemplating the verities of faith.[36] Its meritorious attainment in this world would be succeeded by the reward of the clear vision in the next world.[37] It is only sin which prevents man from inclining to faith by making him blind to its truth; but such a defect is itself extraneous to his true nature. For that reason man was not bound to believe solely on the authority of Catholic faith. Here Wyclif cited Hugh of St. Victor's statement that Adam and Eve in their state of innocence had had intuitive infused faith.[38] This constituted one of the three ways in which faith could be held, the others being through the senses or by probable conjecture. Since in his original condition there was no one who could verbally instruct Adam, God at that time instructed both humans and angels by means of internal inspiration and not by words transmitted sensibly. But men can also be naturally convinced of truths like the Incarnation and other articles of faith from the working of miracles. Thus, even fallen man can with effort be brought to know them without infused faith; not to be able to do is a great penalty which goes against man's nature. Hence reason complements faith.[39]

Indeed Wyclif regarded them as inseparable; some degree of faith is inherent in all knowledge, for no one can know unless he also believes in what he knows. This applies not only to the articles of faith but to natural facts such as the existence of Rome as a city. We can know of it without either intuitive, i.e., direct, experience or a process of reasoning. Hence such knowledge is a species of faith and *e converso*.[40] Any intuitive knowledge presupposes a similar prior disposition which in no way derogates from faith, as can be seen from the example of St. Paul or the Apostles, each of whom believed intuitively before seeing evidence for God.[41] Accordingly Wyclif concludes that intuitive knowledge is compounded of sensation and credulity, which precedes faith as such, because faith also includes denying what does not belong to it. Thus faith is properly consonant with clear knowledge;[42] as a quality in its own right it does not exist accidentally.[43]

Faith, then, is the result of man's inner light moving the intellect to assent to what it experiences intuitively through the senses. It goes beyond the knowledge of the object deposited as an image in the mind.[44] Consequently, it is possible for a theologian to demonstrate that God is triune; his syllogism will give knowledge which was previously lacking, for it is founded upon adherence to infallible truth. What begins from authority becomes fuller knowledge through the agency of reason.[45] Man can therefore believe that he is demonstrating what is necessary; for he possesses within him images and traces of God's truth which are naturally demonstrable. Hence to establish conclusions about matters of faith is not of the same order as in the case of natural phenomena, for we can be in error over the latter, whereas what belongs to faith is necessarily true. It therefore does not demand the same dependence upon all media as in a natural demonstration.[46]

Wyclif has accordingly sought to show where faith and reason converge while reserving for faith what is distinctive to it. By making it accessible to natural experience in its different modes he has allowed reason a far fuller role in theology than the majority of medieval thinkers have.

Finally, there is the question of what can be said about God's nature other than that he is a trinity. Only in heaven can we have direct intuition of him. What belongs to this world is an imperfect and indistinct knowledge, inferior to that which we have of sensible objects.[47]

Wyclif thinks it probable that in our present condition there is no name for God which enables us to describe him directly, because every common name applies to many things; hence it signifies not only God but also inferior beings which come under it. In the same way, any singular term denotes the specific properties of that which it designates; but we can now know God only abstractly — a mode which does not provide pure knowledge of him. Accordingly we only seize God indirectly, in proportion to our own knowledge. Thus the name God does not primarily signify an uncreated being or indeed that God is first being, although God is absolutely necessarily such a being. Such simple terms as "first being," "highest good," and so on, do not express God primarily. For that they must be composite, including also negative aspects; as, for example, the term "uncaused being," which connotes a being which cannot be better. For that reason God is treated analogically — and not purely univocally — from a comparison with what exists in creation.[48] All such divine attributes as God's knowledge, will, ordinance, refer principally to his relation to his creatures and not primarily to his own nature.[49] Accordingly what we can say of God is from the aspect of creation in contradistinction to God's own simple nature. Although Ockham and his disciples had also reached a similar conclusion about the divine names, Wyclif differed from them in investing these terms with reality, namely, in referring to what actually existed. The abstract concepts that we could form of anything signifiable referred to what was signified, as we have seen earlier.[50]

This examination has shown the close connexion between Wyclif's conception of being, knowledge, and faith conceived within an Augustinian framework. The universality of essence, and the unity between the natural and the supernatural flowing from it, led him to treat them as complementary. Already he was going further — in finding a rational support for revealed truth — than most of his predecessors. Within a few years his notion of being and the certainty it gave to scripture was to become absolute.

NOTES

1. E.g., J. A. Robson, *Wyclif and the Oxford Schools* (Cambridge, 1961); G. A. Benrath, *Wyclif's Bibel-Kommentar* (Berlin, 1966); G. Leff, *Heresy in the Later Middle Ages*, Vol. II (Manchester, 1967), pp. 494–558; and bibliographies in these works; and B. Smalley, "The Bible and Eternity: John

Wyclif's Dilemma," *Journal of the Warburg and Courtauld Institutes*, 27 (1965), 73–89.

2. Johannis Wyclif, *Tractatus de Trinitate*, ed. A. du P. Breck (Boulder, Colorado, 1962), to which all references belong.

3. J. A. Robson, *op. cit.*, 133. For a discussion of the work's place in Wyclif's *Summa de Ente, ibid.*, 122 ff.

4. Necesse est animam intellectivam esse trinam propter tres res, scilicet memoriam, racionem, et voluntatem, quarum quelibet est essencia eadem singularis. Sed illa non potest esse trina nisi natura divina ipsam exemplans sit trina cum par sit ratio utrobique; igitur natura divina est trina [*De Trinitate*, pp. 2–3].

5. Cf. Robson, *op. cit.*, especially, pp. 141–95. Also my *Heresy in the Later Middle Ages*, Vol. II, pp. 500–516.

6. *De Trinitate*, p. 3.

7. Proporcionabile vero habet quelibet natura completa ut corpus habet materiam loco potencie, memorie, vel mentis recipientis, et habet formam loco rationis, noticie, vel sapiencie, et habet unionem istorum adiuncto loco voluntatis, amoris, vel quietacionis delectantis. Et sicut tres res increate sunt eadem essencia singularis, sic materia, forma, et composicio sunt eadem essencia singularis [*ibid.*, 61]. Also, *ibid.*, 68–69.

8. *Ibid.*, 64, 68–69.

9. See my *Richard FitzRalph, Commentator of the "Sentences"* (Manchester, 1963), pp. 23 f., 82 ff.

10. *De Trinitate*, pp. 67–68.

11. *Ibid.*, 71.

12. *Ibid.*, 70.

13. Et ista cogitacio est notabilis mihi quo ad philosophiam naturalem vel moralem et quo ad intellectum Augustini [*ibid.*, 71].

14. *Ibid.*, 70.

15. E.g., *ibid.*, 9.

16. *Ibid.*, 45. My rendering of the passage is fairly free.

17. Ad primum dicitur quod quelibet res mundi est signum in gradu suo. Nec est distincio entis in opposita per signum et signatum [*ibid.*, 47].

18. *Ibid.*, 60.

19. *Ibid.*, 143.

20. *Ibid.*, 129.

21. *Ibid.*, 22.

22. *Ibid.*, 24.

23. Stat enim simul videre rem creditam in lumine naturali et in lumine fidei quia sine dubio vis in qua cognoscitur veritas est lumen in quo videtur, et de quanto cognoscitur, de tanto est evidenter cognitum per evidenciam proporcionalem [*ibid.*, 24].

24. *Ibid.*

25. *Ibid.*, 2 and 31. E.g., "Sufficit enim ad demonstracionem naturalem quod a signo vel a posteriori in natura regulariter syllogistice deducatur conclusio necessaria, cui assentitur plene per talem deduccionem. Aliter enim non demonstraret naturalis philosophus deum esse per motum celi, ut signum naturale inducens in eius noticiam. Non enim est racio signanda quare ista

est demonstracio naturalis. Impossible est aliquid moveri nisi moveatur ab alio; sed mundus iste necessario movetur; ergo necesse est ipsum moveri ab alio . . . igitur necesse est primum motorem esse quem deum dicimus" (*ibid.*, 2).

26. For an account, see A. C. Crombie, *Robert Grosseteste and the Origins of Experimental Science* (Oxford, 1953).

27. Ymmo ut credo omnis veritas est demonstracione noscibilis cum iuvamine luminis supernaturalis [*De Trinitate*, p. 31].

28. *Ibid.*, 6.

29. *Ibid.*, 32.

30. *Ibid.*, 95.

31. *Ibid.*, 4.

32. Ideo impossibile est aliquid quidquam distinctum ab eo videre sine proporcionali evidencia [*ibid.*, 5].

33. *Ibid.*

34. *Ibid.*, 7.

35. *Ibid.*, 6–7.

36. nam viator est ordinatus naturaliter ad cognoscendum in via huiusmodi veritates. Sed natura nihil ordinat nisi quod naturaliter potest esse; igitur potest esse quod viator cognoscat naturaliter huiusmodi veritates. Assumptum patet ex hoc, quod finis ad quem naturaliter ordinatur homo est felicitas que consistit in contemplacione fidei veritatum [*ibid.*, 9].

37. *Ibid.*

38. *Ibid.*, 11.

39. *Ibid.*, 11–12.

40. Sic enim cognoscimus Romam esse civitatem et multa talia que non naturali racione convincimus nec intuemur; cum ergo talis noticia sit una species fidei . . . sequitur quod concomitata est noticia intuitiva tamquam prius ea naturaliter [*ibid.*, 12].

41. *Ibid.*, 12.

42. *Ibid.*, 13.

43. *Ibid.*, 14.

44. *Ibid.*, 15.

45. *Ibid.*

46. *Ibid.*, 16.

47. *Ibid.*, 113.

48. *Ibid.*, 115–16.

49. *Ibid.*, 120.

50. P. 32, above; cf. also *De Trinitate*, p. 114.

A Collection of Decretal Letters
of Innocent III in Bamberg

Stephan Kuttner

THE TWENTY LETTERS of Innocent III in MS. Bamberg Patr. 132 (Q. VI. 42) fol. 110r–118r were briefly identified in 1903 by H. Fischer in his *Katalog*;[1] more recently, the present writer suggested that this collection deserved the attention of canonists as a link in the history of papal decretals.[2]

Bamb. Patr. 132 is a composite manuscript, *saec.* xiii, beginning with Robert of Flamborough's Manual for Confessors (fol. 1–64v), followed by penitential canons based on Burchard's *Corrector* (fol. 65–80v).[3] My knowledge is limited to microfilm reproductions of fol. 81–118r, containing in a formal book hand the text of the seventy constitutions of the IV Lateran Council together with the constitution *Ad liberandam* for the Crusade and the quasi-official notice[4] on the participants of the Council (fol. 81–110r); after which, without any interruption, the same scribe copied the collection of twenty decretal letters from Innocent's years xiii–xviii which we shall call *Collectio Bambergensis secunda*;[5] they alone are our concern here. Notes in a cursive hand on fol. 119 pertain to the conciliar controversies of the fifteenth century. The codex formerly belonged to the cathedral library; beyond this, we have no indications of provenance.

It is obvious that after the promulgation of Pope Innocent III's official collection of decretals — completed during his twelfth year, in the summer of 1209 and commonly known in the schools as *Compilatio tertia* — there existed a practical need for supplementing the official book with decisions and responses from the pope's later years. This need accounts for the private circulation of small collections arranged in a roughly chronological fashion, such as the three interrelated texts which Professor C. R. Cheney analyzed some years ago (*Pragensis, Palatina I,* and *Abrincensis II*).[6] A common core can be isolated in these three, which points to a process of selection of letters from Innocent's years xii and xiii by canonists in the Chancery; this core was subsequently added to in various ways. It is also apparent that these collections are connected, "though in an indeterminate and unproved way," with the *Compilatio quarta,* where most of their material reappears.[7] It has been argued elsewhere[8] that Johannes Teutonicus did not work from the papal registers when he composed this systematic arrangement of Innocent's "new" law — conciliar and extra-conciliar — but from intermediate collections. Texts like those of *Coll. Pragensis* and its relatives must have been available at Bologna.

Bambergensis II presents another intermediate collection of the chronological type, a welcome complement to the *Pragensis* group, with which it has only one decretal in common.[9] It provides the full text of fourteen of the thirty papal letters used in *Comp. IV* that can be definitely dated to the period from December 1210 (*Bamb.* 1: 11 Dec. 1210) to Innocent's eighteenth year.[10] Together with another nine letters from *Coll. Pragen.*[11] this accounts for all but seven decretals of this period in *Comp. IV.*[12] In addition, *Bamb. II* contains three letters (Nos. 9, 12, 14) which are not in *Comp. IV* but later reappeared in the decretals of Gregory IX: presumably Raymond of Peñafort, like our collector, took these from Innocent's registers. Only three of the twenty letters in Bamberg (Nos. 10, 17, 18) did not find their way into any of the standard compilations. No. 10 is otherwise known from the register (*Reg.* xvi. 3: PL 216. 786); Nos. 17 and 18 are printed below: they come from the seventeenth year, for which the register is lost. No other copies seem to exist, although another trace for No. 17 is found in the *Indice* 254 of the Vatican Archives.

The letters of *Bamb. II* present a strictly chronological order. This points to the origin of the collection — not necessarily of its Bamberg copy — in the circles of the Chancery. Also, addresses are in general closer to the register than those of either *Comp. IV* or *Liber Extra.* A few examples must suffice.[13]

> *Bamb.* 1 (*Reg.* xiii. 187) "Innocentius iii. Placentino [Palentino *Reg.*] et Burgensi episcopis et abbati de arnundo [Morimundo *Reg.*] Cistersiensis ordinis" shows some confusion. But Palencia is likewise confused with Piacenza in MSS. of *Comp. IV* and *Extra,* with others (and *Extra ed.*) giving Valencia. "de arnundo" becomes "de ar." in *Comp. IV* and "de N." in *Extra.* *Bamb.* 4 (Reg. xv. 6) "Idem G. [S. *Comp. IV*] de uallibus, magistris [magistro *Reg. Comp. IV Extra*] G. et P. de fumiis [Fimiis *Reg.*] canonicis laudunensibus." "G. de uallibus" omitted in *Extra*; "de fumiis can. laudun." becomes "de Fimiscano," "de Fumiscano," "de Firmisca," etc., in *Comp. IV* and *Extra.*

> *Bamb.* 5 (*Reg.* xv. 118) "Idem lingonensi [Legionensi *Comp. IV*] episcopo"; no address in *Extra*.
> *Bamb.* 8 (*Reg.* xv. 191) "Idem episcopo Gebenensi et Vienensi sacriste": the sacristan of Vienne is either omitted or distorted in *Comp. IV* ("et Vienen. vel Ateste") and *Extra* ("et N. Valentinensi," etc.).[14]
> *Bamb.* 11 (*Reg.* xvi. 26) "Idem Slewirensi [Sleswicensi *Reg.*] episcopo": the several sections appear inscribed to "Vicensi" or "Seuicensi" in *Comp. IV*, to "S." or "Senonensi," or without address in *Extra*.
> *Bamb.* 13 (*Reg.* xvi. 118) "Idem archiepiscopo lundensi apostolice sedis legato": in all the sections that appear in *Comp. IV* and *Extra*, Lund is confused with either London or Lyons.
> *Bamb.* 15 and 16 (*Reg.* xvi. 165, 166) "Idem episcopo Wastisslauensi [Wratislaviensi *Reg.*]" and "Idem eidem" reproduce two successive letters of the register; the outlandish name of Wrocław-Breslau is even more disfigured in *Comp. IV* (("Vratismen.," "Veteranen," etc.) and *Extra* ("Veratisamensi").

The texts of the register appear unabridged, with one exception (No. 11, discussed below), as far as the substance of the letters is concerned. Only the conventional, final clauses of chancery usage ("Tu denique, frater episcope . . ."; "Quod si non ambo . . .")[15] are often omitted. The textual quality of the copy is average.[16] Dates are usually in order[17] and given in a slightly shortened form, thus: "Dat'. later. iiii. non. octobris anno xiiii." The fuller ending ". . . pontificatus nostri anno . . ." is written out only once (No. 20). A few dates are omitted or incomplete, but even there the chronological sequence is kept.[18] On the other hand, Nos. 19 and 20 provide dates, from the lost register volumes, that were previously unknown.[19]

As for the date of the collection itself, only a guess is possible. Its last letter (No. 20) was written early in the eighteenth year, 28 March 1215. By contrast, Johannes Teutonicus presented four letters of that year, one from after the close of the Council, while another could be even later.[20] This suggests that *Bamb. II* was completed by the middle of 1215 and that its juxtaposition in the manuscript with the conciliar texts of IV Lateran means no more than that it was convenient to have material of this kind copied into one book. We find the same combination of Council and decretals in the Prague manuscript:[21] yet *Coll. Pragen.* certainly was not composed after Innocent's sixteenth year, of which it includes one letter only.[22]

A single fact could be construed as possibly indicating a post-conciliar origin of *Bamb. II*: No. 11 (Potth. 4722), addressed to the bishop of Schleswig, omits after its third section ("Cimeteria uero") the short piece "Procurationes autem — impendis" (PL 216. 815c2–5), the concluding chancery formula "Tu denique, frater episcope . . . ," and the date. The same omission occurs in *Comp. IV* and *Liber Extra*.[23] Already Baluze observed that this rule on *procurationes* is also found in *IV Later*. c. 33 = *Extra* 3. 39. 23 (*IV Comp.* 3. 18. 2).[24] It stands to reason that *Comp. IV* and *Extra* omitted the clause on *procurationes* in Potth. 4722 in order to avoid repetition.

Reg. xvi. 26	*IV Conc. Later.* c. 33
Procurationes autem quae visitationis ratione debentur, sine manifesta et necessaria causa non exigas, nisi cum personaliter officium visitationis impendis.[25]	Procurationes que ratione uisitationis debentur episcopis, archidiaconis uel quibuslibet aliis, etiam apostolice sedis legatis aut nuntiis, absque manifesta et necessaria causa non exigantur, nisi quando personaliter officium uisitationis impendunt . . .[26]

If the same reasoning is applied to *Bamb. II*, it would argue for composition after the Council. But differently from Johannes Teutonicus — and, later, from St. Raymond of Peñafort — our compiler nowhere else shows any interest in "editing" his texts. He does not shun repetitious material, as can be seen in No. 17 (printed below): thus there exists no conclusive argument for a post-conciliar origin. The inclusion of only one letter an. xviii points rather in the opposite direction.

As for the person or persons who compiled or commissioned *Bamb. II*, it may be tempting to look for clues among the addressees of the letters, in particular of those that are *unica*. But once we admit that the source of our collection must be a choice of texts made in the Chancery, any argument is fallacious in which the accidental loss of a given register volume makes some letters appear — today — as though they came from another source, such as a recipient's archives. For this reason it is inadmissible to deduce, for instance, specific Scandinavian connections from the fact that No. 17, to the archbishop of Lund, is not preserved anywhere else and that *Bamb. II* contains another letter to the same archbishop and one to the bishop of Schleswig (Nos. 11, 13). Like these two letters, No. 17 was once contained in the register (xvii. 6); and with the same logic one could postulate French connections because No. 10, to the archbishop of Reims (Potth.

4678), is not contained in other compilations, and several other letters of *Bamb. II* are addressed to French prelates (Nos. 4, 5, 7, 9, 14, 19).[27] As for the other *unicum*, No. 18, it is true that we have no date and no positive indication that it was ever enregistered; moreover it is the only letter which would seem out of place in a collection of decretals, being a piece of strictly theological teaching. Still, its position between two letters of the seventeenth year makes it unlikely that it should have been copied from a source other than the Chancery records, let alone the difficulty of finding an unequivocal solution for the garbled address "episcopo Ketinensi."

In conclusion, we may classify *Bamb. II* as representing a selection of decretals chosen from the registers by a curial canonist early in the eighteenth year of Innocent III. It adds two pieces to our knowledge of the Innocentian corpus; it adds in no small way to our knowledge of the stuff from which the *Compilatio quarta* was made.

CONCORDANCE OF COLLECTIONS AND PAPAL REGISTER

BAMB.	REG.	DATE	POTTH.	4 COMP.	EXTRA	INCIPIT AND EXPLICIT
1	xiii. 187	1210 Dec. 11	4143	5. 14. 1	5. 38. 10	Noua quedam — celorum commisit.
2	xiv. 107	1211 Oct. 4	4312	5. 6. 4	5. 12. 20	Sicut ex tenore — officio abstinere.
3	xiv. 140	1212 Jan. 10	4360	3. 3. 2	3. 8. 5	Postulasti per sedem — non debet.
4	xv. 6	1212 Mar. 2	4400	1. 2. 2	1. 3. 25	Olim ex litteris — plena fides.
5 (a)	xv. 118	1212 Jun. 7	4523	—	5. 6. 14	Postulasti per sedem — commercia exercere.
(b)	”	”	”	—	—	Consequenter quesiuisti — sustentandum.
(c)	”	”	”	3. 10. 1	3. 31. 21	Tertio quesiuisti — mutare.
6	xv. 162	1212 Sep. 18	4598	5. 12. 3	5. 23. 20	Petisti per sedem — licentia abbatis.
7	xv. 166	1212 Oct. 7	4603	3. 14. 1	3. 40. 6	Ligneis edificiis — denuo consecrari.

BAMB.	REG.	DATE	POTTH.	4 COMP.	EXTRA	EXPLICIT INCIPIT AND
8 (a)	xv. 191	1212 Dec. 20	4628	5. 1. 4	5. 1. 21	Inquisitionis negotium — facere presumatur.
(b)	"	"	"	"	"	Quesiuisti preterea — non existit.
9	xv. 202	1213 Jan. 9	4641	—	5. 39. 45	Contingit interdum — noscitur instituta.
10	xvi. 3	1213 Mar. 14	4678	—	—	Etsi apostolatus — prouocet ultionem.
11 (a)	xvi. 26	1213 Apr. 29	4722	2. 2. 3	2. 2. 14	Postulasti per sedem — facienda.
(b)	"	"	"	"	5. 12. 21	Quesiuisti preterea — duricie imputandum.
(c)	"	"	"	3. 15. 1	3. 40. 7	Cimeteria uero — dedicationibus consueuit.
12	xvi. 93	1213 Aug. 8	4789	—	3. 34. 10	Per tuas nobis — de te factum
13 (a)	xvi. 118	1213 Oct. 3	4820	1. 10. 1	1. 21. 6	Quia circa minima — curauerint continenter.
(b)	"	"	"	—	—	De presbyterorum uero — quod pretendunt.
(c)	"	"	"	5. 15. 1	—	Quesiuisti preterea — exegerit clericorum.
(d)	"	"	"	5. 12. 5	5. 33. 22	Subsequenter etiam — set et futuri.
(e)	"	"	"	—	—	Sane quia contingit — sit subortum.
(f)	"	"	"	—	4. 14. 6	Porro de nobili — scandalum imminere.
14	xvi. 158	1214 Jan. 2	4869	—	5. 34. 16	Accepimus litteras — nostris expressam.
15	xvi. 165	1214 Jan. 8	4873	1. 2. 4	1. 3. 27	Postulasti per sedem — litteris mentionem.

BAMB.	REG.	DATE	POTTH.	4 COMP.	EXTRA	INCIPIT AND EXPLICIT
16	xvi. 166	1214 Jan. 8	4974	3. 2. 3	3. 5. 26	Vacante in quadam — beneficio competenti.
17	(xvii. 6)	1214 Mar. 1	—	—	—	Tua nos duxit — uiderimus expedire.
18	—	(1214 Mar./ Nov.)	—	—	—	Auditis litteris — minime contradicant.
19	—	1214 Nov. 11	—	2. 1. 2	2. 25. 5	Cum inter dilectos — materiam extendatur.
20	(xviii. .)	1215 Mar. 28	5038	5. 7. 1	5. 19. 16	Salubriter conscientie — matrimonii supportanda.

NOTES ON THE CONCORDANCE

The main characteristics of *Bamb. II* as regards addresses, text, and dates have been indicated in the opening pages. A full apparatus of readings should not be expected here; the following notes are only meant to give some information on letters or portions of letters that do not appear in *Comp. IV* and *Extra*. The two letters that were previously unknown will be edited in the end.

Bamb. 5 (b) shows no significant variants from the text as printed in PL 216. 630c5–12. The section deals with a person "qui se falso episcopum asserens altaria consecrauit et alia plura exercuit que ad officium pertinent presulatus." The bishop of Langres is to declare all these acts invalid "et ipsum perpetuo carceri facias mancipari, pane doloris et aqua angustie sustentandum": a penal clause which Innocent used also in Potth. 4683 (*Reg.* xvi. 10, PL 216. 794) and which echoes 3 Regum 22: 27 (cf. Baluze's note col. 630 *ad loc.*).[28]

Bamb. 10: text as in PL 216. 786; a mandate to the archbishop of Reims and his suffragans to suppress the evil practice of blasphemous oaths: many persons in France "non solum per diuinos manus et pedes iurare non metuunt, uerum etiam ipsius Christi et sanctorum eius secretiora membra lingua sacrilega perscrutantes, ea non formidant intimare iurando que nos scribendo sumus ueriti nominare."

Bamb. 13: full text as in the register, printed in PL 216. 914–16 and *Diplomat. Danicum,* I, 5, pp. 58–60 (No. 37). *Comp. IV* and *Extra* omit the final clause, "si uiuere curauerint continenter" of section (a), as well as section (b), in which Innocent cites the rule that priests' sons may not be ordained, except in monastic or regular houses, "ex decreto Urbani ii." (D. 65 cc. 1, 11) and "ex concilio Pictauensi" (*I Comp.* 1. 9. 1 = *Extra* 1. 17. 1), and continues: "de presbyteris autem Suethie certum non possumus dare responsum, nisi uiderimus priuilegium quod pretendunt" (PL 216. 914c10–915a1; *Dipl. Dan.* p. 58. 14–19). The two compilations also omit section (e), which deals with the denunciation of marriages concluded within the forbidden degrees of kindred (PL 216. 915c1–916a1; *Dip. Dan.* p. 59. 15–24); here, the old editions of the register disfigured the rare term *iuramentalis* (compurgator, oath-helper) in the passage "ad denominationem iuramentalium [iumentalium *Reg. ed.*], ut tuis uerbis utamur, procedere . . ."; cf. Skyum-Nielsen, *Dipl. Dan.* p. 57 (introd. to No. 37). The word obviously was unfamiliar to Innocent III; it is therefore interesting to note that the only instances listed by DuCange occur in the *Liber legis Scaniae,* i.e., the Latin version which Archbishop Anders Sunesen of Lund (1201–24; d. 1228) made of the old *Skånske Lov* (*Skånelag*),[29] and that the prelate to whom Pope Innocent wrote about "the appointment of *iuramentales,* to use your expression," should be none but Archbishop Anders.

Bamb. 19, from the lost register an. xvii, provides the address and the date that are lacking in the compilations: "Idem abbati monasterii noui, ph. decano et ph. subdiacono Pictauiensibus. Cum inter . . . Dat. later. iii. Jdus nou. anno xvii." (The inscription "Idem monachis Farfensibus" in the Roman edition of *Extra* 2. 25. 5 is not borne out by manuscripts but due to aberration from c. 6 *ibid.*: see Friedberg's note 2 *ad loc.*) The readings of *Bamb.* generally are closer to *Comp. IV* than to Raymond's text, but at one point *Bamb.* ". . . coram nobis et dil'. n̄." badly distorts the original "coram uobis ex delegatione nostra" which the compilations have preserved.[30]

Bamb. 20, to the bishop-elect of Otranto, likewise presents a previously unknown date; it also gives us the stilted first sentence, which was cut short ("Salubriter, et infra") in the compilations. *Bamb.*: "Idem electo Ydrotinensi.[31] Salubriter conscientie tue consulis sedem apostolicam in dubiis consulendo, que se consulentibus non inconsulte consulere consueuit. Sane generum . . . matrimonii supportanda. Tu denique et cet. Dat. later. kal. aprilis anno pontificatus nostri octauo decimo."

NEW TEXTS

Bamb. 17

Idem Lundonensi archiepiscopo apostolice sedis legato. [1] Tua nos duxit fraternitas consulendos utrum,[a] cum homines prouincie tue proni sint ad periuria et testes aut instrumenta[b] de more terre examinari non consueuerint[c] et uix absque animarum periculo coniugia inter eos qui se in quinto consanguinitatis uel quarto affinitatis gradu contingunt possint rescindi contracta, utrum tibi dissimulare liceat coniugia quinti gradus, si uideris inter eos unanimem cohabitationis consensum aut ex diuortio periculum imminere. [2] Quesiuisti etiam utrum illi presbyteri qui duas successiue focarias habuerunt irregulares existunt, ut cum eis in executione officii ualeas dispensare si promiserint celibatum. [3] Et utrum monachi Omnium Sanctorum uti ualeant priuilegio bone memorie E. predecessoris tui ad episcopales decimas retinendas de possessionibus acquirendis sicut et illo tempore acquisitis; [4] quasdam tam super matrimoniis quam presbyterorum filiis ac dispensatione super matrimonio inter Necui. et N. uxorem eius contracto, falsa[d] suggestione obtenta, et comitatu Alsatie adiciens questiones. [5] Nos ergo fraternitati tue taliter respondemus quod, cum tuam in proximo expectemus presentiam ad concilium generale, supersedendum duximus id ad presens, quoniam auctore Domino super hiis et aliis plenius instrueris. [6] Preterea quesiuisti utrum,[e] cum homines[f] ipsius regni Suetie censum apostolice sedis, prohibente ipsorum rege, tibi iuxta mandatum nostrum soluere non curant, nitentes per census subtractionem ab obedientie iugo subtrahere semetipsos, utrum ipsorum excessus, ne rex Datie offendatur in offensa predicti regis, cum sit ei affinitate coniunctus, debeas tolerare uel in eos censuram ecclesiasticam exercere. [7] Ad hoc autem fraternitati tue taliter respondemus ut, cum tu regni Suetie primas existas, censum sedis apostolice firmiter exigas et diligentia exquisita procures ut census preteriti temporis integre persoluatur et in futuri solutione non adhibeatur aliqua difficultas; [8] Vbsalensem archiepiscopum et episcopos regni illius sollicite commonens et diligenter exhortans et, si necesse fuerit, per censuram ecclesiasticam appellatione remota[g] compellens ut ad concilium ueniant generale, in quo auctore Domino super premissis et aliis statuemus quod uiderimus expedire. Tu denique et cet. Dat'. Rome apud s. Petrum kal. martii anno xvii.[h]

[a] ū *Cod.*   [b] iuramenta *Cod.*   [c] consueuerunt *Cod.*   [d] *leg.* falsi ?   [e] ut *Cod.*
[f] homines *om. Cod.*   [g] ap. se. *Cod.*   [h] xvi. *Cod.* (*sed vide infra in commento*)

Bamb. 18

Idem episcopo Ketinensi. Auditis litteris tuis et intellectis que dilectus filius abbas Casemarij proposuit coram nobis, fraternitati uestre breuiter respondemus quod credendum est pariter et docendum sanctorum animas etiam ante iudicii diem in celo regnare cum Christo, ad quod probandum inter alia testimonia scripturarum, que pro multitudine subticemus, sufficere potest quod Dauid legitur prophetasse de Deo, "Ascendens in altum captiuam duxit captiuitatem." [a] Ipse quidem descendens ad inferos [b] in sanguine testamenti sui uinctos suos emisit de lacu in quo non erat aqua,[c] captiuitatem illam sanctorum ducens in altum captiuitatem [d] captiuam. Haut dubium quin in celum, ubi est ad dexteram Dei sedens. Vnde cum per mortem eius ianua uite sit aperta, dubitare te nolumus quin, etiam cum nunc patrie porta sit reserata, talium anime a peccatorum nexibus et penarum uinculis absolute in celum cum Christo regnature transmigrent, quemadmodum desiderat Apostolus dicens, "Cupio dissolui et esse cum Christo." [e] Quecumque igitur auctoritates aliud forsitan innuere uideantur, ita sunt exponende ut huic sentencie minime contradicent. Dat'. lateran'.

[a] c. d. c. *Cod.*—*Ephes. 4:8 (ex Ps. 67:19)*   [b] *cf. Ephes. 4:9*   [c] *cf. Zach. 9:11*
[d] captiuitate *Cod.*   [e] *cf. Phil. 1:23*

NOTES ON THE NEW TEXTS

Bamb. 17 (fol. 116v–117r), to Archbishop Anders Sunesen of Lund, is recorded in *Indice* 254 of the Vatican Archives as c. 6 of an. xvii:[32] "In primis quod archiepiscopus Lundensis est primas regni Suetie. Vt legitur 'Tua nos' etc." Accordingly, the date of *Bamb.* (". . . anno xvi.") has been corrected above. 1 March 1214 (not 1213) is also required by the reference to the archbishop's presence at the future General Council, the summons to which had gone out only on 19 April 1213 (Potth. 4706).

The letter, which we have divided for convenience into eight sections, consists of two main parts. Sections 1–4 recite a number of queries to which the pope proposes to reply later when the archbishop will be in Rome (section 5). In the second part (sections 6–8) the pope turns to matters on which he prefers to give immediate instructions. Now it is very strange that the first four sections repeat queries which Innocent III had, for the most part, already answered on 3 October

1213 in his decretal letter Potth. 4820, our No. 13, "Quia circa minima"
(= Q):[33]

> Sec. 1 "Tua nos — imminere": though differently formulated, *Bamb.*
> *13* (e) likewise deals with the problem whether to proceed or not to
> proceed against marriages among *consanguinei* and *affines* (see
> notes on No. 13 *supra*); Q 59. 15–24.
> Sec. 2 "Quesiuisti — celibatum": cf. *Bamb. 13* (a); Q 58. 4–7, 11–
> 14; *Extra* 1. 21. 6.
> Sec. 3 "Et utrum monachi — acquisitis": cf. *Bamb. 13* (d); Q 59.
> 5–14; *Extra* 5. 33. 22. The "predecessor E." is Archbishop Eskil,
> 1138–77.
> Sec. 4 "quasdam tam super matrimoniis": no parallel in Q.
> ——— "quam presbyterorum filiis": cf. *Bamb. 13* (b); Q 58. 7,
> 14–17; see notes on No. 13 *supra*.
> ——— "ac dispensatione — obtenta": cf. *Bamb. 13* (f); Q 59. 25–
> 60. 3; *Extra* 4. 14. 6.
> ——— "et comitatu Alsatie": no problem concerning the county
> of Holstein is mentioned in Q.

Have we to do, then, with two papal responses to one inquiry, because
of inefficiency in chancery procedures? Or did Archbishop Anders not
receive the first letter (Potth. 4820) and therefore write again to Rome?
One can only speculate on this, and on the reasons for the pope's
almost brusque refusal (sec. 5) to enter into the substance of the questions from Lund. It is a most unusual reply for Pope Innocent, who
always loved to teach in his decretals — especially if we consider that
the Lateran Council, at which the archbishop would "soon" (*in proximo*) receive his instructions, was still twenty months away.

In the opening of the second part (sec. 6) emendation of the text
was required by grammar and borne out by the parallelism with the
sentence structure of section 1.[34] Collection of Peter's Pence (*census
apostolice sedis*) in Denmark and Sweden was the responsibility of
Lund ever since Paschal II had raised the see to metropolitan rank
in 1104;[35] the *mandatum nostrum* in the present text is Innocent's
letter of 6 November 1204 to Archbishop Anders (Potth. 2320).[36] The
actual controversy with King Eric of Sweden over the payment of the
census and its political implications here alluded to ("lest the king of
Denmark take offense") must be left to the investigation of Swedish
church historians;[37] Pope Innocent seems to have returned to the
matter in a lost letter to all the faithful in Schleswig, May or June 1216
(Potth. 5291).[38]

Section 8, "Vbsalensem archiepiscopum . . . ," is an admonition tacked on to the papal response that has nothing to do with the archbishop's inquiry. We can sense how strongly Innocent must have felt about the presence of the Scandinavians at the future council if he sent this reminder to Lund only eight days after his letter of 21 February 1214 (Potth. 4900), in which he had rebuked the archbishop for seeking an excuse from attending and ordered him to convey the papal exhortation also to Upsala and its suffragans.[39] The new letter differs only in that it adds the authority for Archbishop Anders to enforce compliance by ecclesiastical censure.

Nonetheless, attendance from the northern countries was very poor at the Lateran Council. The only extant list gives one bishop *de Dacia*.[40] But it has been argued with good reason[41] that Archbishop Anders, after all, did come to the Council and that he stayed in Rome until the spring of 1216. The *rubricellae* of *Reg. Vat.* 8A for the lost registers an. xviii/xix include the record of a privilege granted to him of collating to the vacant bishopric of Roskilde (Potth. 5289, 5290).[42] On 25 January 1217, Honorius III confirmed this right, which ". . . dudum *cum esses apud sedem apostolicam constitutus*, b. m. Innocentius papa predecessor noster fraternitati tue interuenientibus nobis indulsit" (Potth. 5432).[43] The original indult, with a batch of other letters on Danish matters, belongs to the last months of Innocent III (May/June 1216).[44] By the testimony of Honorius III, the archbishop was then in person at the Curia. It would be unreasonable to assume that this was anything but a continuation of his presence at the Lateran Council.

Bamb. 18 (fol. 117r–v) is undated, but its position in the sequence of letters permits us to assign it to the months between March and November 1214. Identification of the addressee is less certain. The name as written, "episcopo Ketineñ.," would most likely be a misspelling for "Katinensi" — which may mean Catania in Sicily (Gr. *Katanē*) or Caithness in Scotland: the adjectival form *Catinensis* is attested for either of these sees. Pope Innocent's letter gives no clue as to which of the two bishops might have sent the inquiry. Since the abbot of Casamari (in the diocese of Veroli) is mentioned as having spoken before the pope — apparently he was the bearer of the letter of inquiry — one would be inclined to decide for a bishop from the South. On the other hand, an abbot of Casamari (the same?) had been Innocent's legate to France and England in 1203–4.[45] Connections between Scotland and the abbey were at least possible. A year after the present letter, both bishops attended the Lateran Council, according to the only known list of participants,[46] although the Chronicle of Melrose does not mention Bishop Adam of Caithness among the four prelates who traveled from Scotland to Rome *generalis concilii gratia*: he thus would have been one of the *ceteri* who merely sent their proctors.[47]

But whoever was the bishop to whom Innocent III wrote this piece of doctrinal teaching, it deserves the historian's attention. The controversy over the state of the blessed souls prior to the Last Judgment was to erupt into a serious crisis in the days of John XXII, over a hundred years later.[48] The letter of Innocent indicates an early phase of this theological controversy, and an interesting papal effort to resolve it with an uncommon scriptural exegesis.

NOTES

1. H. Fischer, *Katalog der Handschriften der königlichen Bibliothek zu Bamberg*, I, 1. 3 (Bamberg, 1903), p. 520.
2. S. Kuttner, "Notes on Manuscripts," *Traditio*, XVII (1961), 536; *ibid.*, XXIV (1968), 507.
3. *Katalog*, p. 519.
4. See S. Kuttner and A. García y García, "A New Eyewitness Account of the Fourth Lateran Council," *Traditio*, XX (1964), 118, where MSS., editions, and a possible trace in the register are briefly discussed.
5. The well-known *Bambergensis* (see, e.g., W. Deeters, *Die Bambergensis-gruppe der Dekretalensammlungen des 12. Jhdts.*, Bonn, 1956) should henceforth bc called *Bamb. I*.
6. C. R. Cheney, "Three Decretal Collections before Compilatio IV," *Traditio*, XV (1959), 464–83. For the date of completion of *Comp. III*, see S. Kuttner, "Johannes Teutonicus, das vierte Laterankonzil und die Compilatio quarta," *Miscellanea Giovanni Mercati*, V (Studi e Testi, 125; Città del Vaticano, 1946), 621.
7. Cheney, *Trad.*, XV, 469.
8. *Miscell. Mercati*, V, 622.
9. *II Bamb. 8 = II Abr. 1 (IV Comp. 5. 1. 2)*. This decretal is also entered as an addition in the appendix to Rainer of Pomposa, Reims MS. 692, fol. 31v; cf. Kuttner, *Repertorium der Kanonistik* (Studi e Testi, 71; Città del Vaticano, 1937), p. 310; Cheney, *Trad.*, XV, 472, n. 32.
10. A. Potthast, *Regesta Pontificum Romanorum* (Berlin, 1874–75), Nos. 4143 (an. xiii); 4312, 4360 (an. xiv); 4400, 4523, 4598, 4603, 4628 (an. xv); 4722, 4820, 4873, 4874 (an. xvi); *IV Comp. 2. 1. 2* (Potth. —; an. xvii), and Potth. 5038 (an. xviii) = *II Bamb. 1–8, 11, 13, 15, 16, 19, 20*. For details, see the Concordance, *infra*.
11. Potth. 4163, 4164, 4174 (an. xiii); 4195, 4379 (an. xiv); 4401, 4577, 4614

(an. xv); 4844 (an. xvi) = *Prag.* 14, 13, 15, 20, 19, 18, 17, 25, 34; see Cheney's tabulation, *Trad.*, XV, 473–75. It is possible, though unproved, that five more letters, covered by *Coll. Prag.* but undated, equally belong in this time span: Potth. 2360, 5022, 5025, 5028, *IV Comp.* 2. 7. 2 (Potth. —) = *Prag.* 16, 24, 21, 23, 22 (cf. the tabulation and Cheney, pp. 477–78). If so, our figures would be: thirty-five letters, of which fourteen in *II Bamb.* and fourteen in *Prag.*

12. Potth. 4337 (*IV Comp.* 3. 19. 1), 4587 (2. 11. 1), 4847 (3. 2. 3), 4956 (2. 10. 2), 4989 (1. 3. 2), 5009 (5. 5. 1), 5298 (3. 9. 3: an. xviii/xix). This list does not include *IV Comp.* 1. 18. 2, which Potthast 4957 dates 1214–15 (an. xvii): actually the decretal is of uncertain date, perhaps 1208–15 (if the archbishop of Pisa here addressed was Lotharius the Glossator).

13. The readings here given from the registers (*Reg.*) are those of the Migne text in PL; readings of *Comp. IV* and *Liber Extra* are taken from Friedberg's text and apparatus, checked for *Comp. IV* against Antonio Augustín's edition (Lérida, 1576). — *II Bamb.* 3, 5, 9, 12, 14, 16, 20 have no addresses in *Extra*; the address of No. 19, from the lost register an. xvii, was previously unknown (see Notes on the Concordance, *infra*).

14. The address is correct in Reims 692 (n. 9 *supra*), but garbled in *II Abr.* 1: "Innoc. iii. tenm [with suspension marks: cenomanen ?] episcopo et dilecto filio sacriste uianensi."

15. A convenient list of these common forms will be found in C. R. Cheney and Mary G. Cheney, *The Letters of Pope Innocent III (1198–1216) Concerning England and Wales* (Oxford, 1967), pp. 195–96.

16. Some poor readings will be found in the texts edited below; see also Notes on the Concordance for No. 19. The opening word of No. 14 is "Accepimus" as in *Extra* 5. 34. 16, where the register, at least in the edition, has "Recepimus." At No. 4 the rubricator blundered and made "Cum" out of the initial "Olim" of Potth. 4400.

17. The following differ from the registers: No. 1 "iii. idus nouembris [decembris *Reg.*] an. xiii"; No. 7 "non. kal. [non. *Reg.*] octobris an. xv"; No. 9 "v. kal. [v. id. *Reg.*] ianuarii an. xv"; No. 12 "v. [vi. *Reg.*; vii. *Gall. christ.*] id. augusti an. xvi." But it should be remembered that *Reg. Vat.* 8, which covers the years xiii–xvi, is not the original register but a copy made under Urban V (1362–70).

18. Nos. 11, 14, 18 (undated); No. 15, "Dat. Later."; No. 16, "Dat." ("Dat. ut supra" *Reg.*)

19. Notes on the Concordance, *infra*.

20. Potth. 5009 (*IV Comp.* 5. 5. 1) of 14 December 1215; Potth. 5298 (3. 9. 3) an. xviii or xix. The other two are Potth. 5038 (5. 7. 1) = *II Bamb.* 20, and Potth. 4989 (1. 3. 2) of July 1215.

21. Prague, Univ. MS. XXIII. E. 59 (*ol.* Lobkowitz 439), fol. 2r–23v, 24r–45r.

22. *Prag.* 34: Potth. 4844 of 6 November 1213.

23. *IV Comp.* 3. 15. 1, *Extra* 3. 40. 7; both cite the beginning of the letter wrongly as "Consuluisti et infra. Cimeteria . . ." ("Proposuisti" *Reg.*, *Bamb.*).

24. PL 216. 816, notes 37, 38. See also Niels Skyum-Nielsen, *Diplomatarium*

Danicum, Ser. I, Vol. 5: *1211–1223* (Copenhagen, 1957), p. 52, in his introductory note to the critical edition of this letter (No. 33).

25. PL, *ut supra* (Baluze's text); *Diplomat. Danicum* I, 5, p. 54, lin. 3–5 (from the archival tradition, collated with the register).

26. Text established by A. García y García for the forthcoming edition in the *Monumenta Iuris Canonici*. Variant readings in the vulgate editions (from Crabbe to Mansi): lin. 1 "visitationis ratione"; lin. penult. "praesentialiter" (for "personaliter") — noted as a false reading already by Baluze, see PL 216. 816, n. 38. *Comp. IV* and *Extra* agree with the correct readings. (I am indebted to Fr. García for the permission to use his text.)

27. Laon (4), Langres (5, 14), Besançon (7), Thérouanne (9), Poitiers (19).

28. Had Friedberg, in his edition of the *Liber Extra*, been consistent in his efforts to restore the portions of the text omitted by Raymond of Peñafort and by the respective *Compilationes antiquae*, then the text of PL 216. 630c5–12 should have been printed in italics and included in brackets at the end of *Extra* 5. 6. 14. But Friedberg arbitrarily decided to drop all the passages that appear at the end, rather than in the middle of a decretal (cf. his *Prolegomena*, col. xlv). This makes no sense in a case where the "end" actually occurs in the middle of the original text, as here or as in *II Bamb.* 13 (b) and (e), which are likewise bypassed in Friedberg.

29. DuCange, *Glossarium*, IV, 452 col. *b*, s.v. *iuramentum*. See *Lex Scaniae* 5. 6 ". . . testes totidem quam iuramentales"; 6. 10, 13; 7. 4. 9; 15. 3 ". . . et duodecim iuramentalibus"; also 7. 2, 3, 5, 13; 16. 3: ed. P. G. Thorsen, in *Skånske Lov* (Nordiske Oldskrifter, XVIII; Copenhagen, 1854), pp. 133, 155–56, 159–62, 166, 169, 199. I have not seen the edition by S. Aakjaer and E. Kroman in *Danmarks gamle Landskabslove*, I, 2 (Copenhagen, 1933), 467 667. The original title seems to be "Liber legis Scaniae" as in the colophon (p. 204 *ed.*), not "Lex Scaniae provincialis" as chosen by Thorsen.

30. In Antonio Augustín's edition of *IV Comp.* 2. 1. 2 the word "nostra" (not "delegatione nostra," as Friedberg, n. 6 ad *Extra* 2. 25. 5, asserts) is lacking; it is present in the MSS. Also, Friedberg's n. 14 *ad loc.* should be corrected: all MSS. read "debeat," not "abeat."

31. "Ydotonen." and other variants in *IV Comp.* (garbled in *ed.*); no address in *Extra.*

32. A. Haidacher, "Beiträge zur Kenntnis der verlorenen Registerbände Innozenz' III.," *Römische historische Mitteilungen*, IV (1960/61), 58, No. 1 with note 1; cf. Kuttner, *Trad.*, XXIV (1968), 507.

33. Q (= PL 216. 914–16) will be cited here by page and line numbers in Skyum-Nielsen's edition, *Diplomat. Danicum* I, 5, 58–60.

34. Sec. 6 would lack a subject without inserting "homines"; the reading "ut[rum] cum . . . , utrum . . ." is needed in both sections in order to tie together the long recital of facts with the actual question: an unusual sentence structure, perhaps, but an effective one.

35. Ph. Jaffé, *Regesta Pontificum Romanorum* . . . , ed. 2 (Berlin, 1885–88), No. 6335; for text and date see P. Fabre and L. Duchesne, *Le Liber Censuum de l'Église Romaine* (Paris, 1889–1910), I, 227; L. Weibull and N.

Skyum-Nielsen, *Diplomatarium Danicum*, I, 2 (Copenhagen, 1963), p. 67, No. 30. Also, for Sweden, Anastasius IV on 28 November 1154, Jaffé (ed. 2) 9938.

36. PL 215. 461; N. Skyum-Nielsen, *Diplomat. Dan.* I, 4 (1958), p. 194, No. 94.
37. The issue is not mentioned in Y. Brilioth, *Den påfliga beskattningen af Sverige intill den stora schismen* (Uppsala, 1915), which deals specifically with papal taxation in Sweden.
38. For the date, see *Dipl. Dan.* I, 5, No. 77.
39. PL 216. 965; *Dipl. Dan.* I, 5, No. 41: ". . . unde plurimum admiramur quod te super hoc excusare aliquatenus uoluisti" (p. 64. 23–24).
40. J. Werner, "Die Teilnehmerliste des Laterankonzils vom Jahre 1215," *Neues Archiv der Gesellschaft für ältere deutsche Geschichtskunde*, XXXI (1906), 586, from Zurich MS. Car. C. 148; also in R. Foreville, *Latran I, II, III, et Latran IV* (Histoire des Conciles Oecuméniques, VI; Paris, 1965), p. 392. The authentic list, in the register an. xviii, No. 234, is lost; cf. Kuttner and García (n. 4 *supra*), pp. 118, n. 18, 122.
41. Skyum-Nielsen, *Dipl. Dan.* I, 5, p. 92 (introd. to No. 59).
42. *Ibid.*, Nos. 75, 76 (*Reg. Vat.* 8A, fol. cxviii).
43. *Ibid.*, No. 102 (p. 149f).
44. Cf. *Dipl. Dan.* I, 5, Nos. 74–83, 85–90 (Potth. 5107–8, 5110, 5114, 5116, 5118–19, 5121, 5263–64, 5289–94.
45. See Cheney and Cheney, *Letters of Pope Innocent* (note 15, *supra*), Nos. 484–87, 506–11, 531–32, 555–56, 569 (Potth. 1921–22, 2009–12, 2081, 2181, 2275); cf. H. Tillmann, *Die päpstlichen Legaten in England* . . . (Bonn, 1926), pp. 90–92.
46. Werner (n. 40 *supra*), pp. 587, 592: Foreville, pp. 392, 395.
47. *The Chronicle of Melrose*, from the Cottonian Manuscript, . . . introd. by A. O. and M. O. Anderson, index by W. C. Dickinson (facsimile edition, London, 1936), p. [61]=fol. 32r: "profecti sunt de scotia ad curiam romanam generalis concilii gratia. . . . Ceteri uero prelati personaliter romam non adierunt, set legatos suos miserunt." Cf. A. Bellesheim (tr. Dom. O. H. Blair), *History of the Catholic Church of Scotland*, I (Edinburgh-London, 1887), 339.
48. The documentation in H. Denifle and E. Chatelain, *Chartularium Universitatis Parisiensis*, II (Paris, 1891), 414–42, and in the article by X. Le Bachelet, "Benoît XII," *Dictionnaire de Théologie catholique*, II, 1 (Paris, 1910), 653–704, remains fundamental. For theologians immediately preceding Innocent III, see Le Bachelet, p. 690 f.

The Tale of the Captive
Bird and the Traveler

NEQUAM, BERECHIAH, AND CHAUCER'S
SQUIRE'S TALE

Albert C. Friend

THERE IS A PATTERN in stories of captive birds which has come down to us from stories told by men who were writing in England in the late twelfth century: Alexander Nequam and Berechiah haNakdan. These stories may give us a clearer understanding of the background of the episode of the captive falcon in Chaucer's uncompleted *Squire's Tale* of the fourteenth century.

Chaucer's tale breaks off with the story of the falcon who has lost its mate and complains about its plight to the princess Canacee, who brings the bird home to her father's palace and puts it in a cage. Canacee discovers that she is able to communicate with the bird through the use of her magic ring.

H. S. V. Jones has called attention to an episode in the Indian romance, the *Kadambari*, of the seventh century as an analogue to *The Squire's Tale*.[1] The episode involves a captured myna bird who is angered at her mate, a parrot, who she feels has been unfaithful to her, and she tells the princess Kadambari her tale of woe. Jones goes on to point out stories from the *Arabian Nights* in which a princess takes the complaint of a bird to be an omen that she too may be unhappy in love, and so she avoids any romantic attachment to men. This theme had been previously explored by Haldeen Braddy, who suggested that if Chaucer had continued with his tale, he would have more or less followed the same pattern: the captive bird's complaint appears to serve as a warning to the princess Canacee that she too would be unhappy in love.[2] Whereas Jones and Braddy have concerned themselves with the story of the princess Canacee, this paper deals primarily with the caged bird which has been used down through the ages as the theme of a story which emphasizes separation and reunion through the aid of a traveler.

Just before the end of Part Two of *The Squire's Tale*, Chaucer promises that he will explain how the caged falcon will find its mate again by mediation of Prince Cambalus:

> Thus lete I Canacee hir hauk kepyng;
> I wol namoore as now speke of hir ryng,
> Til it come eft to purpose for to seyn
> How that this faucon gat hire love ageyn
> Repentant, as the storie telleth us,
> By mediacioun of Cambalus,
> The kynges sone, of which that I yow tolde.[3]

[F 651–57]

The poem, however, breaks off abruptly, and we are obliged to speculate as to Chaucer's conclusion.

A possibility as to how the falcon would come to find its mate again appears in a tale told by Alexander Nequam. The story deals with a captive bird, a parrot, who by a stratagem finds release from its cage through the mediation of a noble messenger, a knight, and goes to seek its mate. The tale appears in *De Naturis Rerum*, an encyclopedic work which Nequam compiled probably in England between circa 1197 and 1204, a text which an educated man of the fourteenth century might very well have known.[4]

Nequam is asserted to have been the foster-brother to King Richard I, and, after his education in Paris, Nequam went on to study theology at Oxford in the last years of the twelfth century.[5] He had an elementary knowledge of Hebrew and more than a passing acquaintance with Jewish interpretation of the Bible which enabled him to compile *De Naturis Rerum*, a Latin prose work representing the first two books of his commentary on Ecclesiastes; unfortunately, the last three books remain unpublished.[6] In the section on birds, chapters thirty-six and thirty-seven deal with the parrot, and chapter thirty-seven concerns the plight of a bird in captivity in England and tells the story of its escape.

There was a knight in Great Britain who had a parrot to whom he was greatly attached. And once during a journey, *peregre autem proficiscens*, in the vicinity of the mountains of Gelboa, he came upon a parrot which reminded him of the bird he had left at home, and he said, "We have a bird like you at home in a cage who sends you greetings." Upon hearing this the bird dropped down as if dead. The knight was saddened, for he was deceived by the bird's deathlike appearance. When he reached home, he told to the household what he had seen,

and the caged parrot listened intently to every word. Not long thereafter the grieving parrot dropped from its perch as if dead. The entire
household mourned its apparent illness, and the knight directed that
the parrot be taken from its cage and placed in the open air. Once
freed, the bird took wing and flew away leaving behind the members
of the household, at first saddened by their loss and then angered by
the ruse of the distant mountain bird.[7]

There is also another tale which can be considered a parallel to the
story of a captive bird who seeks its mate. This is found in the Hebrew
Fox Fables, Mishle Shualim, a collection of tales by the great medieval
Hebrew scholar and writer Rabbi Berechiah ben Natroni Krespia
haNakdan (the Punctuator).[8]

While there has been much controversy as to the date of the *Fox
Fables,* the early extant manuscripts were written before Chaucer's
time, and Cecil Roth suggests that Berechiah compiled his collection
in the late twelfth century in England and drew at least in part on
Arabic sources. He can perhaps be identified with the Berechiah who
is recorded as contributing a Donum at Oxford for King Richard in
1194.[9]

Berechiah's Fable 71, "Starling and Princess," which corresponds to
the theme to be found in Nequam's story from *De Naturis Rerum,* is
as follows:

STARLING & PRINCESS *

A Man Filled with Wisdom and
Knowledge Hath an Observant
Eye and an Attentive Ear.

A Princess raised a starling and taught him to speak plainly and
brought him to her chamber in her father's house, in her youth. In
clear speech and pretty wit the starling was cleverer than all the birds,
and he understood, when he heard news, that there is a time for speaking and a time for remaining silent. But he could not go and come,
and his heart grieved. She had made him a cage of iron reeds, and
amongst the reeds his voice was heard. One day a knight who intended
to cross the sea came to the court of the king and queen and com-
mended his house and sons and land to the queen. Her palate was
smoother than oil, and she said: "I will surely hearken to thy voice
and keep mine eye over all that is thine." The starling understood that

* Translated by Moses Hadas, in *Fables of a Jewish Aesop* (New York and
London: Columbia University Press, 1967), pp. 128–30. Reprinted by permission of the Columbia University Press.

the knight sought to cross the sea and as he passed his cage called him by name and said to him: "Lo, thou wilt cross the sea; I shall speak glorious things of thee. If thou see a bird in my form and likeness, be mindful of me and give him greeting in my name, and graciously and mercifully ask him counsel how I may go forth from my barred prison. My soul is wearied of it, for I am surrounded by hedge and wall. Neither have I offended here, but I was stolen from my family and shut up amongst men. Deal with me in kindness and truth. He that is pent in prison is considered as one dead; I am pent and cannot go forth, and my food will have no savor until I am free. Then will I lift up my head. Therefore I adjure thee to recall me to thine acquaintance and upon thy return to tell me the words of his responses." The knight departed thence and went down to the sea. Flying toward him was a bird of the form of him that had spoken to him, and before he approached, he raised his voice and said to him: "A bird of your form and likeness who dwells amongst men and is pent up in their barred gaol sends you his greeting. He hath adjured me to ask counsel of thee how he may redeem his soul and go forth from his prison cell. Deliverance will not fail him if he can again appear in the forest and change his prison garb." When he had finished speaking, the bird folded his wings and fell upon the knight in a swoon, as if death had swept him away. The knight took him up and put his eyes to his own, to restore his breath, and sprinkled fresh water upon his face, and then put him in his bosom; mayhap he would grow warm. When he saw there was no hope he threw him away; his heart grieved, and he knew not what had ailed him. Then he departed quickly to proceed to his desired destination, and returned to his family in the city of his dwelling. The king received him joyfully on his return and embraced and kissed him. As the starling paced back and forth he perceived that the knight was returned from his journey and asked him whether he had remembered his life of sorrow, whether he had found a bird of his likeness, what he had done and what he had said to him. The knight recounted all that had befallen: that it had been a day of wrath for the bird when he heard his words — how his plans were cut short, for with no hunter or fowler he had fallen dead on the field; that he had sprinkled him with water, to return his breath, and covered him with garments, without his growing warm; that before his stink and ill savor should come up, he had cast him away in revulsion. The starling listened attentively. When the princess came to her chamber and did not hear the bird chirping, her wrath burned in her. She opened the cage and saw him, and sent her handmaiden to take him up. He was lying as one dead, and she was vexed when she saw that he stirred no wing, as if paralysis had seized him; where he crouched, there he lay. She threw water upon his head: perchance she could restore his soul; and she took him and put him in her lap. But he neither rose nor moved, and she abode in silence. Then she cast him from her hands to the ground, wet her face with the tears of her eyes, bewailed and lamented him, and departed from his side weeping. When the bird heard that she had gone, all his wishes were attained; he spread his wings and flew, and his pinions wearied not of flight.

The parable: A man filled with wisdom and knowledge hath a seeing eye and an attentive ear. He hears what men say abroad, and his eyeballs look straight before him. Before others perceive his plans he is quick to begin and complete them, in give and take, in purchase and sale. Like the starling he will be diligent and prosper. He who reflects in his wisdom and proceeds accordingly, cometh forth from prison to reign.

> And I plied my poesy and said:
> A man of sense is praised for his sense; and a fool,
> reviled for his folly.
> There are wise men who are so openly, not in riddles,
> And there are simpletons wrapped in a cloak of folly.
> Folly fits close, and moves not, though continually
> reviled;
> But a hint suffices for the course of the perceptive,
> And his understanding is proven by his acts.
> So the starling fell as one slain and won his life for
> his prize.

Here we find a starling who was kept in a cage against its will by a princess and, through the aid of a friendly knight, learned the ruse of shamming death and thus made an escape to search for its mate. The immediate source of Berechiach's Fable 71 has not yet been found.[10] While it is evident that the plot of the story is the same in both Nequam and Berechiah, the story in *De Naturis Rerum* deals with a parrot, while Berechiah's fable concerns itself with a starling of which one species is the Asiatic myna bird known for its ability to imitate the human voice. The Hebrew version is embellished by a more detailed exposition and clearer characterization. One specific difference in format is the point of view of the storyteller at the end of the tale. The conclusion of the tale in Nequam is expressed by the knight and his household in their lament over the loss of the bird, while in Berechiah the ending is recounted in terms of the action of the bird.

Franz Rosenthal of Yale, whose field is Arabic studies, has called my attention to two Persian stories which, although they cannot be considered sources, are closer to Berechiah and Nequam than any parallels as yet discovered in Indian literature or folklore. One of the Persian tales appears in the poem *Assrār Nāme* (*The Book of Secrets*) by Farīd-ad-dīn Aṭṭār, who died at an advanced age between the years

1220–30:[11] An Indian sage came to visit the court of a prince in Turkestan. The prince held captive in a cage a parrot who asked that the sage, on his return to India, learn from other birds of his species how the parrot might escape his imprisonment. Instead of answering the question, the parrots fell from the trees as if dead. On his return to Turkestan, the sage told what had happened. The parrot understood and later himself shammed death and was taken from his cage and thrown on a heap of refuse from which delighted he fled home to India.

A later version of the tale appears in the *Mathnawi*, a lengthy poem by Jalāl-ad-dīn Rūmī, which he wrote after the year 1250. The story differs in a few aspects: A merchant owned a caged parrot who, heartbroken, was filled with longing. It was the merchant who traveled to India and there gave a parrot news of its absent mate, whereupon the bird fell to the ground as if dead, and the merchant, returning home, told his strange experience. The caged bird understood the silent message and shammed death to gain its freedom.[12]

The story of the caged falcon in *The Squire's Tale* and Chaucer's statement that there will be a reunion with its mate through the mediation of Prince Cambalus suggests that Chaucer, had he finished the story, may have planned to use a plot the outline of which we can see in the two Persian tales, as well as in Nequam and Berechiah.

The two Persian stories point clearly to the fact that the theme of the caged bird's reuniting with its own kind by way of a human messenger was prevalent in Muslim countries. This suggests that the stories may have had a Persian source, perhaps transmitted through Arabic, and it is possible that a lost Arabic tale was known to Berechiah. We can conclude that our earliest recorded version of the story appears in England in Berechiah and in Nequam at about the time of the first King Richard.

This raises the question of whether Nequam, compiling *De Naturis Rerum* before the year 1204, was familiar with the *Fox Fables* of his contemporary Berechiah, or whether they both drew from a story derived from the Arabic and carried back to England at the time of the Third Crusade. Like much of the rest of Chaucer's *Squire's Tale*, the episode of the caged falcon derives from Eastern stories which had found their way to England.

NOTES

1. *Sources and Analogues to the Canterbury Tales*, ed. W. F. Bryan and G. Dempster (Chicago, 1941), pp. 374–76.
2. *MLR*, XXXI, 1936, 11–19.
3. F. N. Robinson, *The Works of Geoffrey Chaucer*, 2d ed. (Boston, Mass., 1957).
4. M. Manitius, *Geschichte der Lateinischen Literatur des Mittelalters*, III (Munich, 1931), 784–87. The text is printed by Thomas Wright in *Chronicles and Memorials of Great Britain* (London, 1863), pp. 87–89.
5. A. B. Emden, *A Biographical Register of the University of Oxford*, II (Oxford, 1958), 1342–43; J. C. Russell, "Alexander Neckam in England," *English Historical Review*, XLVII, 1932, 260–68; but see also Sir Maurice Powicke, "Alexander of St. Albans, A Literary Muddle," in H. W. C. Davis, *Essays presented to Reginald Lane Poole* (Oxford, 1927), pp. 255–56.
6. Emden, *op. cit.*, and Raphael Loewe, "Alexander Neckam's Knowledge of Hebrew," *Medieval and Renaissance Studies*, The Warburg Institute, IV, 1958, 18–28; Beryl Smalley, *The Study of the Bible in the Middle Ages*, rev. ed. (Oxford, 1952), p. 235; for a study of Alexander's Commentary, see Mario Esposito, "On Some Unpublished Poems Attributed to Alexander Neckam," *English Historical Review*, XXX, 1915, 462.
7. The translation is my own from *Alexander Nequam*, in the edition of Thomas Wright, *op. cit.*, p. 89:

> Erat igitur in Britannia Majore miles psittacum habens magnae generositatis, quem tenerrime diligebat. Peregre autem proficiscens miles, circa montes Gelboe psittacum vidit, et sui quem domi habebat recordatus inquit, "Psittacus noster cavea inclusus te salutat, tibi consimilis." Quam salutationem audiens avis, morienti similis corruit. Indoluit miles, fraude deceptus aviculae, et itinere peregrinationis completo domum revertens, visa retulit. Militis vero psittacus diligenter relationi domini sui aurem adhibuit, et dolorem simulans e pertica cui insidebat morienti similis cecidit. Miratur tota domus familia, super casu repentino ingemiscens. Jubet dominus autem sub divo reponi, ut salubri aura frueretur, quae temporis nanciscens opportunitatem evolat [evolavit] perniciter haud reversura. Ingemuit dominus, et se delusam esse tota domus conqueritur. Reducunt ad memoriam multiplex solatium quid eis psittacus conferre consueverat, et avi montanae tantae fraudis repertrici saepius imprecantur.
>
> Erubescere debet rationale animal eo quod totiens a rebus rationis expertibus seducitur. Docet autem eventus jam scripto commendatus, non semper gestibus exterioribus fidem esse adhibendam. Vultus namque, etsi quandoque speculum seu certus videatur esse mentis nuntius, nonnunquam proditor esse solet.

8. Translated by Moses Hadas, *Fables of a Jewish Aesop* (New York and London, 1967). Hadas reflected the elaborate rhymed prose of the Hebrew based on the critical text edited by A. M. Haberman, *Mishle Shualim* (Jerusalem, 1945–46. The first edition was printed in Mantua, 1557–58; the text

also appeared with a Latin translation by Melchior Hanel in Prague, 1661).
9. "The Intellectual Activities of Medieval English Jewry," *British Academy, Supplemental Papers*, VIII, 1950(?), 48–50.

A dispute has evolved as to the date of the *Fox Fables, Mishle Shualim*. According to Joseph Jacobs, Berechiah compiled his fables in England at the end of the twelfth century. Jacobs identifies him as Benedict *le puintur* (haNakdan) of Oxford who contributed to the Northamptonshire Donum of 1194 (haNakdan is the title given to the scholars of the Middle Ages who furnished the vowel-points to the Hebrew biblical texts). One of the questions involved is whether Berechiah wrote before Marie de France. As Jacobs pointed out, of Berechiah's fables at least thirty bear a close resemblance to the fables of Marie, who said she was translating into French the English work of Alfred, a collection now lost. Jacobs went on to assert, with, however, little evidence to substantiate his hypothesis, that Alfred was assisted by Berechiah, who translated material from Arabic. Joseph Jacobs, *The Fables of Aesop as first printed by William Caxton*, I (London, 1889), 169–77. Jacobs reiterated his statements in his article on Berechiah in *The Jewish Encyclopedia*, III (New York, 1916; reprinted in 1925), 53–55.

While A. Neubauer agreed that Berechiah lived and wrote in the last quarter of the twelfth century, he found there was insufficient evidence that Berechiah wrote his fables in England and denied that he knew Arabic. *Jewish Quarterly Review*, II, 1890, 331.

Moritz Steinschneider was of the opinion that Berechiah could not have written before the first years of the thirteenth century, and, according to him, the evidence is too sketchy to presume that Berechiah wrote in England or that he knew Arabic. He felt strongly that Berechiah made use of Marie's collection of fables and repeats that Berechiah says in his Prologue that his fables were drawn from oral tradition and books in many languages. The source of several of his fables, including Fable 71, is yet undiscovered. M. Steinschneider, *Die Hebraeischen Übersetzungen des Mittelalters und die Judens als Dolmetscher* (Berlin, 1893; photo-offset, Graz, 1956), pp. 958–62.

There have been other scholars who expressed their opinions on the chronology with very little evidence. According to Lazarus Goldschmidt, the author lived before 1250, possibly in France. *Die Fuchsfabeln des Berekhja ben Natronay* (Berlin, 1921). Meyer Waxman suggests an even later date for the fables — 1260 — for he found a manuscript dated 1286. *A History of Jewish Literature*, II (New York, 1933), 597–600.

Cecil Roth has come forth to support the hypothesis of Jacobs that Berechiah lived in Oxford where he contributed to the Donum of 1194. Roth concludes that although Berechiah was not a native of England, he wrote his *Fox Fables* there before 1186 and points out that the oldest extant manuscript of the thirteenth century, MS. Bodl. 135, was written in England. Cecil Roth, *op. cit.* In another article, Roth states that Berechiah, belonging, as it would appear, to the culture prevalent in northern France, undoubtedly visited England, for in the Prologue to the *Fox Fables* he expressed his disappointment in the lack of interest in literature shown by the Jewish residents of that island. His own interest in work compiled by an Englishman is evident in his Hebrew translation of the *Quaestiones Naturales* of Adelard of Bath. He had an understanding of Arabic as well as of French and Latin. Cecil Roth, "The Jews of Medieval Oxford," *Oxford Historical Society*, N.S., IX (Oxford, 1951), 10, 118–19.

For further information on Berechiah's sources and style, see A. Chaikin, *Apologie des Juifs* (Paris, 1887), pp. 162–65. A clue to Berechiah's evident knowledge of Arabic appears in his Fable 68, "The Man Chased into a Pit by a Lion." To this story, which can be traced to the apologue in *Barlaam and Josaphat* (*Man and Unicorn*), *Catalogue of Romances in the British Museum*, II [London, 1893], 123), Berechiah added an allegorical interpretation found only in the Arabic version.

10. I am indebted to Dr. Haim Schwarzbaum of Jaffa, Israel, who is engaged in publishing a study of the sources of Berechiah's *Fox Fables*. He wrote me that, although he has found several parallels in the literature of India to the theme of a captive bird's shamming death to escape a fowler's net, he finds that a direct link between Berechiah and the Indian stories has not been established. This theme in the folklore of India is acknowledged by Stith Thompson, *Motif-Index to Folk Literature*, 2d ed. (Bloomington, Ind., 1957), K 522.4; and A. Aarne and Stith Thompson, *The Types of the Folktale*, 2d ed. (FF Communications, Helsinki, 1961), 233A. See also Stith Thompson and Jonas Balys, *The Oral Tales of India* (Bloomington, Ind., 1958), K 522 and K 522.4. They refer to M. B. Emenau, *Kota Texts* (Berkeley, 1944–46), "The Karumba Warrior in the Parrot's Body," based on the theme of transmigration of souls. See also Stith Thompson and W. E. Roberts, *Types of Indic Oral Tales* (Helsinki, 1960), 233A.

The theme appears earlier in the *Suskasaptati*, the Sanskrit *Tales of a Parrot*, collected in the fourteenth century and translated into German by Richard Schmidt (Munich, 1913), pp. 110–11; hamsas (swans) escape a net by shamming death. I am obliged to Professor Francis Utley for calling my attention to the following late variant version of our tale in *North Indian Notes and Queries*, Vol. 48, June, 1895. A parrot was owned by a banker who kept him imprisoned in a cage. One day a Sadhu, or holy man, chanced to visit, and the parrot asked him how he might free himself. The Sadhu went to consult his guru, or teacher, who, on hearing the problem, fell to the ground with his limbs outstretched in a dead faint. The Sadhu immediately poured water over him and revived him. The next day the Sadhu told the parrot the strange thing that had happened to the guru, and the parrot then lay still in the bottom of his cage. His master, thinking him dead, threw him to the ground, whereupon the bird arose and flew away. Retold by W. H. D. Rouse, *The Talking Thrush* (New York, London, 1899), p. 127, and cited by Laurits Bødker, *Indian Animal Tales* (Helsinki, 1957), No. 508.

11. Tale summarized by Hellmut Ritter, *Das Meer der Seele* (Leiden, 1955), pp. 583–85, from MS. F 446 in the University Library at Istanbul.

12. Jalāl-ad-dīn Rūmī, *Mathnawi*, edited and translated by R. A. Nicholson, Text, I, 95 ff.; Trans., II, 85 ff.; and Commentary, VII, 112 (London, 1925–40).

Rhythmic Architecture in the Music of the High Middle Ages

Theodore Karp

THE STUDY OF PATTERN is of course central to all artistic disciplines. Indeed, one might claim that, in essence, stylistic awareness consists of an awareness of patterns — of patterns of expression, some subtle, others pronounced, which in individual constellations distinguish the work of one man, one school, one nation, or one period from that of another. For the medievalist the study of pattern is of especial importance, because during the Middle Ages the conscious employment of standard patterns within the creative process was at a significant peak. The scholar concerned with medieval music is among those most deeply concerned with such study since — in comparison with the roles of symbolism and realism — the role played by abstract pattern is greater in the realms of music and architecture than in most of the sister arts. Individual tones and intervals hold little significance for Western man, for within our tradition both creator and observer are concerned primarily with motion, with progression. Even the least sophisticated listener automatically perceives musical structure in terms of groups of tones arranged in a hierarchy of increasing size. It is this sense of hierarchy of construction, of complementary and opposing tonal blocks, that I refer to in the title as rhythmic architecture. The present study is concerned chiefly with ways in which awareness of pattern may influence our views regarding both interrelationships between different repertoires and the structural principles of individual repertoires, as well as our analyses and re-creations of specific works.

The earliest polyphony concerning which we have precise knowledge — the examples of organum contained in the late ninth-century treatises *Musica Enchiriadis* and *Scholia Enchiriadis*[1] — arose as an elaboration of a preexistent melody which served as the pattern for the new creation. In these examples the added part or parts were primarily

---

An earlier version of this paper was read before the 1969 meeting of the Mediaeval Academy of America as part of a symposium under the chairmanship of Professor Edward Lowinsky, the general topic being "New Creations in Old Patterns: Working Methods of the Mediaeval Artist."

duplications of the *cantus prius factus* at different pitch levels. While a slow tempo was recommended for the performance of these organa, there was no bar to the retention in the polyphony of the general flow of the chant serving as structural base.[2] As composers began to realize the creative possibilities inherent in polyphony, the added voice attained greater independence of motion during the eleventh century and began to influence more and more the shape of the polyphonic complex. By the twelfth century it was possible for the composer to treat the *cantus prius factus* not as a living melody in its own right, but as an abstract pattern. On the one hand, because only few harmonic intervals could be employed at points of structural importance, the pattern was an active force that channeled the composer's imagination into predetermined directions. On the other hand, the pattern was also passive material, to be reshaped as part of the creative process. By changing rhythm and phrasing, it was possible to alter the original melodic drives of the *cantus prius factus* for the structural purposes of the polyphonic complex.[3] An extreme example of the reshaping of germinal material may be observed in a small work based on a melisma over the word *Dominus*. In this particular clausula the composer has disregarded the liturgical function of his pattern, has ignored the significance of the text, and has reworked the material by reversing the original series of notes; a rubric with a reversed order of syllables, *Nus mi do*, provides the clue that led to the discovery of this early use of retrograde motion.[4]

Obviously, surviving monuments of medieval polyphony are not evenly distributed in terms of genres, periods, and locales. But if we assume that those monuments that survive are reasonably representative of the sum total that once existed, we can state that just as the Gothic spirit is strongest and purest in the North, so too do we find the greatest interest in the constructive potential of musical patterns among Northern musicians, specifically those residing in or having cultural ties with the Île-de-France.

Because of difficulties posed by the notation, which affords no direct information regarding rhythm and incomplete information regarding harmonic structure, we are just beginning to examine in detail twelfth-century polyphony created in southern France or influenced by southern French tastes. If one goes over those aspects of the musical skeleton that can be reasonably determined, certain noteworthy elements of pattern emerge. In most ages, cadential articulations tend to involve progressions that cover small rather than wide spans of pitch space. But in the liturgical polyphony contained in the Codex Calixtinus of Santiago de Compostela, one finds cadences where the melodic motion of the upper voice does not proceed to the closest stable point, but plunges boldly downward past three points of relative stability to achieve an asymmetrical resolution on a still lower level. The point that concerns us is not the unusual nature of the harmonic motion, but the fact that while the basic harmonic pattern is quite frequent, the details of the melodic configuration almost always display elements of individuality. While the structural framework is closely dictated by standard pattern, the artist's immediate concern is for originality of detail. A similar concern may be manifested in a troubadour or trouvère poem that is otherwise shaped by standard patterns of structure and rhetoric. Given the fact that very little Italian polyphony survives from before 1325, and that we are actively trying to account for the sources for the brilliant musical efflorescene of the Trecento,[5] it is significant, I think, to observe in the madrigal, the earlier of the two main genres, the same harmonic formulae found in Calixtine polyphony, handled in the same spirit and with the same emphasis on originality of detail.

In the North, pattern was treated with greater strictness. I propose therefore that we turn our attention to a central repertory of Northern polyphony, the Notre Dame organa dupla, and to two important genres that developed therefrom, the clausula and the motet. According to present consensus, the central corpus of these organa — two-part settings of responsories, graduals, and alleluias for major feasts of the Church year — was created by the Parisian composer Leonin during the decade 1160–70. Rather than deal directly with working methods themselves, I shall treat three areas of interpretation that are dependent upon our awareness of patterns. As will become apparent, in many cases "interpretation" may be equivalent to actual reconstruction. Of course, scholars dealing with early music do not have available living monuments, the counterparts of surviving buildings, sculpture, paintings, and literary texts. The objects of our study are closer to fossil remains that must be restored through recourse to available data, logic, and even scholarly intuition. (In somewhat similar fashion, the art historian may seek to bring to life architectural monuments, such as the old basilica of St. Peter in Rome or the castle of Coucy, that survive only in sketches or written descriptions.) Often the musical data may lend themselves to sharply differing reconstructions. Before proceeding to the main task at hand, a summary of the ways in which various patterns function in the organa may be apropos.

The first element of predetermined pattern lies in the use of a *cantus prius factus*, taken from the liturgy. The creative elements lie in the arrangement of the preexistent pattern and in the newly composed upper voice. The second main element of predetermined pattern lies in the overall architectural structure of the organa. The chants employed alternated sections for soloists with sections for choir, and it was twelfth-century practice to set polyphonically only those portions sung originally by soloists. Therefore the large outlines of the organa follow a common pattern formed by the alternation of polyphony and monophony. Polyphony is provided for the opening of the respond and the greater part of the verse. Occasionally the first half of the Lesser Doxology and sometimes even the repeat of the respond may be set. Within the chants themselves there are contrasts between sections in which each syllable is set to one or a few notes and others in which a few syllables are each set to many notes. Each of these two styles generated a different polyphonic texture. The tones of the syllabic sections are drawn out to support flowing arabesques of various lengths in the newly created part. But where the chant itself is florid, the composer orders both voices in strict rhythm with less contrast between the flow of each. These sections are termed clausulae. In the accompanying schematic representation of the *Alleluia* and verse, *Dies sanctificatus* (Example 1), the heightened areas represent polyphonic sections and the striated portions thereof, clausulae. (No attempt has been made to represent the relative lengths of the different sections.)

The architectural features of these works were by no means immutable. On the contrary, the balance displayed in the originals was often modified by later artists. Counterparts to such modifications are of course familiar in the realm of architecture; the cathedrals of Chartres and Strasbourg come to mind readily as examples. But whereas a cathedral obviously can have only one final form, there are organa that survive in several, representing various degrees of modification of the original. The trend followed was to replace sections of flowing arabesques over a sustained tenor with more tightly organized clausulae, more dependent upon patterned construction.

Just as the large architectural shape of the organa was determined by pattern, so too was the rhythmic microcosm. During the twelfth century, composers began increasingly to channel their rhythmic impulse into a small group of simple patterns similar to poetic meters. While medieval theorists were not in full agreement regarding the number of patterns to be codified and the proper order of their presentation, in modern practice we speak of six rhythmic modes.[6] To the medieval composer these modes represented abstractions of infinite extension that were transformed into realities by breaking the normal flow through the introduction of a rest, thus defining the length of the musical gesture. Elements of rhythmic individuality could be attained either through control of phrase length or through the use of certain

EXAMPLE 1.

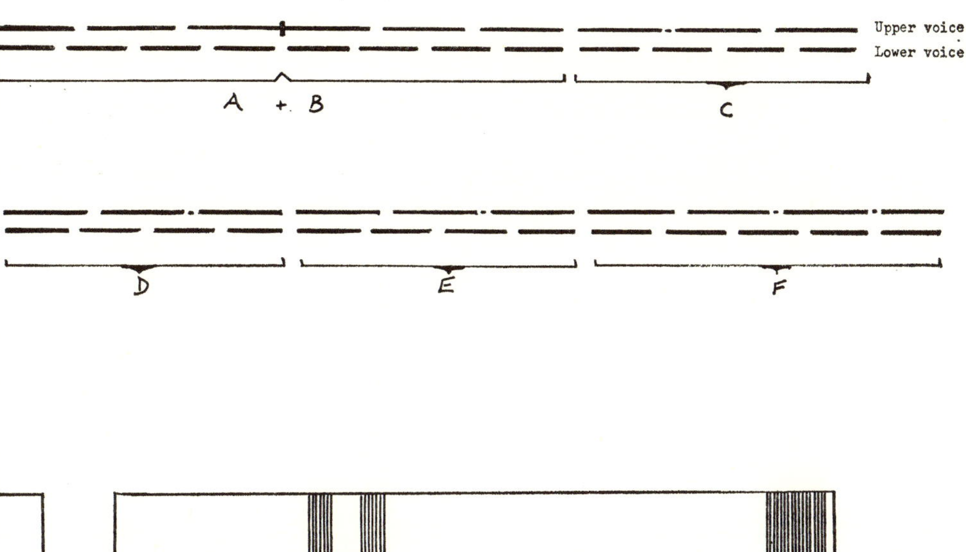

exceptions permissible within the modal system. A composer might divide a given time value among two or more notes, thus providing a faster than normal decoration. Or, he might fuse two values into one larger whole, thus providing rhythmic emphasis through added length. In the organa we may observe various stages in the evolution of modal rhythm, from the rather vague and free beginnings to the strict governance of the rhythmic impulse.

Lastly, not even in the melodic construction of the upper voice did the composer seek maximum freedom. Instead he drew extensively on preexistent material, whether in the form of common melodic formulae or of entire phrases, or groups of phrases, that could be borrowed deliberately from one work for use in another. The composer's contribution lay in the sections of new material that he created and in the specific configuration given to the assembled material. In this regard, one might draw certain analogies between these procedures of musical construction and the use of stereotyped imagery, situations, and even of quotations in medieval literature.

In what ways may an awareness of pattern help us to a better understanding of this music? Given the fact that the notation of the earlier works is often ambiguous, that significantly different interpretations may satisfy the broad rules of the theorists, the study of pattern may be one of the chief means of determining the structure of the musical thought. If we examine the published transcription of an early version of the responsory, *Gaude Maria*, (Example 2),[7] we shall observe that the polyphony for the respond consists of three main sections, each built of a number of small motives.

The first and third terminate in small codettas, while the second and third develop the same material. If we follow the edition and the recorded performance based on it, we are likely to conclude that the first codetta was designed to form an unbroken link with the section following. Even though the final interval (just preceding the third "comma" in the example) is the stablest possible, and even though the editor shows that there is a division mark in the MS., we are apt to regard this interval as a point of tension, driving the music forward to the beginning of the new section.[8]

However, an investigation of patterns reveals an opposite story. This codetta is one of the innumerable standard phrases found in the organa. The same pattern of melodic motion, harmonic context, and notation is to be found in six other works.[9] In these the pattern functions as the conclusion either of the polyphonic portion of the respond or the equivalent portion of the verse. We may infer, therefore, that the pattern itself was associated with the feeling of finality. Thus it appears that the final tone sung to the word *Gaude* is not the means to a goal, but the goal itself, a major point of relaxation. The division mark in the MS. apparently should be interpreted as a rest, thus reinforcing the feeling of finality developed by association of context and harmony. Such an interpretation is fully in accord with the notational practice,

EXAMPLE 2.

From William Waite, *The Rhythm of Twelfth-Century Polyphony*. Reproduced by permission of Yale University Press.

even though not every division mark signifies a rest. The first tone setting the word *Maria* is not a goal, but a fresh beginning. This is borne out by the fact that the music immediately following also forms a pattern, employed elsewhere in the responsory *Concede*. In setting the respond of *Gaude Maria*, the composer did not construct an unbroken chain, but juxtaposed two entities, each setting one word.

The difference between the interpretations outlined may not seem too great at first, but the difference is nevertheless vital. Furthermore, just as the study of pattern may occasionally incline us to separate sections that might otherwise be thought to belong together, so too will it reveal passages that ought to be treated as continuous ideas rather than as groups of smaller fragments.[10]

Since medieval compositional procedures permitted the composer to reshape his preexistent material, we need consider not only the larger aspects of construction, but also the inner rhythmic organization bestowed on the new creations. This involves awareness of subtle patterns of progression that might lead the listener to perceive regular series of two or three pulses each, or more complex or irregular groups. Most existing transcriptions of organa and clausulae seem to suggest that the editors felt either that no hierarchy of beats obtained or that the music was organized, with occasional exceptions in duple patterns. While it is true that such patterns play an important role in the organa and are still more predominant among the clausulae, we may nevertheless consider with profit the possibility of a higher percentage of asymmetrical elements in musical construction and also of patterns that group beats by threes.

Once we begin to look from this point of view, we discover a much richer variety of inner organizations than was previously thought to exist. We find, for example, that the composer of the *Alleluya Justus germinabit* observed that at one point, twelve notes of his preexistent tenor formed a fourfold varied statement of a pattern comprised of three descending notes. He chose to bring out this fact by means of a varied sequence organized in triple rhythm.[11]

A more extensive example of triple organization is found in one of the many clausulae to *Regnat*, the melisma that concludes the polyphonic portion of the *Alleluya Hodie Maria*. Through the addition of text to the upper voice, this clausula later became the motet *Deus omnium*. Against a steadily progressing chant, the composer has created a series of three-beat motives. These are each subjected to immediate repetition and form good harmonies on both their first and second statements (Example 3).

This play on repeated patterns takes on added fascination when we find a very similar technique employed in another clausula on the same tenor, later converted to the motet *Infidelem populum*. This time

EXAMPLE 3.

the patterns are formed of four or eight beats and the first two repetitions take place on pitch levels different from those of the original statements (Example 4).

In these two clausulae we find one form of rhythmic pattern used throughout. But the medieval composer did not always desire such consistency. There is a clausula common to both the *Alleluya Christus ascendens* and the *Alleluya Judicabunt sancti* that became the motet *Se quis ex opere*. Here the composer begins with patterns of threes, as in the first of our *Regnat* clausulae, but breaks off shortly. There is more than one way of construing the main body of the piece, but it appears that the organization is primarily duple, with occasional groups of threes (Example 5).

EXAMPLE 4.

Although these examples reveal some of the richness of medieval musical construction, they are not representative of the main line of development. Patterns dependent upon melodic repetition or harmonic regulation were not deemed sharp enough to be satisfying. The clarity required was achieved by cutting the chant that served as structural foundation into small segments through the insertion of rests.

By far the most important of the rhythmic patterns employed in clausulae and early motets is one consisting of three equal notes of moderate length, followed by an equivalent rest. In a frequently employed variant, the first two values of alternate groups are fused into one larger value, the ensuing compound pattern occupying twice the length of the normal one. Numerous other patterns were also possible.[12] Just as there are entire families of clausulae and motets built on the

EXAMPLE 5.

same chant fragment, so there are numerous families built on the same rhythmic pattern, though using different chants. Furthermore, since repetition of the chant fragment was often required in order to achieve the length desired for the polyphony, there was opportunity for imaginative interplay between melodic and rhythmic patterns. If the number of notes in the chant constitutes an even multiple of the number of notes in the rhythmic pattern, the fragment retains its original rhythmic profile upon repetition. But if the chant fragment contains an odd number of notes, rather than alter the rhythmic pattern when the end of

77

the melodic statement is reached the composer often preserves the rhythmic regularity. The first note of the repeat thus enters at the middle or end of the rhythmic statement, resulting in a shift of all subsequent material. This shift in turn disguises the presence of the melodic repetition.

The clarity and rigor of rhythmic construction gained through the employment of patterns delineated by rests are obvious. But these advantages entail also certain problems. The structural foundation for the music is lacking in continuity. Some way must be found to bridge the constant gaps in motion if the music is not to be excessively shortwinded. In studies of other early repertories of polyphony[13] we have not yet observed any instance in which the phrase length of the upper voice differs from that of the lower. With the advent of the clausula with modal tenor (i.e., with short patterns defined by rests), the two voices are often disparate in structure. The building of a greater sense of continuity in the polyphony and the delineation of larger structural entities were achieved variously. The upper voice might be organized as rigorously as the lower one, though in different patterns. Sometimes these patterns might be an even multiple in length compared to those of the lower voice. On the other hand, in the motet *Face de moi*, on the tenor *Domino*, the upper voice is organized in phrases of four pulses each, save for the last, while the lower follows a pattern that spans only three pulses. In this fashion, five larger sections of twelve pulses each and a concluding section of fifteen pulses are formed. Another equally simple method of increasing continuity consisted in alternating the motion between voices, as may be observed in the opening of the motet *Ad veniam*, which was formed by the addition of a text and a third voice to a two-part clausula on *Tanquam* (Example 6).

Phrasing of the sorts described above is also limiting, and composers realized that there was no vital need for the upper voice to be constructed with a rigor equal to that of the lower voice. On the contrary, they often sought to balance the strictness of the patterns of the structural foundation through the employment of varied patterns in the upper voices. There was one further problem in musical architecture to solve. A strong interest in three-part writing arose during the late twelfth century. The earliest three-part motets employ the same structure and the same text for both upper voices. It appears that the medieval musician found that the resultant polyphonic structure was topheavy, that the importance of the structural foundation was weakened by the combined weight of the paired voices. This writing technique was abandoned, and the third voice was endowed with an individual structure that might now parallel that of the second, now that of the lowest, and at other times follow neither. Because the structure of a motet text had to accord with that of the music, the upper-

EXAMPLE 6.

most voice was provided with a text of its own. Thus the motet encouraged the development of a particularly keen sense of architectural balance among the several voices, rivalling the balancing of thrust and support achieved in the Gothic cathedral. Within this musical genre, the control permitted by the use of rhythmic patterns continued to develop and to be refined until the early fifteenth century, when composers turned to other means to delineate musical architecture.

NOTES

1. In these treatises polyphony is not referred to as a recent innovation. There are imprecise passages in earlier writings that have been interpreted by some as showing awareness of polyphony, but such interpretations have been disputed.
2. Cf. Gustave Reese, *Music in the Middle Ages* (New York, 1940), p. 265.
3. In contrast to this procedure, the Renaissance composer drawing on a voice part of a chanson or motet as the basis for a cantus-firmus Mass would normally preserve the rhythmic relationships present in his model although lengthening the actual time values by some multiple, often two or four.
4. Cf. Friedrich Ludwig, *Repertorium organorum recentioris et motetorum vetustissimi stili*, I[1] (Halle, 1910), 80, No. 36.
5. See, for example, Kurt von Fischer, "On the Technique, Origin, and Evolution of Italian Trecento Music," in *The Musical Quarterly*, XLVII (1961), 41–57.
6. The rhythmic values of these modes (the counterparts of the poetic trochee, iamb, dactyl, anapest, spondee, and tribrach) are given in numerous publications; cf. for example, Reese, *op. cit.*, 272.
7. William Waite, *The Rhythm of Twelfth-Century Polyphony* (New Haven, 1954), transcriptions, pp. 14–19.
8. See also the close analysis of this work by Felix Salzer ("Tonality in Early Medieval Polyphony," in *The Music Forum*, I [1967], 35–98, esp. 67–71).
9. These are: *Concede, Ecce sacerdos, In columbe, Inter natos, Propter veritatem* (second setting), and *Timete.*
10. One might compare, for example, three transcriptions in Waite, *op. cit.*: the passage in *Sint lumbi,* beginning on page 43, system 1, measure 3, with a similar passage occurring later in the same work (page 43, system 4, measure 7), and with a third passage in *Regnum mundi* (page 47, system 5, measure 1).
11. See *ibid.,* page 244, system 1, measure 3 ff. where, however, the passage is barred in duple rhythm.
12. Cf. Yvonne Rokseth, *Polyphonies du XIIIe siècle* (Paris, 1939), IV, 144–51.
13. These repertories include the organa of the Chartres 109 fragment, the proses and versus of St. Martial, the repertories of the Codex Calixtinus and the eleventh fascicle of Wolfenbüttel 677 (W_1), as well as the Notre Dame conductus *sine caudis* and the texted portions of other conductus.

The Tuscan Town in the Quattrocento

A DEMOGRAPHIC PROFILE

David Herlihy

THE ITALIAN CITY of the Middle Ages and the Renaissance, its vigorous economy, complex society, sophisticated politics and brilliant culture, have all been subject to the minute examination of generations of fascinated historians. Only recently, however, have scholars begun the systematic exploration of one fundamental aspect of the Italian urban community: its demography and demographic behavior, the patterns of births, marriages, and deaths which circumscribed and defined the lives of its people.[1] This present paper is an effort to review, in necessarily preliminary fashion, some of the fruits of this recent research, and to point out a few of the salient characteristics of the town populations of Renaissance Italy, especially those of Tuscany in the fifteenth century. We shall also advance some suggestions concerning the influences which demographic factors and demographic experiences may have exerted upon Italian urban culture in the Quattrocento. The latter part of our survey will take us at times across treacherous terrain, and our remarks may appear to some readers too hazardous, too speculative, too uncertain. But the effort to correlate demographic and cultural phenomena still seems, in this writer's estimate, worth making. We know a fair amount about Renaissance society, much about its politics, a good deal about its educational methods and formal scholarship. But we know very little about the vital events — marriages, the

An earlier version of this paper was delivered at a conference devoted to the Renaissance town, held at the Newberry Library in Chicago in April, 1968. Research for the paper was begun at Florence in 1966–67, when the author held a study fellowship from the American Council of Learned Societies. Computer time and technical advice needed in the preparation of the article were made available through the support of the University of Wisconsin Foundation and the Graduate Research Committee of that university. Further research in this area will be made possible through a grant from the National Science Foundation. To all these foundations the author would like to express his gratitude.

birth and rearing of children, the inroads made by death — which were continuously acting upon urban society and its constituent families. The city was in part always dying, and in part always being replenished, and this substitution of new members for old inevitably affected its social structure and colored its social experience. Still more intimately and emotionally, the separate families were the constant witnesses of births and burials, and were themselves constantly shaped and reshaped by these vital changes. Could these events have come and gone, and left no mark on the values, the attitudes, the behavior of the people? To deepen our appreciation of the social milieu of the artistic and cultural Renaissance, we should know more precisely than we do what it was like to live, to raise a family, and to meet with death in the Quattrocento. We need to investigate better than we have the statistical odds presiding over life and death with which, and against which, every man was playing.

This gap in our knowledge of Renaissance social life is the more deplorable as it does not result from any dearth of documents.[2] Whether we measure them by their bulk or by their quality, Italy's documentary archives relevant to demographic history must be called extraordinary and nearly unique for their age in Europe. From the fourteenth century, the Italian communes attempted to register and record vital events. Florence, for example, has preserved from 1385 *Libri dei Morti*, or Books of the Dead, which oddly included marriages too, and which were intended to aid in the regulation of the grain supply.[3] So also, from 1378, we have the first surviving registrations listing the years of birth of Florentine citizens.[4] This information was needed to determine age and eligibility for office. These early registrations of vital statistics, at Florence and elsewhere, are of course crude and incomplete. In 1429, for example, the Florentine *Libri dei Morti* recorded only 747 deaths.[5] Since the city's population was about 38,000, this would mean a yearly death rate of only 20 per 1000 — probably only one-half of the true figure. Moreover, these registers do not include in their purview the rural communities. But even the countryside is not completely closed to demographic investigations. From the middle and late thirteenth century, we possess scattered but revealing tax surveys, *estimi* or *catasti*. These would usually list the families resident in a village or city, and assess their relative wealth.[6] The best of them constitute true censuses of the population and open a wide window onto Italian society in the late medieval and Renaissance periods.

And the best of these surveys, or at least the most famous of them, is the cadastre, or Catasto, which the commune of Florence redacted in 1427 and subjected to several subsequent revisions over the course of the fifteenth century, until a new system of direct taxation, the Decima della Repubblica, replaced it in 1498.[7] This first Catasto survey of 1427, and the subsequent surveys too, included not only the city and countryside of Florence but the towns and territories subject to it — Arezzo, Pistoia, Prato, San Gimignano, Pisa. Of all major social groups, only the clergy and nuns are omitted from it. The document thus attained vast proportions. Geographically, it comprehended the entire range of the Arno valley; in numbers, it included some 50,000 families and upwards of 200,000 people. For each family, the tax officials recorded residence, of course, the status of the household head (whether immigrant to the area or residing elsewhere), the names and ages for all household members, the marital status of women, occupations, and even physical and mental disabilities. The officials further inventoried in detail the family's possessions, in land, animals, commercial investments, or shares in the public debt. Allowance was then taken for all outstanding debts, and a final reckoning made of the household's taxable wealth.

Several scholars have recently examined the technical character of the document and have attempted to judge its accuracy.[8] They seem to be agreed on this: wherever it is possible to judge from comparisons with other documents, the comprehensiveness and level of accuracy of the Catasto's data appear to be of a remarkably high order. Less gracefully perhaps than the great monuments of Quattrocento art and thought, but no less dramatically, the Catasto makes manifest the extraordinary cultural level then attained by Florentine and Italian society — its love of precision, and its will to base decisions of policy upon a sound statistical foundation.[9] Data of this volume and this detail are not to be found elsewhere in contemporary Europe. Even Florence itself could not, or at least did not, continue this massive collection of precise statistical information into the sixteenth century, at least not with the rigor evident in the Catasto survey. We know more, or could know more, of the Florentine population, and its demographic peculiarities, in the fifteenth century than we can know for the next several hundred years.[10]

The sources left to us by the statistically-minded Florentines and other Italians constitute a priceless treasury of data, but there are problems in exploiting its riches. The chief of these problems is certainly this: the documentation is so enormous as to surpass by far the time, energy, and resources which an individual scholar could devote to its collection and analysis. Here, surely, there is opportunity for co-operative research. Here also, in confrontation with an enormous mass of data, is a chance to enlist in the service of history the ingenious techniques of data storage, retrieval, and analysis, which modern computer technology has made available to those who work with numbers.

To analyze this documentation with the thoroughness and sophistication it richly deserves, a team of American, French, and Italian scholars was formed two years ago, specifically for the purpose of gathering the principal demographic and economic data contained in the Catasto of 1427, for its entire population of more than 200,000 persons.[11] The project has subsequently secured the support of the French Centre National de la Recherche Scientifique and the American National Science Foundation. We are at present preparing a partial, machine-readable edition of the Catasto, and hope to finish this work of coding in another year. In its final form, the "edition" will be on magnetic tape, and duplicate copies of the data will be available to scholars both at Paris and at Madison. At the date of this writing (June, 1969), the data for the some 10,000 households of the city of Florence, 3,800 from the city and countryside of Pistoia, and 1,000 from Impruneta, in the Florentine countryside, have been entered onto tape. Once the data from the entire survey have been translated into a form readable by machine, we should be able to manipulate the amount of information easily in spite of its gigantic size, to turn it by computer over and under and upside down, in the search for statistical patterns.

To consider the urban populations of Tuscany in the late Middle Ages and Renaissance is at once to be struck by this, probably their most astonishing quality: their sheer size, in relation to the numbers of the surrounding rural peoples. According to the calculations of Josiah C. Russell, the ten principal cities of the Tuscan region included by the end of the thirteenth century some 26.3 per cent of the population — a figure which Professor Russell calls "really stupendous."[12] In England, for example, in 1377, only 10 per cent of the population — two fifths of the Tuscan figure — were residing in boroughs or cities with a population greater than 3,200 people.[13] It is of course difficult to form a reliable estimate of the population of the entire province of Tuscany, but a consideration of the separate cities in relation to their rural territories makes the figure of about 26 per cent seem quite likely. At Florence in the early fourteenth century, the ratio of the city population to that of the *contado*, or countryside, seems to have been about 1:2.8, or slightly more than 26 per cent.[14] At Pistoia, even before 1250, the urban-rural balance was probably also 1:2.8, or again 26 per cent.[15] The ratio at Siena could not have been much different, and was perhaps even more heavily weighted in favor of the city.[16]

In the wake of the massive depopulations which struck Tuscany with and after the Black Death of 1348, the percentage of city dwellers held fairly firm, or in some areas even increased. In San Gimignano, for example, the relative proportion of city dwellers gained slightly between 1332 and 1427, as it did also at Pistoia over the same approximate period.[17] The reason for this seems clear enough. Depopulations were emptying the poorer sections of the countryside of their people, who flocked to more favored areas or to the city, where better opportunities for employment, in large measure opened by death, attracted them. In 1427, the Florentine contado (not including the subject towns or their territories) contained about 125,000 persons, as against some 38,000 in the city.[18] The percentage of urban dwellers was, in other words, 22 per cent. In truth, however, the urban proportion is here much underrepresented. The figures for the Florentine countryside include communities — Empoli, Montevarchi, San Giovanni Valdarno, and even Prato — which could hardly be considered peasant villages. These small towns supported a large artisan population and many notaries and professional persons. They were in fact halfway stations between the small, authentically rural villages and the great cosmopolitan city. They were able to provide, and did provide, to the large towns a stream of immigrants who already possessed the skills and experience needed in staffing the businesses, industries, and government of the city. The economic and social importance of these communities of middling size has gone largely unappreciated by social historians and remains largely unknown, and yet they supplied, as we shall see, many of the leading figures in the cultural Renaissance.

The support of so large a portion of its people settled in cities presented a severe economic challenge to the region of Tuscany. We are told that by the early fourteenth century the Florentine countryside could provide the city with grain sufficient for only five months of the year.[19] Simply to survive, the population had to develop the non-agricultural sectors of the economy, to create large industries and to trade vigorously in foreign markets for raw materials and for food.[20] The severe contraction in the urban population over the fourteenth century probably helped alleviate this pressure, but the numbers of rural producers were falling too. Tuscany in the fifteenth century still required strong industries and a vigorous commerce to support so many of its people within cities. This challenge undoubtedly affected the culture of the city, as it placed a premium on education, literacy, and the maintenance of a high level of business skills.

The presence of so large an urban population seems also to have created demographic pressures, which worked subtly but powerfully to shape urban society and perhaps also to influence its culture. To understand what those pressures were, we must first compare the two sectors of the population, rural and urban, in regard to their demographic characteristics. As the basis of such a comparison we shall chiefly consider the city of Florence, the small neighboring town of Pistoia, and two rural areas: the *pieve* or "people" (plebes) of Impruneta, which lay just south of Florence in the direction of the Chianti hills; and the countryside of Pistoia, including its mountains.[21] In a region so varied as Tuscany, it is impossible to assume that any rural area is typical or representative of the whole. For example, many of the residents of Impruneta were *mezzadri* or sharecroppers. They were poorer than most inhabitants of the contado; 43 per cent (420 out of 977 households) bore no tax assessment in the Catasto. The countryside of Pistoia was larger, wealthier (at least according to its tax assessment), and its people practiced a more varied agriculture. But its economy and society may have been affected by its status as a territory subject to a foreign commune. We therefore cannot pretend that these examples are representative of all rural areas in Tuscany, and conclusions suggested here may have to be modified as more data become available. But in a gross way at least, they should still help illustrate some contrasts in family life between city and countryside.

The most evident demographic contrast between city and countryside is in the size and structure of the household. Table I shows the average size of households and the average size of the "nuclei" or family units within them. In redacting the table we counted as nuclei or family units all married couples, with or without children, and all widows or widowers with children. However, the widowed parent of a household head was not taken to be a separate family unit within the household.[22] Household heads who were also bachelors were considered to form a single family unit together with all unmarried brothers, sisters, cousins, or widowed parents who were living with them. This means that all households contain at least one family unit, no matter what the marital status of the household head.

As Table 1 illustrates, households in the city were quite small, and this seems characteristic of other urban populations as well. At Bologna in 1395, the average household size was even smaller than these samples — only 3.5 persons.[23] The larger size of the rural household is partially to be explained by the tendency of peasant families to live together. In our two examples, roughly 20 per cent of the rural house-

TABLE 1. URBAN AND RURAL HOUSEHOLDS

	CITY OF FLORENCE	IMPRUNETA	TOWN OF PISTOIA	COUNTRYSIDE OF PISTOIA
Number of Households	9,836	977	1,245	2,528
Number of Persons	37,420	4,968	4,431	11,778
Number of Persons per Household	3.80	5.08	3.56	4.65
Number of Nuclei	10,738	1,235	1,411	3,259
Number of Households with only one Nucleus	9,074	770	1,106	1,964
Per Cent	92.3	78.8	88.3	80.0
Number of Persons per Nucleus	3.48	4.10	3.13	3.61
Children, Ages 0–4	5,499	839	805	2,558
Children per Household	0.56	0.86	0.65	1.01
Children per Nucleus	0.51	0.68	0.57	0.78

holds contained more than a single family unit, as opposed to approximately 10 per cent within the towns. If we calculate the average size of the family nuclei, the contrast between city and countryside is modified but does not disappear. In spite of the large numbers of fiscal paupers at Impruneta, who bore no tax assessment, its families remained substantially larger than the city's, and a similar contrast divided the rural from the urban population at Pistoia. Upon still closer inspection, the basic reason for the small size of both the household and family within the city appears to be the paucity of children. If we compare our two largest populations (in the city of Florence and the countryside of Pistoia), there were in the peasant families three children within the age range 0–4 for every two within the urban families. In the early fourteenth century, Dante had complained in his *Comedy* that the households of his native Florence were "empty of family" (*case di famiglia vuote*).[24] The data from the Catasto strongly suggest that this scarcity of children continued to characterize the urban households a century later.

Why were the urban households and families so poor in children? It is of course possible that child mortality was considerably higher in the city than in the countryside. The towns were certainly more vulnerable to plague and disease, and these killers claimed their most frequent victims from among the young and the weak. Unfortunately, we have no way of measuring mortalities whether in the city or the countryside at any age level. But it should at least be noted that there were some compensating factors working to make life safer in the city, even for children. The standards of living were generally higher than in the countryside; city people, or many of them, enjoyed throughout their lives a superior diet which perhaps lent them greater immunity against infection. The town governments worked strenuously to feed their populations, even their poorest citizens, in periods of famine, and charitable distributions were both more frequent and more generous in town than in country. By the early fifteenth century, all the Tuscan cities were supporting half or less of the populations they had contained 150 years before; it would be hard to call them overcrowded. When prosperous (and many were in the city), the citizens could afford nursing when they or their children were ill; if this care seems woefully inadequate by our standards, it was still better than sheer neglect. Affluent residents had the further option of fleeing with their children to the countryside in times of mass infection, of imposing on themselves a quarantine which was probably the best defense against the plague. The chroniclers give no consistent impression that death imposed higher tolls upon the cities than it demanded from rural communities. In describing the Black Death of 1348, Boccaccio says that the surrounding countryside was "spared nothing."[25] These remarks are only impressions, but we can at least say this: there is, at least at present, no certain evidence that either of these two areas, town or countryside, offered consistently greater protection against the ravenous plagues of the late Middle Ages. Death, the great equalizer, seems to have taxed rural communities and urban communities with equal severity.

In seeking to explain the emptiness, as Dante called it, of the urban household, we would do well to consider the explanations which contemporaries offered for this phenomenon, of which they were well aware. One of the most perspicacious of these commentators and an exact contemporary of the Catasto was the Franciscan preacher Bernardine of Siena. He laid the blame primarily on the low fertility of the urban population, and once devoted an entire sermon to the theme that "the multiplication of peoples was very much declining." [26] Bernardine compared the society of his day (and there is no doubt that he had urban society foremost in mind) to Sodom and Gomorrah and the Dead Sea; his contemporaries, he believed, were similarly barren. [27] A fiery man and a great preacher, Bernardine undoubtedly exaggerated what he took to be the moral aberrations and the social ills of his day. But it would be foolish to maintain that he completely misrepresented, for his listeners and for history, the social problems and the moral behavior of his own society.

According to Bernardine, the chief cause for the declining population were the "vanities" or luxuries so beloved by urban society, which in turn exerted a nefarious influence upon marriages within the city. [28] Many young men, because of the great expenses in supporting a wife and family in sufficient comfort, either did not marry or married too late in life to raise a numerous progeny. Another contemporary of Bernardine and the Catasto, the Florentine Leon Battista Alberti, in his books on the family, similarly remarked on the reluctance of young men to marry. "I counted a few days ago," one of the participants in his dialogue remarks, "no less than twenty-two young members of the Alberti house, living alone without a mate, not having a wife, none less than sixteen and none older than thirty-six years of age." [29] Still according to Bernardine, the reluctance of young men to marry, and the high dowries they demanded, forced the fathers of young girls into several deplorable practices. "Similarly," he protested, "many parents, who are not able to provide enormous dowries for their girls, keep them at home sterile, and would that they remained modest virgins! And what is more cruel, if at times they have three or four daughters, not being able to endow them according to their desires, they give in marriage one or two of the prettiest ones with the largest dowries. But the other girls, sometimes deformed, lame or blind, they give to a convent, as if they were the scum and the vomit of the world. Would that they were offering them to God and not to the devil! From these things it is apparent to all that the procreation of children is ending." [30]

Through the Catasto we can investigate rather precisely the marriages of the Tuscans, and Bernardine's description of their marital practices stands up remarkably well. Table 2 shows the percentage of the population in our four communities which was married at various age levels. It should be stated that for technical reasons it is not possible to distinguish in the census bachelors from childless widowers, and some such widowers may be counted among the unmarried men. But childless widowers were undoubtedly very few at these age levels, and the difficulty should have no effect at all upon the contrasts between city and countryside. The figures are also slightly distorted by a tendency on the part of the persons surveyed to give their ages in round numbers, especially 15, 20, 25 and so forth. To offset this, the age categories are arranged to place the preferred age at the midpoint.

It should be noted that the Catasto does not include clergy or nuns and does not therefore directly reflect the loss of persons to the religious life.

TABLE 2. PERCENTAGE MARRIED IN CITY AND COUNTRYSIDE

	CITY OF FLORENCE	IMPRUNETA	TOWN OF PISTOIA	COUNTRYSIDE OF PISTOIA
A. Men				
Ages 13 to 17				
Number of Men	1,763	169	162	387
Married or Widowed	0	0	0	3
Per Cent	0.0	0.0	0.0	0.8
Ages 18 to 22				
Number of Men	1,471	206	165	471
Married or Widowed	82	25	29	109
Per Cent	5.5	12.1	17.6	25.3
Ages 23 to 27				
Number of Men	1,468	140	131	421
Married or Widowed	360	70	80	295
Per Cent	24.5	50.0	61.1	70.1
Ages 28 to 32				
Number of Men	1,517	161	124	375
Married or Widowed	738	124	88	291
Per Cent	48.6	77.0	70.1	77.5

	CITY OF FLORENCE	IMPRUNETA	TOWN OF PISTOIA	COUNTRYSIDE OF PISTOIA
		Ages 33 to 37		
Number of Men	1,161	116	111	300
Married or Widowed	760	108	91	266
Per Cent	65.5	93.1	82.0	88.5
		B. Women		
		Ages 13 to 17		
Number of Women	1,342	163	126	383
Married or Widowed	234	19	37	105
Per Cent	17.3	11.7	29.4	27.2
		Ages 18 to 22		
Number of Women	1,228	177	148	426
Married or Widowed	1,044	144	141	401
Per Cent	85.9	81.0	95.3	94.2
		Ages 23 to 27		
Number of Women	986	143	136	346
Married or Widowed	938	140	134	340
Per Cent	95.1	97.9	98.6	98.3

(Percentages in subsequent age periods remain in the high nineties.)

The tardiness with which the male Florentine entered marriage seems readily apparent from Table 2, especially when the population of Florence is compared with our largest rural sample, the inhabitants of Pistoia's countryside. Between ages 23 and 27, only a quarter of the Florentine men were or had been married, as against 70 per cent of Pistoia's peasants. Not until the age range 32–37 were more than half of the Florentine men married; the male residents of Pistoia's countryside had passed that level more than ten years earlier in their span of years.

In contrast to the males, the girls of the city and countryside do not show such great divergences in regard to marital customs. It appears, however, that girls in the cities married at a slightly younger age than girls in the countryside, and that young women in the provincial town and region of Pistoia were younger at marriage than their counterparts at Florence. But everywhere, brides at their first marriage were very young. At Florence in 1427, the average age of marriage for the bride in her first wedding was only 17.6 years, and her groom was on the average some 13.6 years older.[31] We have, unfortunately, for technical reasons no comparable figures from our other regions, but the percentages married at the various age levels would suggest that the age difference between bride and groom was substantially less.[32] Table 3 gives the average age difference between husband and wife in all marriages in which the ages of both partners are stated.

TABLE 3. DIFFERENCE IN AGE BETWEEN SPOUSES

	CITY OF FLORENCE	IMPRUNETA	TOWN OF PISTOIA	COUNTRYSIDE OF PISTOIA
Number of Marriages	6,104	1,032	945	2,674
Average age difference between husband and wife in years	12.7	10.2	11.5	9.3

Why did most male Florentines delay marriage until their thirties? Bernardine of Siena, as we have mentioned, blamed the influence of the city's "vanities"; to paraphrase his argument, young men feared that the expenses of marriage and a family would compromise their social position and standard of living. There is no doubt that in the city the taking of a wife and the beginnings of a household required that the young man possess some economic means and a measure of economic independence. But means and independence came late in most urban careers. To gain substance and an income sufficient to maintain a family usually required long years of apprenticeship, sometimes travel abroad, careful saving, and sometimes also waiting patiently for an inheritance. The situation was doubtlessly further aggravated by the unsettled economic times of the fourteenth and fifteenth centuries. Moreover, the rich urban families followed a policy of great caution in allowing their sons to marry; they wanted a sufficient number of heirs to continue their lineages, but not so many heirs as to fragment the patrimony and threaten the wealth and social position of the house. Giovanni Morelli, writing in the early fifteenth century, in his family memoirs urged his male descendants to marry young, but also to consider the economic implications of their decision to take a wife. "Don't penalize yourself by haste," he advised, "I mean to say that if you think you can improve your estate in any way by delaying until the age of thirty . . . you should delay."[33] Leon Battista Alberti claimed that the reluctance of young men to marry, by reason of their supposed poverty, was threatening the existence of the Alberti line.[34] He pleaded with their older and wealthier relatives to provide them the means they required, and thus to purchase, as he phrased it, the survival of their house.

Economic conditions in the countryside, on the other hand, favored early marriage for the male. A young man could rather easily find a farm or *podere* to lease and his landlord would typically give him the animals, stock, seed, and even loans which he might need to work it well. In his agricultural labors, a wife and children were assets. The landlords themselves often insisted that the man who leased their farms be married, as the help of family members insured good husbandry.

Oddly, the same economic forces which worked to delay marriage for urban males seem to have had the opposite effect upon marriage for girls. Already in the early fourteenth century, Dante suggested that the desperation of fathers led them to marry their daughters at an unreasonably young age, and for an unreasonably high dowry.[35] For this reason, the birth of a daughter struck terror into the heart of her father. A century later, Giovanni Morelli similarly cautioned his descendants against too much haste in giving their daughters in marriage, and too much extravagance in offering or demanding dowries; fathers should wait until their daughters were at least in their fifteenth year before allowing them, or forcing them, to marry. Like Dante too, Morelli believed that the excessive haste in marrying young girls had not been characteristic of older Florentine society. In the twelfth century, girls supposedly married not at 15, but between the ages of 24 and 26.[36] Bernardine of Siena, as we have seen, similarly noted and condemned the intense competition of fathers to marry their daughters, so much so that they were likely to favor with elegant clothes and high dowries their prettiest girls, while committing the homely or the sick to convents; in Bernardine's phrase, they were the vomit of the world.

But for all the condemnations of the moralists, from Dante to Bernardine, the fathers of daughters had ample cause for desperation. The ruthless shrinking of the age pyramid guaranteed that there would have to be fewer men in their thirties than girls in their teens. To judge from the distribution of ages, probably a sixth or more of the girls had no statistical chance of finding a mate.[37] As Bernardine noted, the response of many fathers, who were probably well aware of the odds against them, was to commit their daughters to convents; Table 2 shows quite clearly that in no Tuscan region did the families keep spinster daughters in the household in any considerable numbers past their early twenties. The commitment of young women to convents seems to have been especially common in Florence, where marriage for men was especially delayed. It also seems to have been a phenomenon most characteristic of the middle and upper levels of Florentine society; even the convents demanded a dowry. The loss of young women to the lay world, and hence to the Catasto census, seems indirectly reflected in the marked diminution in the relative number of women between ages 13 and 17, and ages 23 and 27 respectively, in the urban population. Utilizing the absolute figures already presented in Table 2, and taking the number of women between 13 and 17 as equivalent to 100, that decline is as follows:

TABLE 4. RELATIVE NUMBER OF WOMEN IN THE AGE PYRAMID

	CITY OF FLORENCE	IMPRUNETA	TOWN OF PISTOIA	COUNTRYSIDE OF PISTOIA
Ages 13–17	100.0	100.0	100.0	100.0
Ages 23–27	73.4	87.7	108.0	91.0

The illustration is of course crude, but it would be hard to believe that a mortality peculiar to the women of Florence, and inoperative in these other communities, could explain the pronounced diminution in the relative number of women at these two levels of the age pyramid. The chief explanation for this disproportionate contraction in the number of young women seems to be the greater tendency of Florentine fathers to place their daughters into convents, once it appeared that they could not be married.

The contention of Bernardine of Siena, that men in the city married late and that consequently many girls could not marry at all, thus finds support in the Catasto. He also claimed that late marriage for men limited the fertility of the urban community. Here too, he seems to be correct, for two principal reasons. Because of the relatively advanced age at which most urban males took a wife, a considerable number of young girls had no statistical chance of finding a husband and were forced to remain sterile, as Bernardine noted. So also, the husband, some twelve or thirteen years older than his wife, would usually precede her in death by a lengthy period. The number of relatively young widows in the urban population proliferated, and many of them never remarried. In the age bracket 33 to 37, 11.2 per cent of the Florentine women recorded in the Catasto were listed as widows, and more than a quarter (25.2 per cent) were widows between the ages 43 and 47.[38] The great age difference between husband and wife thus condemned many women to perpetual spinsterhood, usually spent in a convent, and for many others it limited their years of child bearing to only a part of its full biological span.

The comparatively low fertility of women within the city seems reflected by another indicator: the average age at which women gave birth to their babies. When that age is low, it suggests that women in the latter part of their fertile years were reproducing at levels below their biological potential; low average age of motherhood is characteristic of societies which, by one means or another, are limiting the fertility of women. Table 5 gives the average age of mothers who appear in the Catasto with babies less than one year of age, for both babies originally recorded in the Catasto and those added to the document after the completion of the census. As is evident from the size of the figures, peasant women and provincial women were much less conscientious than urban mothers at Florence in notifying the commune of babies born once the census had been completed. But the figures remain large enough to give a fairly reliable average age.

The low average age (between 25 and 26 years) at which Floren-

TABLE 5. AVERAGE AGE OF NEW MOTHERS

	CITY OF FLORENCE	IMPRUNETA	TOWN OF PISTOIA	COUNTRYSIDE OF PISTOIA
A. Babies Less than a Year in 1427				
Number of Mothers	918	128	163	416
Average Age	26.6	28.4	27.9	29.1
B. Babies Added to the Census				
Number of Mothers	731	22	47	50
Average Age	25.7	30.6	25.6	27.3

tine mothers gave birth to their children suggests that the fertility of these women declined quite remarkably during their thirties. Again, the great age difference which divided them from their husbands seems to have limited the fertility of older women. The death of many of these older husbands cut short the child-bearing years of their spouses. Moreover, older men, declining in years and in vitality, probably were losing their own fertility or their own interest in fathering children.

The fertility of urban women within marriage merits special attention and this is examined in Table 6.

TABLE 6. FERTILITY OF MARRIED WOMEN AT FLORENCE ACCORDING TO AGE IN 1427

	TOTAL MARRIED WOMEN	TOTAL BEARING BABIES (1426–27)	BABIES PER 100 WOMEN
Ages 13–17	232	29	12.5
Ages 18–22	1,032	286	27.6
Ages 23–27	901	235	26.1
Ages 28–32	1,026	210	20.5
Ages 33–37	636	99	15.6
Ages 38–42	685	85	12.4
Ages 43–47	489	14	2.8

The low fertility of very young wives (ages 13 to 17) is slightly deceptive, as most of these girls at the time of the redaction of the Catasto were still new brides in their first months of marriage. If we base the calculations on babies added in 1427–28, the group would contain 52 mothers, for a ratio of 22.4 babies per 100 women. But the principal fact illustrated by the table is the rapidity with which the fertility of married women declined after their late twenties. Again, this is a pattern to be expected of a society in which strong limitations were being imposed upon fertility, even within marriage.

To explain the barrenness of the town, Bernardine of Siena cited not only late marriages for men, and the reluctance of some to marry at all, but also contraceptive practices within marriage, which he equated with the sin of sodomy.[39] There is no doubt that Bernardine considered such practices widespread. Of 1,000 marriages, he maintained, 999 were of the devil, because of this moral failing.[40] Dante also clearly alluded to such acts, to explain the "empty houses" of the Florentines; Sardanapalus, he claimed, the symbol of refined lust, had instructed the people of the city "what one can do in the bedroom."[41]

In the fifteenth century, St. Antoninus of Florence also condemned husbands who cohabited with their wives in unnatural ways to avoid the conception of children; the excuse they offered was that they could not afford a larger family.[42] At Paris in the sixteenth century, the Florentine Benvenuto Cellini was accused of having had unnatural and sodomitic sexual relations with a young girl; the euphemism used to describe these acts was "the Italian fashion."[43] We also hear of "potions of sterility," and charms, which a woman would wear around her neck, in the hope of avoiding an unwanted pregnancy.[44] The small size of urban families and the rapid decline in the fertility of married women at an early age strongly suggests that Florentine couples were limiting their fertility, although it is nearly impossible to know whether this was done primarily by abstinence or by other means. The problem of birth limitation within urban society, its relation with age, wealth, and social position, is a delicate question which richly deserves, and will be given, a more rigorous examination as more data become available to us.

Although we cannot precisely evaluate the relative roles of births and deaths, the city — especially the great metropolis of Florence — appears to have been considerably less successful than the countryside in the rearing of children. This is not in itself a surprising conclusion; the barrenness of cities has impressed both contemporary observers and modern demographers.[45] Bernardine of Siena singled out both Milan and Siena as "growing less" because of population decline.[46] In 1548 at Lübeck in Germany, a commentator noted that most urban families were not surviving through a fourth generation: "Among all the families of Lübeck there are not three or four in which there is a living member of the fourth generation. It makes you angry . . . that we thus perish, and raging that we must thus disappear."[47]

As we have only samples with which to work, we cannot calculate precisely the replacement deficit of the city in relation to the countryside. But this much at least seems clear: because of contrasts whether in births or deaths, each new generation was not an exact image or projection of the old. Differential fertility (or, perhaps more prudently, differential replacement) changed the composition of the population over time, and required that the society, to maintain needed or wanted services, constantly redistribute its membership among its various socio-economic sectors. This therefore worked to increase both the physical and social mobility of the population.

Of all groups within the community, the urban poor were apparently the weakest in maintaining or replacing their own numbers. The following table offers a comparison between the richest and poorest households in the city of Florence.

TABLE 7. RICH AND POOR AT FLORENCE, 1427

	HOUSEHOLDS WITH NO TAX ASSESSMENT*	HOUSEHOLDS WITH ASSESSMENT OF 801 FLORINS AND MORE*
Number of Households	3,081	1,946
Number of Nuclei	3,286	2,302
Number of Persons	10,427	10,899
Persons per Household	3.39	5.60
Persons per Nucleus	3.18	4.74
Married women, Ages 13–47	1,767	1,236
Babies born, 1426–27	302	263
Babies per 100 Women	16.8	21.1
Number of Children, Ages 0–4	1,628	1,772
Children per Nucleus	0.49	0.77

*Assessment is based on total declared assets minus deductions.

Since those with no tax assessment constituted a substantial 31 per cent of the urban households, the city must have had difficulty maintaining its numbers. This, in turn, would seem to explain the large numbers of immigrants which formed part of the urban population. In considering immigration, it must, however, initially be stated that it is difficult to measure its importance exactly. Many household heads in the census certainly failed to record that they were new arrivals in the city. On the other hand, those who list themselves as coming from a rural or a foreign locale almost never mention the time of their immigration, whether it was ten years or ten months before. For some families, chiefly in the wealthiest class, place of origin served as a family name, even for those born in the city.[48] Finally, some families quite clearly moved back and forth repeatedly between the city and their rural homes, coming to the town when economic conditions were favorable and returning to the countryside when they were not. Urban society, particularly on its lowest levels, was extraordinarily mobile.

The importance of immigration and emigration is at least suggested, although not precisely measured, by the fact that 19 per cent of the Florentine household heads declared themselves to be from a rural or foreign area, or were living in a village while maintaining a residency for tax purposes in the city. At Pistoia, the comparable figure is 10 per cent. Such large percentages, even if not rigorously precise, imply that the city was constantly recruiting men from the more prolific countryside to compensate for its own failure to replace its numbers through natural reproduction.

Although the sources are incomplete and the act of immigration is not always a clear-cut decision, it remains remarkable how many persons in the towns preserve at the least a rural association. At Pisa, for example, in the fourteenth century, fully half of the *anziani*, the "elders" who governed the town and enjoyed a certain social prominence, were associated with rural villages, and most of them were probably true immigrants.[49] Some segments of the urban population, especially the artisans and the professional classes, seem to have been heavily dependent on immigration to maintain their numbers. The artisans lived poorly, married late, and raised few children. At Florence in 1427, one-half the weavers were Germans, and many were immigrants from other regions.[50] Among the professions, the notaries seem particularly dependent upon a sizeable immigration. According to a list of 442 judges and notaries practicing at the city of Florence in 1280 or 1290, between a third and a half were associated with, and presumably immigrated from, a rural village.[51] At Pisa in 1293, out of 98 notaries in the city, some 65 show a rural origin, or at least a rural association.[52] In 1427, in the same city, 41 out of 69 notaries, or nearly 60 percent, are similarly identified. At Florence in 1280 or 1290, or Pisa in 1293 and 1427, without a large influx from rural areas the staff of urban notaries would have been cut by 50 per cent or more, and probably could not have fully met the demand for its services.

The immigration which helped to offset the defective replacement of the urban population through natural reproduction seems also to have been socially selective. Thus, it affixed an unmistakable stamp upon the character of urban society and even, as we would suggest, upon its culture. It was, to begin with, selective in terms of sex. The city of Florence attracted both young girls for household service and young men for employment in its shops and businesses, but in keeping with its industrial importance it seems to have drawn boys more than girls. Together with the loss of young women to convents, this gave the lay population of the city a male preponderance which persisted from adolescence to the middle thirties.[53] On the other hand, the city seems also to have attracted older women from the countryside, chiefly widows who found life more amenable in the town and could afford to move. At the older age levels, the sex ratio at Florence thus swung in favor of women. Table 8 gives the sex ratios of the Florentine lay population according to age. It should again be noted that clergy and religious are not included in the figures; as nuns seem to have substantially outnumbered male religious, their inclusion would have the effect of lowering the ratios in the adult ages. The gyrations of the ratio at the upper age levels (e.g., 85.8 for ages 58–62, and 129.6 for ages 63–67) are primarily due to the tendency of women more than men to state their age in numbers exactly divisible by 10. In spite of this distortion, the overall shift in the sex ratio in relation to age emerges clearly. In this shift, selective immigration seems a factor of first importance.

TABLE 8. SEX RATIOS AT FLORENCE, 1427

AGES	MEN	WOMEN	RATIO (MEN PER 100 WOMEN)
0–2	1,824	1,589	114.8
3–7	2,726	2,356	115.7
8–12	2,273	1,913	118.8
13–17	1,763	1,395	126.4
18–22	1,471	1,240	118.6
23–27	1,468	977	150.3
28–32	1,517	1,149	132.0
33–37	1,161	748	155.2
38–42	1,149	858	133.9
43–47	843	706	119.4
48–52	859	897	95.8
53–57	609	523	116.4
58–62	641	747	85.8
63–67	613	473	129.6
68–72	359	469	76.6
73–77	200	203	98.5
78–82	131	175	74.9
83–87	54	47	114.9
88–92	19	27	70.4
93–97	7	7	100.0

The small towns did not have the large industries to attract and support great numbers of male immigrants. Immigration was therefore of comparatively less importance in shaping the character of the population, and it seems consistently to have involved women more than men. In most of these towns, women came to constitute a majority of the adult population. At Bologna in 1395, through the ages of childhood up to 15, the ratio between the sexes greatly favored men, with 120 boys for every 100 girls.[54] But the ratio swung dramatically in the adult years. Between the ages 16 and 35, women made up a large majority; for every 100 women, there were only 79 males. For the entire population surveyed at Bologna, there were more women than men, 2,448 to 2,366. At Pistoia, too, in 1427, there were more boys than girls registered in the population during the years of young childhood, but women began to outnumber men from age 11 on.[55] Some 21.2 percent of Pistoia's households were headed by a woman. Besides attracting women from the countryside, these small towns may also have been losing young men to the large industrial centers, but this movement unfortunately cannot at present be measured.

Here again, the Tuscan city of the Quattrocento, with its strong attraction for women, shares a peculiarity of urban life widely evident across Europe. In Germany, for example, women held a numerical dominance within the cities even greater than in Italy. At Nuremberg in the fifteenth century, for every 1,000 men there were 1,207 women; at Basel, 1,246; and at Rostock, 1,295.[56]

Variations in the sex ratio seem in several ways to have affected the character of urban culture. At Florence, the large number of young men, most of them unmarried, probably added to the tumultuous tenor of urban life and offered fertile ground for the spread of prostitution and other vices associated with the city. The numerous older women also merit some attention. Many were widows with some economic means, and were able to influence through donations and legacies the direction of what we may call cultural investments. Living alone or in small households, they also had to seek cultural diversion apart from their families and their homes, and thus constituted an important part of the audience at great public and religious functions. The preachers of the age — St. Bernardine, St. Antoninus, even Savonarola — spoke before congregations which would frequently have been composed mostly of women. Could these discerning men have remained unaware of the special character of their audiences? This is not the place for an extended examination of the influence women may have exerted upon Renaissance urban culture, and we shall content ourselves with one final comment. In considering that culture, we should not forget the numerical importance (and for the upper adult ages, the preponderance) which women held in the urban population.

Immigration was selective in other ways. It was certainly selective in terms of wealth, attracting to the city both the very rich and the very poor.[57] The rich were drawn by the comforts and amenities of urban life, and found the city a better place to advance and defend their interests. The poor looked for support to its charities and hospitals, and to the patronage of the great urban families. Immigration also concentrated into the towns large foreign communities. All the major Italian cities played host to large numbers of Germans. At Rome and Venice, they dominated the ranks of bakers, innkeepers and shoemakers; at Florence, they seem to have made up a majority of the weavers working in the city.[58] Everywhere the Germans served as government employees. Standing above the factions, they constituted a more reliable and effective civil service than could be recruited from the native-born. Never as numerous as the Germans, other foreign groups are still much in evidence within the Italian urban populations — Frenchmen, Spaniards, Hungarians, and Slavs, not to mention slaves imported from the east.[59] Most of them placed special skills at the service of the urban economy, and all of them helped lend the Renaissance city its pronounced cosmopolitanism.

Selective in terms of sex, wealth and nationality, this immigration was also, and critically, selective in terms of psychological qualities. The city attracted from the surrounding small towns and rural communities the trained, the talented, the energetic, the ambitious — those equipped and eager to offer their services on the urban market. In a region such as Tuscany, where the urban segment of the population was so large, the human demands imposed upon the countryside were especially heavy. Without constant and large immigration from the villages and the small towns, the staff of notaries at Florence and Pisa would have been drastically reduced, as we have seen, and probably could not have met the needs of the urban economy. Those needs thus generated a powerful draft in the countryside, which took the skilled and the talented, and pressed them towards the city.

This pattern of rural recruitment is readily apparent in the individual careers of many of the Renaissance's cultural leaders. Petrarch's father, Giovanni Boccaccio, Coluccio Salutati, Iacopo di Agnolo da Scarperia, Ambrogio Traversari, Leonardo Bruni, Poggio Bracciolini, Marsilio Ficino, Angelo Poliziano — these men and many others were born in the countryside or small towns. All were immigrants to the great city, satisfying its demand for men and finding their way, as hundreds like them did, to higher social levels. Among the artists too, who are nearly indistinguishable from the artisans, examples of the rural born pressed into the city's service are easily found: Giotto, Masaccio, Desiderio da Settignano, Leonardo da Vinci, and many others.

This recruitment of new men in the countryside had two profound repercussions on the character of urban culture. This was a situation highly favorable to vertical social mobility on the basis of ability and energy, especially among the liberal professions and the artisans. The gifted notary or artisan from a small town or village found ready employment within the city, support for his work, and recognition and reward for his achievements. Under this system of constant recruitment and replacement, the society of the Quattrocento opened wide opportunities for talent, which guaranteed the efficient use of the human resources, the human capital, of the region of Tuscany. Today still, the social historian must marvel how a society so much smaller than our own produced such a plethora of talented men. One reason for the high cultural creativity of the Renaissance town may well be this pattern of replacement. To maintain its numbers and the services it wanted, urban society had to seek, to locate, to support, and to reward the gifted men within its region.

But this is the paradox, and in some measure even the penalty, which massive immigration imposed upon the city. In bringing these men of unusual attributes into the town, this intensive recruitment was also placing them within a milieu which made it difficult for them in their turn to raise large families and replace their own numbers. The pattern of selective immigration, favoring skills and talent, simultaneously created a pattern of selective replacement, which was likely in time to threaten and frequently to erase the lineage of the new arrivals. We are not suggesting that selective immigration and replacement resulted in any kind of deterioration of the biological stock. But it did mean that families with a tradition of skill and a respect for learning could not easily maintain their numbers over many generations. Renaissance society brilliantly used its accumulated human capital, and tended to destroy it.

This erosion of human capital through selective immigration and selective replacement seems most evident in regard to the class of rural notaries. From their ranks came many of the cultural leaders of the Renaissance — Coluccio Salutati, Leonardo Bruni, Poggio Bracciolini, Petrarch, Leonardo da Vinci, and (outside of Tuscany) Vittorino da Feltre. Several historians who have worked in the notarial deposits of the Florentine State Archives have noted that the number of chartularies from rural notaries dwindles, for many regions to the point of disappearing, in the fourteenth and fifteenth centuries.[60] By the fifteenth century, it was rare for a small village to have the services of a resident notary.[61] Immigration seems to have thinned the ranks of the notaries, and this pool of trained men was not inexhaustible.

When data from the entire Catasto of 1427, and perhaps of some later Catasti, have been collected, we should be able to calculate with greater precision the replacement deficit of the urban population in relation with the countryside, and determine the degree to which the city may have been dependent upon surrounding rural areas to maintain its own numbers. But perhaps these samples and these preliminary comments may have illustrated this much at least. Residence, wealth, social position, and probably other factors influenced the ability of the various sectors of the Tuscan population to replace and maintain their own numbers. These sectors did not therefore replace themselves over time at exactly the same rate, and contrasts among them seem especially pronounced in the highly urbanized region of Tuscany. Each new generation, in other words, differed demographically and socially from the generation which produced it. The contrasts between the generations, and the effort of the community to maintain traditional services while its own composition was changing, forced it constantly to redistribute its membership. This favored both physical and social mobility, and added movement and dynamism to social life. We cannot as yet give all the processes involved a full and precise statistical description, but perhaps we have shown that these patterns of replacement, and their social and cultural implications, are indeed worthy of continuing research and thought.

NOTES

1. Among many recent publications with demographic content, special mention should be made of the studies of Enrico Fiumi. See especially his *Demografia, movemento urbanistico e classi sociale in Prato dall' età comunale ai tempi moderni* (Florence, 1968). *Idem, Storia economica e sociale di San Gimignano* (Florence, 1961). *Idem,* "Fioritura e decadenza dell' economia fiorentina," *Archivio Storico Italiano,* CXV (1957), 385–439; CXVI (1958), 443–501; and CXVII (1959), 427–502. *Idem,* "La demografia fiorentina nelle pagine di Giovanni Villani," *Archivio Storico Italiano,* CVIII (1950), 78–158. See also my own study, *Medieval and Renaissance Pistoia: The Social History of an Italian Town, 1200–1430* (New Haven, 1967).

2. The volume of surviving documentation in Italy and widely across Europe expands to huge quantities from the late thirteenth century. For the character of this documentation and a review of some of the statistical uses to which it has been put, see my article "Quantification and the Middle Ages,"

presented to the Conference on Quantitative Data: Western Europe, sponsored by the American Historical Association and held at Ann Arbor, Michigan, November 10–11, 1967. This and other papers presented to the Conference will be published in 1970 as a special number of the journal *Explorations in Economic History*.

3. Archivio di Stato of Florence (henceforth, ASF), Grascia, Vol. 186, "Registro dei morti dell' anno 1385 al 1397," and subsequent volumes. For another inventory of deaths, see ASF, Medici e Speziali, Vol. 244 (1450–1459), "Hic est liber sive quaterna continens in se notificationes mortuorum." For the reliability of these lists, see G. Parenti, "Fonti per lo studio della demografia fiorentina: i libri dei morti," *Genus* (1943–49), who concludes that they greatly understate the numbers of the dead until the eighteenth century.

4. ASF, Tratte, Vol. 39, "Descrizione dell' età dei cittadini fiorentini dal 1378 al 1456."

5. I am indebted for this figure to Mme. Christiane Klapisch, Ecole Pratique des Hautes Etudes, VIe Section.

6. On the nature of these *estimi*, see E. Fiumi, "L'imposta diretta nei comuni medioevali della Toscana," *Studi in onore di Armando Sapori*, I (Milan, 1957), pp. 329–53, and my own "Direct and Indirect Taxation in Tuscan Urban Finance, ca. 1200–1400," *Finances et comptabilité urbaines du XIIIe au XVIe siècle* (Brussels: Centre "Pro Civitate," 1964), pp. 385–405. Both Perugia and Orvieto have preserved such catasti from the late thirteenth century. See G. Mira, "I catasti e gli estimi perugini del XIII. secolo," *Economia e Storia*, I (1955), 75–84, describing the catasti from Perugia of 1260 and 1285. For Orveto, see E. Carpentier, *Une ville devant la peste. Orvieto et la peste noire de 1348* (Paris, 1962), p. 16, and G. Pardi, "Il catasto d'Orvieto d'anno 1292," *Bollettino della Società Umbra di Storia Patria*, II (1896), 225–320. Macerata, in the Marches of Ancona, possesses a catasto from 1268; see R. Foglietti, *Il catasto di Macerata del 1268* (Macerata, 1881). For direct taxation in Lombardy, see G. Biscaro, "Gli estimi del comune di Milano del secolo XIII," *Archivio Storico Lombardo*, LX (1928), 343–496. For Florence and Siena, see U. Sorbi, *Aspetti della struttura e principali modalità di stime dei catasti senese e fiorentino del XIV e XV secolo* (2d ed. Florence, 1962), and the older but still valuable B. Barbadoro, *Le finanze della Repubblica fiorentina. Imposta diretta e debito pubblico fino all' istituzione del Monte* (Florence, 1929).

7. On the technical character of the Catasto and its relationship with both earlier and later methods of direct taxation, see most recently Elio Conti, *I catasti agrari della Repubblica fiorentina e il catasto particellare toscano (secoli XIV–XIX)*, (Rome: Istituto Storico Italiano per il Medio Evo, 1966), pp. 21–130.

8. See especially the researches of Elio Conti, *Catasti agrari*, pp. 87–117, who compares data from the Catasto with those available from other contemporary sources. He concludes, for example, that in regard to the "censimento del numero dei proprietari" the results of the survey of 1427 can be called excellent (p. 106). Conti's published research has so far been limited to the rural surveys, but it is in the countryside where errors and omissions

would likely be most pronounced. On the fiscal character of the document and the influence this exerts on the character of the data, see Christiane Klapisch, "Fiscalité et demografie en Toscane (1427–1430)," *Annales-Economies-Sociétés-Civilisations*, XXIV (1969), 1313–37.

9. On the Florentine love of statistics, see the recent, perceptive remarks of Richard A. Goldthwaite, *Private Wealth in Renaissance Florence: A Study of Four Families* (Princeton, 1968), pp. 3–13.

10. With the new tax system, the Decima della Repubblica, the Florentine government abandoned the effort to register all the inhabitants of its territories. In Conti's phrase (*Catasti agrari*, p. 117), ". . . di fronte a noi si chiude una straordinaria finestra sul mondo contadino."

11. As participants, the group includes Mme. Christiane Klapisch, Ecole Pratique des Hautes Etudes, VIe Section; M. J. Dupâquier, Université de Paris, Faculté des Lettres; and M. Charles de la Roncière, Université de Dakar, Faculté des Lettres; Prof. F. Melis, Università degli Studi, Florence; and Prof. Elio Conti, Università degli Studi, Florence.

12. "Thirteenth Century Tuscany as a Region," *Taius. Texas Agricultural and Industrial University: Studies*, I (1968), 42–52.

13. J. C. Russell, *British Medieval Population* (Albuquerque, 1948), p. 305, Table 11.4.

14. In 1338, the population of the city of Florence was probably about 100,000 (estimates vary from 90,000 to 125,000 inhabitants). The countryside in the early fourteenth century probably included about 280,000 men, based on the figure of 80,000 rural males able to bear arms mentioned by Giovanni Villani. The problem of Florence's population is examined by Fiumi, "La demografia fiorentina," cited in n. 1 above.

15. Herlihy, *Pistoia*, p. 76.

16. According to William M. Bowsky, "The Impact of the Black Death upon Sienese Government and Society," *Speculum*, XXIX (1964), 11, the city population "probably included over 50,000 persons in the city itself, and perhaps more than double that number in the remainder of the state."

17. Fiumi, *San Gimignano*, pp. 153–74. In 1332 the city counted 1,687 households and the countryside 852, a ratio of 2.0:1. In 1427, the comparable figures were 564 and 250, or 2.3:1. For Pistoia, see Herlihy, *Pistoia*, p. 76. For further comment on urbanization in medieval and Renaissance Italy, see Philip Jones, "Medieval Agrarian Society at Its Prime: Italy," *Cambridge Economic History*, I (2d ed.; Cambridge, 1966), 344–46.

18. Cf. Conti, *Catasti agrari*, p. 76.

19. Cf. Georges Duby, *Rural Economy and Country Life in the Medieval West*, trans. C. Postan (Columbia, S. C., 1968), p. 129.

20. Cf. Russell, "Tuscany as a Region," pp. 49 ff.

21. For further comment on these regions, see Herlihy, *Pistoia*, and *idem*, "Santa Maria Impruneta: A Rural Commune in the Late Middle Ages," *Florentine Studies: Politics and Society in Renaissance Florence*, ed. Nicolai Rubinstein (London, 1969), pp. 242–76. Because of the adoption of slightly different editorial conventions concerning such matters as the cancellation of individuals or entire households for reason of death, the addition of persons after the census was completed, the treatment of households

with incomplete data, and so forth, the totals given here sometimes differ slightly from those appearing in the above two studies. The conventions followed in regard to such cases will be explained in subsequent publications; but as the variations are slight and their statistical importance almost nil, we have not considered it necessary to discuss them in detail and at length here.

22. The figures showing household size do not include servants, who if adult were responsible for presenting their own declarations. If children, they appeared in the declarations of their parents, not of their employers. Because of the character of the document, it is usually and unfortunately impossible to learn how many servants might have been employed in a particular household. Slaves, however, are included, as they did not present their own declarations and are listed among the possessions of their masters.

23. Paolo Montanari, *Documenti su la popolazione di Bologna alla fine del Trecento* (Fonti per la storia di Bologna, 1; Bologna, 1966), p. 5.

24. *Paradiso*, XV, 106.

25. *Il Decameron*, ed. Luigi Russo (Florence, 1939), p. 14.

26. *S. Bernardini senensis ordinis fratrum minorum Opera omnia. Studio e cura Pp. Collegii S. Bonaventurae* (Florence, 1950), II, Sermo 46, p. 82. "Quod propter superflua vanitatum cessat plurimum multiplicatio populorum."

27. San Bernardino da Siena, *Le prediche volgari*, ed. Ciro Cannarozzi, II (Florence, 1958), pp. 98–112. "Questa è la predica dello vizio della sodomia." It should be remembered that in contemporary terminology the sin of sodomy included not only homosexual acts, but heterosexual acts in which conception was prevented. "E però Idio manda le pistolenze per la sodomia, perchè tu non vuoli figliuoli, e tu non ai, e quelli che avevi, Idio te li tolle a te e ai tuoi parenti."

28. *Opera*, II, 82. Bernardine repeats essentially the same analysis, specifically to explain the dwindling population of Siena and Milan, in *Prediche volgari*, II, 107. "E pone mente, e considera con questi motivi, quanti figliuoli sarebbono più. Non vedi tu che Siena viene meno, che in Milano, quando frate Bernardino tornò, li fu detto che venti milia fanciulle v'erano da maritare, senza le maritate e quelle che non avevano tempo; e più fanciulli che in tutta Italia?"

29. *Opere volgari*, ed. Cecil Grayson (Scrittori d'Italia, 218; Bari, 1960), p. 34. "Che è questo a dire? — che io annoverava pochi di fa non meno che venti e due giovani Alberti vivere soli senza compagna, non aver moglie, niuno manco che sedici, niuno più che anni trenta e sei."

30. *Opera*, II, 82. "Similiter multi parentes, qui non valent immensas dotes tradere filiabus, in domo steriles, non propter Deum, retinent illas, et utinam virgines et pudicas! Et quod crudelius est, si quando tres vel quatuor filias habent, ad vota non valentes dotare illas, unam vel duas formosiores cum dotibus maximis nuptui tradunt; reliquas vero, quandoque distortas, claudas seu caecas sive quocumque modo deformes, quasi spumam vel vomitum saeculi, monasterio tradunt; illas, utinam Domino, non diabolo dedicantes! Ex his omnibus manifeste apparet quod cessat generatio filiorum."

31. Based on the ages of 73 girls who in 1427–28 were transferred from the declarations of their fathers to those of their new husbands.
32. At Pistoia in 1427, the average age of five new grooms was twenty-six years.
33. Giovanni di Pagolo Morelli, *Ricordi*, ed. Vittore Branca (Florence, 1956), p. 207. "Ma abbi riguardo di non ti disavvantaggiare però pell' affrettarti: vo' dire che se tu pensassi per indugiarti insino in trenta anni avere migliorato tuo istato in che che atto si fusse, per modo da valerne molto di meglio, indugia."
34. *Opere*, I, 34. "Ben mi duole di voi non pochi giovani Alberti, e' quali vi trovate senza eredi, senza avere quanto potresti accresciuta la famiglia e fattola molto populosa." See also *ibid.*, 108–9, in which the entire house is urged to support young men who wish to marry: "Contribuischi tutta la casa come a comperare l'accrescimento della famiglia. . . ."
35. *Paradiso*, XV, 101–5: "The daughter in being born did not then [i.e., in the twelfth century] cause fear for the father; for the time [of marriage] and the dowry did not depart, the one and the other, from the reasonable."
36. *Ricordi*, pp. 111–12. "Del tempo non voglio ti maravigli, perchè allora s'usava così e perchè l'età d'anni ventiquattro o venzei. . . ."
37. The population of girls recorded in the census between the ages of 15 and 19 (the most common marriage ages for women) numbered 1,225. Men between 31 and 35 (the usual marriage ages for men) were 1,002. The difference between the groups was thus 223. If the bulk of the population married in these years, this figure would represent the portion of the girls who would be without mates, about one-sixth of the total. In large measure, they were destined for the convent.
38. 86 women out of 760 and 181 out of 719 respectively.
39. *Le prediche volgari di San Bernardino da Siena dette nella Piazza del Campo l'anno mccccxxvii*, ed. Luciano Banchi (Siena, 1880), III, 270. "Così dico anco a le donne, le quali so' cagione che i figliuoli che hanno già conceputi, si vengono a perdere. Peggio, chè anco so' di quelle che aoperano che non possono generare; e se anno generati, in corpo gli disperdono. Voi (a chi toca, dico), sete più iniqui che non sono e' micidiali. . . . O maldette da Dio, quando ne farai penitenzia? Vedi che tu se' cagione che il mondo manchi, come il sodomitto; da te a lui non è differenzia niuna."
40. *Prediche volgari*, ed. Banchi, II, 95. "Io ho uno grandissimo dubbio di voi, che io mi credo che se ne salvino tanti pochi di quegli che sono in istato di matrimonio, che de' mille, novecento novantanove credo che sia matrimonio di diavolo."
41. *Paradiso*, XV, 108.
42. *Summa Theologica* (Graz, 1959), I, 713. "Contra illud preceptum [the sixth commandment] etiam facit, qui cum uxore vel aliqua extra vas debitum fundit semen, ne scilicet generet, et inde scandalium oriatur, vel ne gravetur in alendo filios, pauper existens. . . ."
43. *The Autobiography of Benvenuto Cellini*, trans. John Addington Symonds (New York: Modern Library, n.d.), p. 836. "They made their minds up to have the law of me, and consulted a Norman advocate, who advised them

to declare that I had used the girl after the Italian fashion; what this meant I need hardly explain." The note reads: "Qual modo s'intendeva contro natura, cioè in soddomia."

44. Cf. Herlihy, *Pistoia*, p. 100, n. 45. On the use of a "brevet," or charm suspended around the neck, see the ribald tale told by Poggio Bracciolini, *The Facetiae*, trans. Bernhardt J. Hurwood (New York, 1968), p. 172.

45. Cf. J. C. Russell, "Late Mediaeval Population Patterns," *Speculum*, XX (1945), 164.

46. See above, n. 28.

47. Quoted in Fritz Rörig, *The Medieval Town* (Berkeley and Los Angeles, 1967), p. 115.

48. The best example of this in Florentine society is probably provided by the Buondelmonti family, which derived from Monte Buono in Impruneta.

49. D. Herlihy, *Pisa in the Early Renaissance* (New Haven, 1958), p. 41.

50. Alfred Doren, *Deutsche Handwerker und deutsche Handwerkerbrüderschaften im mittelalterlichen Italien* (Berlin, 1903), p. 91.

51. Johan Plesner, *L'émigration de la campagne à la ville libre de Florence au XIIIe siècle* (Copenhagen, 1934), p. 149.

52. Herlihy, *Pisa*, p. 41.

53. It should be noted that the apparent influx of young men did not compensate for the shrinking of the age pyramid through deaths, and did not provide a sufficient number of mates for girls of marriageable age. As Table 8 shows, there were substantially more girls (e.g., 1,395 between ages 13 and 17) than men (e.g., 1,161 between ages 33 and 37) in the usual ages for marriage. See also above, n. 37.

54. Montanari, *Bologna*, p. 9.

55. Herlihy, *Pistoia*, p. 83.

56. Rörig, *Medieval Town*, p. 115.

57. The attraction of the city for substantial residents of the countryside was a principal thesis of Plesner's book cited in n. 51 above.

58. On Germans in the Italian towns, see the old but valuable study by A. Doren, cited in n. 50 above.

59. In 1427, the number of slaves recorded in the population of Florence, almost all of them women, was 301.

60. Cf. the comments of Plesner, *L'émigration*, p. 151, specifically regarding the region of Passignano.

61. At Impruneta, we have eighteen chartularies from six rural notaries before the Black Death, and then nothing at all until the late fifteenth century. In 1427, the village of Impruneta had no resident notary.

The University and the Church

PATTERNS OF REFORM IN JEAN GERSON

Steven E. Ozment

THIS ESSAY WILL EXPLORE the relationship between Jean Gerson's program for theological reform within the University of Paris and his program for the unification and reform of the Church. The former program culminates in the development of a mystical theology as the more effective way to salutary knowledge of God. The latter culminates in the enactment of the *via concilii* as the only effective route to the settlement of the Great Schism and as *doctrina* which can assure reform in head and members. Are Gerson's efforts against errant theological "heads," specifically the speculation of the more extravagant followers of Duns Scotus (the "formalizantes"), and against errant ecclesatistical "heads," specifically the popes of Rome, Avignon, and eventually Pisa, fundamentally consistent? Is there a common pattern of reform expressed in Gerson's advocacy of the *via mystica* against the curiosity of scholars and his promotion of the *via concilii* against the obstinacy of Christ's vicars?

André Combes, the most prolific and formidable of the Gerson *experti*, argues that parallels do exist between Gerson's mystical theology and his Pauline ecclesiology, which defines the Church as the Spirit-filled mystical body of Christ. In a general sense, "un principe d'essence mystique" underlies Gerson's ecclesiastical as well as his University reform.[1] Yet, according to Combes, this parallel does not conceal the fact that a major development and a quite radical alteration of perspective occur during Gerson's trek from the lecture halls of Paris to the bargaining tables of Pisa and Constance. Combes summarizes this development and alteration of perspective as a transition from preoccupation with psychology to a concern for pneumatology. "For the University reformer, the structure of the soul is primary; for the conciliar spokesman, it is the Holy Spirit."[2]

This essay will argue that, far from indicating a major development and a radical alteration of perspective, Gerson's preoccupation with anthropology and psychology as spokesman for the *via mystica* and his preoccupation with ecclesiology and pneumatology as spokesman

111

for the *via concilii* are quite logical and unified. As we shall see, both *viae* are invoked for the same reason and as the result of the same pattern of reform.

I

The Pattern of University Reform: The *Via Mystica*

In April, 1400, we find a program for theological reform attached to a letter Gerson writes to his teacher and friend Peter d'Ailly. This short sketch calls attention especially to "useless teachings which are without fruit and solidity," and which cause one to forsake those teachings which are both useful and necessary to salvation.[3] These vain and sterile teachings lead those who are not theologically informed away from truly Christian concerns, transform and corrupt traditional theological vocabulary, cause other faculties to ridicule theologians as *phantastici*, and, generally, never edify but only confuse and scandalize layman and cleric alike.[4]

Among Gerson's reformatory measures are the following. The temptation to speculate can be curbed by directing students away from the first to the second, third, and fourth books of the *Sentences* and also to the Bible. A nontechnical summary of basic religious principles should be constructed for the theologically unlettered, and theologically skilled inquisitors might police places where theological teachings are publicly disseminated. Gerson even suggests an enforced ban on the offensive teachings.[5] In this first draft of a program for theological reform, one notes a strong doctrinal concern in both the censure and the measures suggested for rectification.

What was sketched in April, 1400, is fleshed out two years later in Gerson's two University lectures, *Contra curiositatem studentium* (November 8 and 9, 1402). The scholars Gerson has in mind are his Franciscan colleagues on the theological faculty of the University of Paris, who, having dismissed the good example and the sound teaching of the *Doctor seraphicus*, turn to and fight over "novelties" too insignificant to enumerate,[6] as they multiply *prioritates, instantia, signa, modeitates,* and *rationes* even "beyond Scotus."[7] The biblical text of the two lectures is Mark 1:15: "Repent and believe the Gospel." It is through such repentance and belief that one finds the effective antidote to the offspring of scholarly *superbia*, that is, to the *curiositas*, which seeks what is less useful, unattainable and, indeed, harmful to

112

man, and to the *singularitas*, which devotes itself to "foreign and un-accustomed teachings."[8] "Those who repent and believe the Gospel attend more to the knowledge that edifies than to that which inflates."[9]

In the first consideration,[10] which composes the bulk of the first lecture, Gerson outlines the limits of reason's competence in theological matters. He argues that natural reasoning can progress to the knowledge of God's unity and providential governance of the creation — a concession which owes more to Bonaventure and Thomas Aquinas than to William of Occam.[11] The *articulus Parisiensis* of 1277, which denies that the same proposition can be true for the philosopher but false for the theologian, is invoked to make clear the conviction that no conflict exists between rational and revealed truths.[12] The latter, however, remain within the exclusive domain of revelation and faith, a domain which reason penetrates only on pain and penalty of paralogism.[13] "Is it any wonder," Gerson asks, "that when [philosophical reasoning] tries to transcend those boundaries [of its competence] with prideful curiosity it tumbles down, blindly dashes itself upon the stone of error, and, persisting in its efforts, bashes itself to death."[14] In matters which concern the secrets of the divine nature and activity, it is better to turn to the greater security of humility and say: "I know not, but God knows, and he to whom God has revealed it knows. Believe the Gospel, and let that suffice."[15]

In the second of the two lectures, specific signs of *curiosa singularitas* are enumerated and appropriately censured.[16] As in April, 1400, so here too some practical reform measures are put forth. For example, a unified and uniform theological curriculum; the prohibition of vernacular translations of the Bible; and fewer, or at least a more hand-picked group of, popular preachers. But the point on which Gerson hinges theological reform in the University, and which serves as the systematic leitmotif of both lectures, is the self-confinement of theologians within the perimeters of their discipline.[17] This does not mean that theologians should eschew metaphysics and logic; anything in either the real or the logical sciences which promotes faith, hope, and love is fair game for theologians.[18] Rather Gerson's daggers are directed at those who so concern themselves with grammar, secular history, poetry, the eloquence of ancient orators, and mathematical investigations that the principal subject matter of theology is replaced by what is only an accessory to theology.[19]

Confronted with the natural limitations and the *de facto* errancy of the theological "head," and the consequent danger of a doctrinal obfuscation of the theological enterprise, Gerson turns to the theological "heart" — to the penitential, affective way of mystical theology — for an ultimate solution. He will counteract the unwholesome speculation of the overly curious with simple, penitential affection. The concluding words of his second lecture against the curiosity of scholars announce the project of a mystical theology:

> The clear and savory understanding of those things which are believed in the Gospel is called mystical theology. [This understanding] is to be acquired more through penitence than through human inquiry alone. In this regard, the question will be treated, whether God is known in this life more through penitential affection [*per poenitentem affectum*] than through the inquiring intellect [*per investigantem intellectum*].[20]

Gerson undertakes the scientific project of a mystical theology not to dismiss but to reform and to realize the goal of theological inquiry and speculation. The way of the heart is invoked as the more effective way to the goal of the head: knowledge of God in this life. Gerson reasons so in his sermon *Ad Deum vadit* (April, 1403). In the *via Dei*, the *pes amoris* — i.e., mystical theology — can not only enter regions forbidden the *pes cognitionis*, but it can also draw the *pes cognitionis* into the more remote regions, which are to be known only by a more penetrating light than that provided by the cognitive powers alone.[21]

The penitential, affective way of mystical theology focuses on the things believed in the Gospel, and in this sense establishes the identity — the defining perimeters — of the theological enterprise. The affective way of mystical theology not only reorients the errant intellective powers in this way, but goes still further and enables these powers to overcome their limitations and to reach finally into the most remote regions of theological knowledge and truth.

Gerson's first treatment of the nature of mystical theology, the programmatic treatise *De mystica theologia speculativa* (1402–3), presents a detailed anatomy of the soul. Such, we are told, is prerequisite to a full understanding of mystical theology.[22] The more immediate motive behind these extensive and often tortuous psychological investigations, however, is the fact that Gerson is questing for the "purer" power of the soul. For it is in the purer power of the soul that mystical theology finds its anthropological foundation[23] and point of departure for the ultimate reformation of the theological "head."

When it is seen in its full complexity, the soul consists of three cognitive and three affective powers. Each of these powers possesses an appropriate function or activity. The following diagram summarizes the situation:

Cognitive Powers	Activity	Affective Powers	Activity
1) *sensualitas*	*cogitatio*	*appetitus sensualis*	*concupiscentia*
2) *ratio*	*meditatio*	*appetitus rationalis*	*contritio*
3) *intelligentia simplex*	*contemplatio*	*synderesis*	*dilectio extatica*

According to Gerson, these two sets of powers are arranged in a correlative, reciprocal relationship. This point is of maximum importance for understanding the reform potential of mystical theology. Gerson writes:

> Every effect, especially immanent effect, produced by this rational nature [i.e., the soul], is said to acquire some light either in the form of clarity in the cognitive powers or of heat in the affective powers, or to acquire both simultaneously (*aut simul utriusque*). For it is difficult to find a cognition which is not formally or virtually a certain affection, just as it seems quite impossible to find an affection which is not a certain experiential knowledge. Indeed, neither power causes its effect without the other, for an affective power concurs in the emergence of a cognition, just as a cognitive power concurs in the generation of an affection [*neutra potentia effectum suum causat sine altera, quoniam ad cognitionis causationem affectiva potentia, sicut ad affectionem generandam cognitiva concurrit*].[24]

The practical consequence and importance of this relationship becomes evident when Gerson turns to a discussion of the effects of original sin upon the soul. He finds these effects to be much greater with the cognitive than with the affective powers. "Woe to us now," he laments, "for [the eye of contemplation] is almost totally extinct, just as the eye of reason is darkened and the sensitive eye almost corrupted."[25] Although sin has also had its detrimental impact upon the affective powers,[26] their greater purity is attested by Gerson's location of mystical theology in the highest affective power of the soul: the *synderesis* — the "virginal portion of the soul"[27] — and its activity, ecstatic love.[28]

In the greater purity of the affective powers, specifically the affective *synderesis*, the possibility for the reformation of the whole soul (i.e., the fulfillment of the possibilities of the cognitive as well as the affective powers) is found.[29]

On the one hand, the existence of this correlative, reciprocal relation between the "head" and the "heart" means that the errancy of the former can threaten the health of the latter. On the other hand, this relation insures that the reforming power of the heart cannot and will not be without salutary effect upon the head, once the *via mystica* is entered. In the resources of the heart (*affectus*) lies the power to initiate the rectification of the head (*intellectus*). And that is the reason why Gerson urges the *viri scholastici* to read and to practice mystical theology, even though they are not yet experientially privy to such ecstasies.[30] For regardless of the errant extremes of the cognitive powers, resources requisite to the reformation of the whole soul lie in the *apex mentis* — the affective *synderesis*.

II

The Pattern of Ecclesiastical Reform: The *Via Concilii*

Gerson did not quickly adopt coercive conciliar action as the solution to the Schism. The period between 1391, when he first addresses himself to the Schism, and roughly 1407–8, when he has become a firm advocate of the conciliar way, is marked with caution and optimistic faith in the good will of the contending popes.[31] His position in this period is fairly, if somewhat generally, characterized by a comment made in a February, 1404, sermon on the same biblical text which guided the initial phase of his University reform: "Repent and believe the Gospel" (Mark 1:15). "The present Schism," he writes, places no obstacle to repentance, but rather inspires and moves one all the more to repentance as the principal antidote and means for reaching the port of salvation."[32]

Gerson's patience with Benedict XIII and his prolonged defense of the *via cessionis* in this period are clear indications of his commitment to a *via poenitentiae* as the principal antidote and means to ending the Schism. He hopes and expects that a penitent and faithful pope, like a penitent and faithful scholar, will work for the edification and utility of the Church. It was out of deep disappointment with the failure of this *via poenitentiae* that Gerson was driven finally to chart a conciliar course which would compensate for the poverty of papal good will. For despite occasional and apparently sincere intentions, Gregory and Benedict never reached the point of a magnanimous act of mutual cession.

Faced with the errancy of the ecclesiastical "head(s)," Gerson seeks a remedy within the body of Christ, the Church. He looks for resources intrinsic to the very nature of the Church which can empower and authorize a conciliar solution. The direction he will take is adumbrated as he makes manifest his disappointment with the progress produced by human labors with "positive laws":

> Having weighed the duration and continuation of the Schism [and seeing how] perplexity has taken root in the hearts of men and surges forth, as much from action as from the law, even in the hearts of the wise, when now after so many years human labors with positive laws have accomplished nothing or very little, it is expedient to find a means for success elsewhere which has not yet been tried or put into practice. It should be a juridical means, however, in accordance with natural and divine law, and one which may overcome the Schism between the present contenders and insure that the Schism will not be extended further into the generations of heirs to the present contenders.[33]

The way according to natural and divine law is formed and given mature definition in Gerson's three Pisan treatises: the *De unitate ecclesiastica* (January, 1409); the *Propositio facto coram Anglicis* (January, 1409); and the *De auferibilitate sponsi ab Ecclesia*, which was written June–July, 1409, and, significantly, retouched for presentation at Constance in April, 1415.

In the *De unitate ecclesiastica*, a basic contrast is discernible in the second, third, and fifth considerations. On the one hand, there is the mystical body of Christ, the Church, in essential and permanent unity with her Head. This body is capable of representation by a general council. It is authorized by divine and natural law, which no positive law, properly understood, may impede.[34] And the authoritative interpretation of positive law in light of divine and natural law (i.e., the implementation of the principle of equity [*epikeia*]) is "principally" the privilege of "those skilled in theology" — not the canon and civil lawyers.[35]

On the other hand, we find the two contenders for the vicarship of

Christ, Gregory XII and Benedict XIII. They have the direct support of positive law and various other justifications and arguments, as these are presented by canon and civil lawyers favorable to their causes.[36] To summarize, we have:

(1)	(2)
A general council in essential and permanent unity with Christ,	Two popes in contention for the vicarship of Christ,
authorized immediately by divine and natural law,	authorized immediately by positive laws,
to which the *doctores theologiae* are directly privy.	to which canon and civil lawyers are directly privy.

It is through an analysis of the nature of the connection between the general council of the Church and its divine authorization that Gerson unfolds his ecclesiology and unveils its intrinsic charter of reform. In a second Pisan treatise, the *Propositio facta coram Anglicis*, the clue to the whole comes through the interpretation of Isaiah 1:9 (= Romans 9:29): "Had the Lord of hosts not left us a seed (*semen*), we would have become like Sodom and Gomorrah." This biblical text, which can also serve as a primary locus for the *synderesis voluntatis et rationis* in the sphere of theological anthropology,[37] indicates to Gerson a resource intrinsic to the very nature of the Church, which can empower and authorize the action of a general council to unify and to reform the Church in head and members.[38]

The biblical text of this address to the English delegation at the Council of Pisa is Hosea 1:11: "The people of Judah and the people of Israel shall be gathered together, and they shall appoint for themselves one head" — words of self-evident appropriateness to the inchoate council. During the course of the address, Gerson finds occasion to appeal repeatedly to the *semen* of Isaiah 1:9. He tells his audience that the formal cause, which inspires and prepares the celebration of the council, is "the living and efficacious *semen Dei*, the *semen Spiritus Sancti*, which has the power to form and to reform the whole body of the Church. . . ."[39] "The congregation of the sons of Israel and Judah together receives its efficacy and power from a divine *semen* which is *radicaliter* and *inseparabiliter* placed within and diffused throughout the ecclesiastical body as life-giving blood."[40]

It may happen that the *respublica Ecclesiae* finds herself in imminent danger of destruction with no salutary leadership forthcoming from Christ's vicar. It may occur that the pope has permanently lost the use of his reason or has become depraved by heresy or scandalous morals.

The circumstance may arise, as indeed it has in the present, that a pope, sufficiently petitioned and even admonished, refuses to authorize a council, since he does not want to listen to the Church. And it could be that such a pope nowhere receives obedience and support from the faithful which is sufficient to ensure the safety of the whole Church. "In such and similar cases," Gerson writes, "the ecclesiastical congregation [i.e., a general council of the Church] assumes the authority and power to unify itself *ex divino semine*, which is diffused throughout its body. . . ."[41]

Regardless, then, of the errant and even irredeemably wicked extremes to which the ecclesiastical "head," the pope, may go, the Church by definition, and that means by her very ontological constitution, has a resource sufficient to the unification and reformation of the whole. It is on the basis of this resource — an indestructible *semen Dei* placed within and diffused throughout the ecclesiastical body — that the sacramental,[42] the hierarchical,[43] and the magisterial authority and continuity of the Church abides without interruption. The latter, the magisterial authority and continuity of the Church *ex divino semine*, is the ultimate theological justification of conciliar power over the occupant of Peter's chair. Gerson summarizes:

> Christ, the bridegroom of the Church, cannot be taken away from the Church in such a way that the Church would not always have within herself a life-giving *semen* by which she is able to continue herself in her whole body and especially in her official members through succeeding generations. . . . In this regard, the apostle [Paul] in Romans 9 [:29] brings forth the text of the evangelical prophet, Isaiah 1 [:9]: "Had the Lord of hosts not left us a *semen*, we would have become like Sodom and Gomorrah." What else should be understood by this *semen* than a spiritual power and a kind of life-giving capacity (*ars*) which is engrafted into the whole body of the Church and through which the hierarchical order is able to continue until the end of time. And from this it is concluded that the Church or a council representing the Church is able to institute, elect or appoint the highest pontiff to the sacred chair of Peter.[44]

The authority which a council of the Church may wield over the occupant of Peter's chair does not entail the creation of a lay Church,[45] nor does it threaten a Marsilian disestablishment of the official dignity of Peter's chair.[46] Gerson is consistently careful to distinguish between conciliar jurisdiction over the *usus* or *executio* of papal power by particular occupants of Peter's chair and conciliar supremacy over Peter's chair per se.[47]

In the ninth and tenth considerations of his most detailed exploration of this topic, written after the conciliar triumph at Constance, the 1417 treatise, *De potestate ecclesiastica*, Gerson reasons in the following way. It was precisely in order to avoid schism that Christ, "with the consent of the whole primitive Church or a general council," limited the *usus* of ecclesiastical power to Peter. By taking this action, Christ and the Church took measures to insure the continual unity of faith.[48] What Christ and His Church have freely given for the sake of a specific end, they may "moderate and regulate" so that this end is indeed achieved. It is "pestiferous and most pernicious *doctrina*" to argue in the midst of a prolonged schism that a council of the Church cannot assemble without papal consent and take fully authoritative measures for the regulation of the *usus* of the plentitude of papal power. Constance is, for Gerson, God's liberation of His Church from such disastrous teaching.[49]

III

The *Via Mystica* and the *Via Concilii*: A Common Pattern of Reform

From the foregoing discussion rather striking parallels between Gerson's anthropology and his ecclesiology are discernible. The *synderesis* anthropology is to the *via mystica* and the reformation of the soul what the *semen* ecclesiology is to the *via concilii* and the reformation of the Church. The affective *synderesis* is a given structure in the soul, which is naturally oriented and receptive to the Spirit of God. It is the very place where Christ is Spiritually born in the soul.[50] Psychology and pneumatology coalesce in the *via mystica*. The *semen Dei* metaphorically describes a given structure in the body of Christ, which is naturally oriented and receptive to the Spirit of God. Empowered by this *semen Dei*, the council becomes the place where the Spirit's will is made known in the Church.[51] Ecclesiology and pneumatology coalesce in the *via concilii*. The affective *synderesis* is the anthropological, the council the ecclesiological, mouthpiece of the Holy Spirit.

The errancy of the theological "head" (*intellectus*) adversely affects the soul as a whole, inclusive of all its powers and activities. The errancy of the ecclesiastical "head" (the pope) likewise endangers the whole body of Christ, inclusive of all her members. But in both psychology and ecclesiology, the reverse is also true. The affective powers, because of the *synderesis*, have salutary effect on the errant cognitive powers. And the council, because of the *semen Dei*, has salutary effect on the errant vicarship of Christ.

The activity of the affective powers, empowered and guided by the *synderesis*, neither suspends nor in any way threatens the structural integrity of the cognitive powers of the soul. The activity of the council, empowered and guided by the *semen Dei*, preserves in full the structural integrity of Peter's chair. Indeed, the goal of the affective powers becomes identical with that of the inerrant cognitive powers: salutary knowledge of God. And the goal of the council becomes precisely that of the inerrant vicar of Christ: the edification and utility of the Church.

As University chancellor and as conciliar strategist, Gerson executes a fully unified pattern of reform. Against the curiosity of theologians his ultimate appeal is to intrinsic resources of the soul. Against the obstinacy of Christ's vicars, his ultimate appeal is to resources intrinsic to the Church. Both *viae* — the *via mystica* and the *via concilii* — seek an immanent foundation and authorization for reform.

With the coming of Luther's Reformation, this pattern of reform will be broken. Luther, unlike Gerson and medieval theology generally, will be unable to find a *habitatio iustitiae* in either psychological or institutional structures. He will introduce a concept of reform based on the conviction that man ultimately cannot be reformed, only forgiven.

NOTES

1. André Combes, *La théologie mystique de Gerson: Profil de son evolution*, I (Rome, 1963), 278; cf. *ibid.*, 266–77.
2. *Ibid.*, 377; cf. *ibid.*, 356, and *ibid.*, II (Rome, 1964), 149.
3. *Jean Gerson. Oeuvres complètes*, ed. P. Glorieux (Paris, 1960–) [=Gl.], II, 26. For specific examples of propositions drawn from *doctrinae inutiles*, see *ibid.*, 27; cf. *infra*, n. 16. Regarding the dating of works cited in this section, see P. Glorieux, "L'enseignement universitaire de Gerson," *Recherches de Théologie ancienne et médiévale*, XXIII (1956), 88–113.
4. Gl., II, 26f.
5. *Ibid.*, 27f.
6. *Contra curiositatem studentium*, Gl., III, 231.
7. *Ibid.*, 242. Here Gerson has John of Ripa particularly in mind. In a subsequent consideration, he laments that Ramon Lull "habet . . . terminos a nullo doctore usitatos." *Ibid.*, 245.
8. *Ibid.*, 230.

9. *Ibid.*, 243. Cf. the discussion of *poenitentia* and Franciscan reform by G. B. Ladner, "Reformatio," in *Ecumenical Dialogue at Harvard: The Roman Catholic-Protestant Colloquium*, ed. S. Miller and G. E. Wright (Cambridge, Mass., 1964), pp. 172–90.

10. This first consideration appears in annotated translation together with other selections from Gerson's works in this period in my Latin-English edition of *Jean Gerson: Selections from A Deo exivit, Contra curiositatem studentium and De mystica theologia speculativa, Textus minores*, XXXVIII (Leiden, 1969).

11. *Contra curiositatem studentium*, Gl., III, 231: "Ductus itaque ratiocinationis naturalis ad hoc pertingit ut sciatur esse unus Deus, princeps et rector omnium, qui dedit omnibus esse et vivere; his quidem clarius, illis vero obscurius; 'invisibilia enim Dei a creatura mundi per ea quae facta sunt intellecta conspiciuntur, sempiterna quoque virtus ejus et divinitas' (Rom. 1:20)." For Occam, the unity and essential attributes of God are articles of faith. Cf. P. Boehner, "Zu Ockhams Beweis der Existenz Gottes," in *Collected Articles on Ockham* (St. Bonaventure, N.Y., 1958), pp. 399f. Compare Bonaventure, *Itinerarium mentis ad Deum*, II, 12.

12. *Contra curiositatem studentium*, Gl., III, 231f: "Qua in re concludimus cum articulo Parisiensi, articulos fidei nullo modo esse contra philosophiam naturalem; eidem potius consoni sunt, quamquam eos attingere et invenire [sua] non est, praesertim nisi praevia fidei revelatione quae tales veritates subministret." Cf. H. Denifle and E. Chatelain, *Chartularium universitatis parisiensis*, I (Paris, 1889), 543.

13. *Contra curiositatem studentium*, Gl., III, 233.

14. *Ibid.*, 231.

15. *Ibid.*, 233.

16. The censured *signa* are: (1) scorn for teachings which are fully disclosed and discussed and zeal for those which are unknown and unexamined (*ibid.*, 238); (2) the appropriation and defense of particular theologians and teachings simply out of school allegiance (*ibid.*, 239); (3) preoccupation with purely logical or philosophical subject matter to the point that the nontheological sciences no longer subserve and embellish what promotes faith, hope, and love (*ibid.*, 239f); (4) finding greater joy in the defense of one theologian than in the attempt to harmonize the teachings of the Church (*ibid.*, 240ff); (5) predilection for inventing new terms, especially in the speculative sphere of the Trinitarian life of God (*ibid.*, 244); (6) the theological appropriation and implementation of *fundamenta* taken from pagan philosophers (Plato, Aristotle, Origen, Avicenna, Algazel) (*ibid.*, 245ff); (7) disdain for clear and established teachings because they seem so unchallenging (*ibid.*, 247ff).

17. *Ibid.*, 248f.

18. *Ibid.*, 240; cf. *ibid.*, 241. Cf. Gerhard Ritter, *Studien zur Spätscholastik*, II, *Via Antiqua und Via Moderna auf den deutschen Universitäten des XV. Jahrhunderts* (Heidelberg, 1922/Darmstadt, 1963), pp. 31ff.

19. *Contra curiositatem studentium*, Gl., III, 248.

20. *Ibid.*, 249.

21. *Ad Deum vadit*, Gl., V, 7: "Pes amoris in via hac Dei saepe intrat ubi

cognitionis pes foris stat; quamvis itaque ambulando in via Dei modo prae-
tacto dum pede fidei praeposito subsequitur pes dilectionis, trahi possit
consequenter pes cognitionis ad ulteriora, propinquiori luce cognoscenda,
eundo sic pede post pedem; attamen pes amoris dexter sublimius semper
extendi potest pro hac via quam sinister. Haec est theologia mystica. . . ."

22. *De mystica theologia. Tractatus primus speculativus* in *Ioannis Carlerii de
Gerson. De mystica theologia*, ed. A. Combes (Lugano [1958]) [=*De
myst. theol. spec.*], cons. 9, 22.6ff.

23. *Ibid.*, *cons.* 19, 46.4ff: "Inter sex potentias prenominatas [see *infra* in
text], quanto aliqua fuerit purior et luminosior tam ex se quam ex adjuncta
illuminatione, tanto fit ad theologiam misticam aptior."

24. *Ibid.*, *cons.* 17, 39.17ff. For a more detailed assessment of this important
passage and my differences with André Combes' interpretation of Gerson's
anthropology and the development of his mystical theology, see my study
*Homo Spiritualis: A Comparative Study of the Anthropology of Johannes
Tauler, Jean Gerson and Martin Luther (1509–16) in the Context of Their
Theological Thought* in *Studies in Medieval and Reformation Thought*, VI
(Leiden, 1969), 59–71, esp. 64f; 79–82. An important parallel in Thomas
studies to my effort to highlight the correlative, reciprocal relation be-
tween *affectus* and *intellectus* in Gerson is the recent book by Tibor Hor-
váth, S.J., *Caritas est in Ratione: Die Lehre des Hl. Thomas über die
Einheit der Intellektiven und Affektiven Begnadung des Menschen* 1. *Beiträge zur Geschichte der Philosophie und Theologie des Mittelalters* 45
(Münster/Westfalen, 1966).

25. *De myst. theol. spec.*, cons. 24, 62.42ff.

26. See *ibid.*, cons. 20, 49f.

27. *Ibid.*, *cons.* 14, 34.2ff. Gerson's formal definition of the *synderesis* is "vis
anime appetitiva immediate a Deo suscipiens naturalem quamdam inclina-
tionem ad bonum, per quam trahitur insequi motionem boni ex apprehen-
sione simplicis intelligentie sibi presentati." For the philosophical and theological background of this concept, see Endre v. Ivánka's chapter, "Der
'apex mentis'" in *Plato Christianus: Uebernahme und Umgestaltung des
Platonismus durch die Väter* (Einsiedeln, 1964), pp. 315–51.

28. *De myst. theol. spec.*, cons. 21, 51.8f: ". . . in vi synderesis affectiva re-
ponitur mistica theologia. . . ."

29. *Ibid.*, *cons.* 20, 50.29ff: "In hoc [the reformation of the fallen soul] preci-
pue versatur ipsa, cuius naturam inquirimus, theologia mistica, quam per
penitentiam et credulitatem evangelii adipisci, et non aliter phas habe-
mus. . . ."

30. *Ibid.*, *cons.* 8, 19.4ff: "Expedit scolasticos viros etiam devotionis expertes
in scripturis devotis theologie mistice diligenter exerceri, dummodo credant
eis."

31. Cf. James L. Connolly, *John Gerson: Reformer and Mystic* (Louvain,
1928), 169ff; John B. Morrall, *Gerson and the Great Schism* (Manchester),
1960), pp. 30–69; André Combes, *La théologie mystique de Gerson*, I, 251,
276.

32. *Poenitemini et credite evangelio*, Gl., V, 465.

33. *Acta quaedam de schismate tollendo* (Dec., 1406–Jan., 1407), Gl., VI,

97: "Pensata diuturnitate schismatis et extraneitate, cum perplexitate radicata in cordibus hominum etiam sapientum consurgente tam ex facto quam ex jure, ubi jam per tot annos labores humani cum juribus positivis nihil aut modicum profuerunt, expedit reperire modum providendi alias non usitatum vel practicatum, juridicum tamen secundum naturale jus et divinum, ut vel tollatur schisma viventibus contendentibus, vel saltem non ultra per generationes et generationes contendentium continue substitutorum jugiter protendatur." In *propositiones* 6–8 Gerson argues vigorously that no positive law shall stand in the way of union sought "conformiter ad jus divinum vel evangelicum." *Ibid.*, 98. In the *Propositio facta coram Anglicis*, Gerson laments that "nulla hactenus profuerunt efficaciter humana remedia" to end the Schism. Gl., VI, *cons.* 1, 128. The *via cessionis* is a legal and human remedy for Gerson; it has failed. The *via concilii* which is to replace it is, in a sense, "extra-legal," yet a divinely sanctioned remedy.

34. *De unitate ecclesiastica*, Gl., VI, *cons.* 2, 137: "Unitas Ecclesiae essentialis semper manet ad Christum sponsum suum; nam caput Ecclesiae Christus, in quo sumus omnes unum secundum Apostolum. Et si non habet vicarium, dum scilicet mortuus est corporaliter vel civiliter, vel quia non est probabiliter exspectandum quod unquam sibi aut successoribus suis obedientia praestetur a christianis, tunc Ecclesia tam divino quam naturali jure cui nullum obviat jus positivum rite intellectum potest ad procurandum sibi vicarium unum et certum, semet congregare ad concilium generale repraesentans eam, et hoc non solum auctoritate dominorum cardinalium, sed etiam adjutorio et auxilio cujuscumque principis vel alterius christiani."

35. *Ibid.*, *cons.* 5, 138: "Auctoritas vero doctrinaliter utendi epikeia residet principaliter apud peritos in theologia, quae est architectoria respectu aliarum, et consequenter apud peritos in scientia juris canonici et civilis prout ex principiis juris divini et naturalis habet accipere fundamenta." Cf. Aristotle, *Ethica Nichomachea*, V, 10.

36. *De unitate ecclesiastica*, Gl., VI, *cons.* 2–3, 137.

37. According to the *sensus tropologicus* or "moral" interpretation, the *semen* is the *synderesis*. See, for example, Luther's early sermon, *De propria sapientia et voluntate* (Dec., 1514), *WA*, I, 32.1ff.

38. A possible connection between the *synderesis* anthropology of the *via mystica*, outlined above, and the *semen* ecclesiology of the *via concilii*, to which we now turn, is Gerson's description of the advocates of the conciliar way as "viri spirituales et eruditi non innitentes soli litterae, ascendentes de terrenis affectibus et in liberum atque purum aether lucidissimae veritatis desideriorumque splendidorum sese attolentes"; it is because such men have not been listened to that the general council of the Church has been so long in coming. *Propositio facta coram Anglicis*, Gl., VI, 130. Gerson's description of the conciliar advocate parallels his earlier description of the mystically purged and enraptured. "Raptus," he writes, "est fortis actuatio et vehemens in superiori potentia, unde cessent inferiores potentie vel ita debilitantur et ligantur, ut superiorem in sua operatione nequaquam impediant." *De myst. theol. spec.*, *cons.* 36, 95.8ff. Cf. the larger discussion, *ibid.*, *cons.* 35–39, 94–102.

39. *Propositio facta coram Anglicis*, Gl., VI, 126.
40. *Ibid.*, 131.
41. *Ibid.*, 134. Cf. *Ambulate dum lucem habetis* (Oct., 1415), Gl., V, *cons.* 3, 44: "Ecclesia habet potestatem. . . ex vivifico germine sibi insito per Spiritum Sanctum. . . ."
42. *Propositio facta coram Anglicis*, Gl., VI, 131; cf. *De auferibilitate sponsi ab Ecclesia*, Gl., III, *cons.* 4, 295f.
43. *Ibid.*, *cons.* 5, 296; *Propositio facta coram Anglicis*, Gl., VI, 132.
44. *De auferibilitate sponsi ab Ecclesia*, Gl., III, cons. 6, 297. Cf. Johann Altensteig, *Lexicon theologicum*, ed. Tytz (Cologne, 1619), p. 836. In his sermon *Prosperum iter faciat* (July, 1415), Gerson grants the council authoritative power over papal bulls and all positive laws of former popes and councils: "Concilium generale sic est super leges omnes positivas vel a summis pontificibus vel a generalibus conciliis editas quod eas potest interpretari, mutare vel tollere pro quanto viderentur impedimento vel scandalo esse ad iter ecclesiasticae unionis." Gl., V, *pars prima, directio* 4, 475. Further, Gerson makes it equally clear that the council is superior to Scripture alone: "Concilium generale potest et debet damnare propositiones multas vel assertiones hujusmodi [sc. haereticas et erroneas in fide et moribus] quamvis non possent ex solo et nudo textu expresso Sacrae Scripturae patenter reprobari seclusis expositionibus doctorum vel usu celebri Ecclesiae et ceteris." *Ibid.*, *pars secunda, directio* 4, 477. This is directed immediately against Wyclif and Hus. Cf. Paul de Vooght, "Jean Huss et ses juges," in *Das Konzil von Konstantz. Festschrift für Hermann Schäufele*, ed. A. Franzen and W. Müller (Freiburg, 1964), pp. 167ff.
45. *De auferibilitate sponsi ab Ecclesia*, Gl., III, *cons.* 7, 298. This is directed most probably against Occam. Cf. G. II. M. Posthumus Meyjes, *Jean Gerson: zijn Kerkpolitiek en Ecclesiologie. Kerkhistorische Studiën*, X (The Hague, 1963), 292f.
46. *De auferibilitate sponsi ab Ecclesia*, Gl., III, *cons.* 8, 298f. Gerson is explicit in his criticism of Marsilius of Padua. See further A. Franzen, "The Council of Constance: Present State of the Problem," in *Concilium 7: Historical Problems of Church Renewal* (Glen Rock, N.J., 1965), pp. 50, 54f.
47. *De auferibilitate sponsi ab Ecclesia*, Gl., III, *cons.* 14, 304. Cf. *Prosperum iter faciat*, Gl., V, *pars tertia, directio* 2, 477f. It is to be emphasized that this position forms the "fundamentum reformationis" for Gerson: "Ecclesia vel generale concilium quamvis non possit tollere plenitudinem potestatis papalis a Christo supernaturaliter et misericorditer collatae, potest tamen usum ejus limitare sub certis regulis ac legibus in aedificationem Ecclesiae, propter quam papalis auctoritas et altera hominis collata est; et in hoc est totius ecclesiasticae reformationis stabile fundamentum." *Ambulate dum lucem habetis*, Gl., V, *cons.* 8, 45.
48. *De potestate ecclesiastica* (Feb., 1417), Gl., VI, *cons.* 9, 226: "Et forte quoad usum vel exercitium potestatis ecclesiasticae sic evenit ipsis etiam Apostolis et discipulis quod post immediatam concessionem utriusque, scilicet potestatis et usus, factam a Christo postmodum crescente numero fidelium fuit ad tollendum schisma et ad exemplar dandum posteris, limita-

tio facta talis potestatis quoad usum, et hoc per Petrum summum pontificem de consensu totius Ecclesiae primitivae vel generalis concilii, ut non quilibet posset in quemlibet uti potestate sua, attenta Christi ordinatione primaria qua voluit Ecclesiam suam regi principaliter sub uno et ab uno monarcha, sicut est una fides, unum baptisma et una Ecclesia, unitate capitis tam primarii quam vicarii; quoniam iste [sc. concilium generale] est optimus principatus, praesertim in spiritualibus ad conservationem unitatis fidei ad quam obligantur omnes." Cf. *Propositio facta coram Anglicis*, Gl., VI, *cons*. 9, 133: ". . . claves datae sunt Petro auctoritative et exercitative sed Ecclesiae universaliter et susceptive; vel datae sunt Ecclesiae ut in actu primo et Petro ut in actu secundo." Compare the second condemned proposition of Marsilius on this point, Denzinger, *Enchiridion Symbolorum* (32d ed.), § 951, 291.

49. *De potestate ecclesiastica*, Gl., VI, *cons*. 10, 229: "Benedictus autem Deus qui per hoc sacrosanctum Constantiense concilium illustratum divinae legis lumine, dante ad hoc ipsum vexatione praesentis schismatis intellectum, liberavit Ecclesiam suam ab hac pestifera perniciosissimaque doctrina qua semper manente perseverasset semper schisma nutritum ab ea. Declaratum nempe decretumque est quod et sine papa generale concilium convocari et a concilio papa judicari certis casibus potest; quod insuper habet auctoritatem generale concilium praescribere leges seu regulas secundum quas plenitudo potestatis papalis non quidem in se, quae semper eadem est, sed in usu suo moderanda regulandaque est." Cf. *Prosperum iter faciat*, Gl., V, *pars prima, directio* 1, 474.

50. Writing in September, 1416, Gerson summarizes: "Sed ad quid ista de synderesi [sc. voluntatis]? Certe ut ostenderemus eam [sc. animam] semper virginem esse quae dum caret obumbrante et foecundante Spiritu Sancto manet infeliciter sterilis; dum autem adest idem Spiritus visitans, gratificans et foecundans, fit ipsa verbigena, hoc est verbum pariens et hoc sine corruptione quia non ex sanguinibus corporalium phantasmatum, neque ex voluntate carnis desideriorum sensualium, neque ex voluntate viri hoc est ex potestate liberi arbitrii, sed ex Deo est quidquid hic natum est. Nec tamen excluditur synderesis rationisque consensus; sed dum nuntiatrix gratia afflatu secreto et intimo veluti clauso super animam ostio suggerit adventum verbi in mentem, respondet synderesis humili genuflexione: 'ecce ancilla Domini, fiat mihi secundum verbum tuum' [Luc. 1, 38]." *Jacob autem genuit Joseph*, Gl., V, *cons*. 4, 359f.

51. *Prosperum iter faciat*, Gl., V, *directio* 2, 479: ". . . in concilio papalis potestas includitur quamvis sit aliter haec potestas in papa, aliter in concilio; sicut aliter claves Petro traditae sunt, aliter Ecclesiae. Unde concilium in multis quae papam respiciunt, habet auctoritatem consiliativam et dictativam, papa exercitativam et executivam. . . . Ad ipsum [sc. concilium] spectat circa haec hujusmodi [sc. quae papam respiciunt] consulere vel dictare, cujus dictamini qui repugnat contumaciter repugnat Spiritui Sancto cujus est ipsum concilium in dictando vel consulendo dirigere." Cf. *Ambulate dum lucem habetis*, Gl., V, *cons*. 6, 44.

Epistola Cuthberti
De Obitu Bedae

A CAVEAT

W. F. Bolton

DOCUMENTS IN THE HISTORY of Anglo-Saxon England are so few that they prompt gratitude before skepticism among modern students, and it is often only after one such document has served researchers for generations that it begins to appear too good to be true.[1] In addition, students are often inclined to make more of a document than its contents really warrant, especially when they are trying to ascertain something useful like the death date of an important figure.[2] When a document of uncertain authenticity gives only indirect testimony of a date, and this testimony is employed in a critique of another source, the assessment is on doubly doubtful grounds. This paper seeks to review the facts about the so-called *Epistola Cuthberti de Obitu Bedae* (*EC*)[3] in order to weigh its authenticity, its evidence on the death date of Bede, and — as a codicil — its role in the controversy about the colophon of the Leningrad MS. of Bede's *Historia Ecclesiastica* (*HE*).

Dobbie has classified the forty-five *EC* MSS. he knew into two groups, the Continental Version (CV) and the Insular Version (IV). His terminology represents distribution: CV MSS. are found in continental libraries, almost all IV MSS. in the British Isles. He believed that most of the CV MSS. ever made had survived in the twelve he studied, but that his thirty-three IV MSS. were only a portion of the original output. (Since he wrote, Laistner has drawn attention to three more MSS. and another now lost.)[4]

Both versions purport to be eye-witness (*[Beda] dixit mihi. . . . curre velociter et presbiteros nostri monasterii adduc ad me. . . .*) accounts of the last days and hours of the Northumbrian master; IV alone identifies the writer as "Cuthbertus" in an opening salutation, and the passage quoted would suit well enough the monk of the same name who was abbot of Wearmouth-Jarrow and who died some time after 767, the earliest date for one of his surviving letters to Lul.[5] The account then would be hardly more than thirty-five years later than the events it describes, conventionally held, on the basis of *EC*, to have taken place in 735. The same abbot Cuthbert elsewhere writes of himself as a *discipulus* of Bede;[6] he is probably not the same man to whom Bede addressed his *De arte metrica* around 701, for Bede called that Cuthbert a *collevita*[7] and employed language that, in Laistner's view, points to a difference of nine or ten years in the two deacons:[8] hence that Cuthbert would have been about eighty-seven in 767. We have, instead, a document written by a man born at the turn of the century that cannot be dated later than 770 or so if it is what it claims to be.

The two versions differ enigmatically, even more so than Dobbie knew, for another MS. with a "mixed text" was published after his study appeared.[9] As he saw the forty-five MSS. he treated, CV had the oldest but the slenderest testimony: twelve MSS. going back to the ninth century, quite probably the end of the first half. IV had the later but more abundant testimony: thirty-three MSS. dating from no earlier than the twelfth century. CV lacks the important opening salutation of IV, *Dilectissimo in Christo lectori Cuthwino Cuthbertus condiscipulus in deo eternam salutem*, but CV alone has a final sentence which is, however, not a formal closing. CV is about ten per cent longer than IV (that is, 100 lines in Dobbie's edition), largely through obvious verbal elaborations of no particular interest, but occasionally in material ways; IV, on the other hand, has very little besides the opening salutation that is not in CV, although one or two details are of importance. Finally, the two versions differ on the date of Bede's death: CV has *VII idus maias* (i.e., 9 May), while IV has *VII kalendas junii* (i.e., 26 May, on which the calendars generally agree).[10]

Other noteworthy differences between the two versions do not consistently favor the readings of one or the other. Where CV, having described the prayers and tears around the dying man's bed, reads,

> In tali laetitia quinquagesimales dies usque ad diem praefatum deduximus, et ille multum gavisus est, et deo gratias referebat quia sic meruisset infirmari, et saepe dicebat. . . ,

IV has instead

> . . . et ille multum gaudebat, et deo gratias agebat quia sic meruisset infirmari. Referebat et saepe dicebat. . . .

The diction of CV is more concise and purposeful, and its reading *gavisus est* is apparently to be preferred, although a case might perhaps be made for IV's *gaudebat*.

Describing Bede's last literary efforts, both versions refer to his excerpts from Isidore of Seville, but IV correctly — it seems — speaks of the *libris rotarum*, an apparent reference to the many circular figures in the MSS. Bede's amanuensis is simply *praefatus puer* in IV, but CV adds *nomine Uuilberch*. IV improves by adding the implied word *sententia* twice where CV has the elliptical *restat adhuc una non descripta* and *modo descripta est*. IV is probably also to be preferred where CV has

> multum me delectat sedere ex adverso loco sancto meo in quo
> orare solebam, ut et ego sedens patrem meum invocare possim

and IV *ut ibi sedens*. But IV appears to be in error where CV has *obitum Bedani* (var. *bede, bedae*) *patris nostri* and IV *beati patris obitum*, possibly through a misreading of the proper name in a MS. form like *bedāi*.

Dobbie believes that the history of the two versions is one that includes long separation after the original, presumably insular, composition. But matters are more complicated than that. To begin with, many copies of IV read *ut et ego* with CV, or something derived from that, in the passage noted above. For another, the Hague MS. of *EC* is basically a CV text but has several IV touches: among the more important are the salutation, the readings *VII kalendas junii* (the "correct" date) alone among CV MSS., the specification of the *libri rotarum*, and the addition of *sententia* in the first (but not the second) of the two places where IV supplies it. In these ways it appears to be a CV text "improved" by reference to the shorter IV, but it falls down badly in naming the *praefatus puer* as *Guthbertus*! For the story of the transmission of the text, its mixed readings are especially noteworthy, for it is one of the earliest CV MSS. (early tenth century) and two hundred years earlier than the earliest surviving IV text. (The implications of its opening address, apparently to Alcuin, will be discussed below.)

There are other features of the relationship between CV and IV that might be mentioned — it is perhaps noteworthy, for example, that the expatiations in CV are generally concentrated in a few passages rather than scattered throughout the letter — but the above account may serve to suggest something of the problem: in matters of both style and content, each version offers some features in which it is preferable to the other. It is on the whole probable that CV was "worked up" from IV, but even their disagreement in matters of fact suggests a particularly elaborate series of phases in this development.

Neither authorial revision nor inadvertent corruption nor both will explain all the divergences. But for the purpose of discussing the circumstances of Bede's last days, it will suffice to deal with IV, which gives the opening salutation, the "correct" date, and the *rotarum* reference in Isidore, and for the existence of which the Hague MS. provides evidence halfway between the earliest IV MS. in Dobbie's list and the alleged date of composition. It is, after all, true, as Dobbie says, that everything points, however strangely, to the priority of IV: and if that is so, then the existence of a CV MS. of the second quarter of the ninth century is further testimony to the early date of IV, even though the earliest pure IV MS. is of the twelfth century. (Dobbie also found a reference to a MS. of *EC* in a catalogue of the second quarter of the ninth century, but the portion of the MS. containing *EC* is lost, and there is no clue to which version it may have been. The catalogue entry omits Cuthbert's name and so hints at CV, which lacks the salutation.)

To begin with, *EC* does not make many references to external events by which it might be assessed. We have seen that as author Cuthbert is not an improbable figure; but equally, his name might have been garnered by anyone who knew anything of the history of Wearmouth-Jarrow; or had read Bede's very popular early work *De arte metrica* with its address to the other Cuthbert; or knew of the man of the same name who was Archbishop of Canterbury until his death in 758; or even knew the common name from legends like that of Cuthbert of Lindisfarne, about whom Bede had written a prose and a verse life and some of the *HE*.[11] In the latter case the connection with the Wearmouth-Jarrow circle would be coincidental. Cuthwine too is a name made of common elements, but his identity is unknown.[12] The point is that the salutation is no guarantee of authenticity in itself, and, indeed, was felt to be dispensable by the mid-ninth century at least, when the first CV appears without it. (Of course, many of the details of the *EC* could be reconstituted from common knowledge or spun out by stylistic elaboration, but if CV stems from a defective MS. of IV lacking the salutation, the defect would be difficult to restore. A single, hypothetical, defective IV MS. would thus account for this feature of CV but would leave other features obscure.)

Secondly, both versions attribute to Bede in his last days a translation of a portion of the gospel of St. John into English and a volume of extracts from Isidore of Seville. They also attribute to him, and in most MSS. give, the short Old English poem called *Bede's Death Song*.[13]

Now the former two works do not survive: there is no volume of extracts from Isidore, and the Old English gospel of St. John is of the wrong date and dialect to be Bede's.[14] If *EC* really stems from Wearmouth-Jarrow around 735, it is remarkable that we should have almost fifty MSS. of it and not *one* of the two works from the same time and place that it alludes to, for if Bede as subject was sufficient to give currency to *EC*, Bede as author ought surely have sufficed at least to preserve either the St. John or the Isidore; so, for that matter, ought the reputations of Isidore and of the Bible, both greater than that of Cuthbert. Imagine it: the works that elicited the final breaths of the dying man, at the height of his reputation in Northumbria, England, and Europe, to which he consecrated those last moments because *Nolo ut pueri mei mendacium legant, et in hoc post obitum meum sine fructu laborent*, written in a monastery that had a fruitful and expert scriptorium with a successful export program[15] — these works have disappeared and left only half a hundred identical references to them. Something is amiss with the third opusculum as well, for the CV gives it in a Northumbrian dialect correctly enough, while IV gives it in a West Saxon dialect. Yet IV is meant to be the original and CV somehow the derivative; so the dialectal origin of the *Death Song* is precisely the reverse of what we should expect. The literary history of these three items as *EC* presents them is indeed difficult to credit.

In the third place, we have the matter of the date. I have insinuated something about the traditional preference for the IV reading, 26 May, by putting inverted commas around "correct." Ascension Day is a movable feast which falls forty days after Easter; since the early limit for Easter is 21 March, there is nothing impossible about an Ascension Day on 9 May. The preference for 26 May arises from the calendars that give that day for Bede, in common with St. Augustine of Canterbury (some later calendars moved Bede on to 27 May, apparently so that he would not have to share the day with another Church figure especially important to the English).[16] Yet the calendars too are late and may well be following *EC* even if *EC* is a hundred years later than it claims to be. The preference for IV against CV for the "correct date" then depends on the authenticity of *EC*, which is precisely the problem at issue.

Another line of approach has been to question the probable year that a commitment to IV or CV would involve, for as Ascension Day is a movable feast, it falls on a specific day of the month only in certain years. The evidence for the age of Bede is this: his remarks in *HE*,

V.24, *usque ad annum aetatis meae LIX*, make it clear that he was at least fifty-nine in 731, when by its own testimony the work was written; these remarks refer to the period of his dedication to writing scriptural commentaries that continued at least as late as 729; so he was probably no older than sixty-one in 731, that is, born about 670. He is last known to have been alive, by the explicit testimony of his *Epistola ad Ecgberhtum*, in late 734 (5 November).[17]

EC refers to Bede's death as having occurred on Ascension Day, but as it was in the evening, *nona hora*, it was liturgically Ascension Day itself while still civilly the day before (unless the author of *EC* is setting this distinction aside and intends to refer to the evening of Ascension Day). With these two possibilities, and the two dates given by CV and IV, and with a terminus *non ante quem* of 734, we can construct the following table of possible years in which the death may have taken place, with Bede's approximate age in parentheses:

	Ascension Eve	Ascension Day
9 May	742(72), 750(80)	none possible
26 May	751(81)	735(65)

It is clear that 735 provides the most reasonable solution to the intersecting possibilities, and this year has attracted the almost unanimous favor of historians. There are, up to this point, two objections to it: the document that enshrines it is under suspicion, and the choice that leads to it is thus circular, for we cannot test the credibility of the document by supporting one of the choices that it offers us when only the document has committed us to those particular choices (and somewhat indirectly at that, what with the two versions of the date and the two possible interpretations of the relation of the date to Ascension Day). Moreover, the connection with Ascension Day which the document suggests is not independently attested — the calendars mention day of the month, not liturgical day [18] — and is open to question as an obvious hagiographical convenience.

Seemingly, the arithmetic which lies behind this rather unstable dating was a problem for medieval chroniclers as well: a "poll" of the *MGH Scriptores* in folio produces substantial support for 724, 730, 731, 734 (*huius* [i.e., Charles Martel] *XVII anno Beda . . . obiit*), 735, 736, 737, and at some time during a longish period ending 742. The number of testimonies of each of these dates is probably of little significance until the interrelationship of all the chroniclers has been worked out, and so I have not given references to each;[19] but there is no overwhelming evidence in favor of 735, and little to suggest that the *EC* either represented or acted as the vehicle for an established tradition. On the contrary, the two dates that can be discerned easily within Bede's books, 725 (*De temporum ratione*)[20] and 731 (*HE*), were commonly mistaken for his death date unimpeded by any other generally accepted notion. (It is interesting that the phrase *Beda scripsit suum librum*, which recurs, is under 725 and alternates with *Beda sacerdos huc usque chronicam suam contexuit* and the like, betraying the chronicler's special debt to — perhaps his exclusive knowledge of — Bede's *De temporum ratione*, with its long appended chronicle,[21] in contrast with the modern opinion that identifies *HE* as *librum suum*.)

Thus far I have attempted to show that *EC* is of doubtful authenticity in itself because of its grotesque textual history, which looks very much like variant fictive iteration without the control of a basis in fact and which excludes any manuscript evidence earlier than a century after the events it describes, and because of the improbabilities surrounding the literary efforts of Bede's last days. I have further tried to show that the dates it offers for his illness and death are contradictory, capable of several interpretations, and unsupported by independent contemporary evidence. Hence, the employment of *EC* to arrive at a date of 735 both relies on an unreliable document and makes unwarranted use of it. I should not be astounded if proof were forthcoming that Bede died in 735 — he mentions in his letter to Ecgberht of 734 that he was unwell — but *EC* is not such proof.

Before leaving the question of *EC* itself, we must look at its connection with the *Vita Bedae*, with Simeon of Durham's *Historia Dunelmensis Ecclesiae*, with other hagiographical materials of the Bede tradition, and with Alcuin.

As Dobbie points out, a number of the exemplars of IV are in twelfth- and thirteenth-century MSS. of the *Vita Bedae*,[22] a short work which begins with some independent material, continues with a lengthy quotation from the "bio-bibliography" of *HE*, V.24, and concludes with *EC*. *Vita Bedae* draws no conclusions about Bede's death date, either from *EC* or otherwise, but it does give a birth date of 677. The materials in *HE*, V.24, however, as we have seen above, suffice to give a *terminus non post quem* of 672 for the birth of Bede; so *Vita Bedae*, by virtue of this unreliability, its late MS. tradition, its silence on the death date, and its lack of independence of *EC*, throws no new light on our investigation.

Simeon of Durham, in his work of the twelfth century, includes IV in his account of the life of Bede.[23] He also gives a death date of 735. Unfortunately, he adds that Bede was fifty-nine at the time of his death, an evident confusion of the material in *HE*, V.24, that would lead to a birth date around 676, similar perhaps to the error which vitiates *Vita Bedae* as a source for the solution of the problem under discussion. Simeon remains important, as does *Vita Bedae*, for the text of IV, but neither tradition goes any way towards solving the difficulties of *EC* as an instrument of dating.

Of the major Latin saints' lives written in England by the mid-eighth century or so, two — the *Vita anonyma Sancti Gregorii*[24] and Eddius' *Vita Wilfridi*[25] — are relatively independent of each other and of the rest. But three, the *Vita anonyma Sancti Cuthberti*, Bede's prose *Vita Sancti Cuthberti*,[26] and Felix's *Vita Sancti Guthlaci*,[27] stood in close connection, for Bede's work is based in substantial measure on the anonymous life, and Felix's draws on them both, as well as on other non-English lives, notably the translation by Evagrius of Athanasius' life of St. Anthony.[28] The borrowings are often extensive and *verbatim*. If *EC* has any part in this "great tradition," however, it is only in a detail of content, not in their common stock of phraseology: its verbal debt is almost exclusively to the Bible.[29] Yet the detail of content is relevant to our inquiry. Bede recorded that Cuthbert died on a Wednesday, and this detail — mostly in Bede's very words — was taken over by Felix.[30] Now *EC* likewise gives us a death date of Wednesday, at least by civil reckoning, and "improves" upon the detail by making it the vigil of the Feast of the Ascension. As this point is, we have seen, essential for the computation of the year of Bede's death, its place in earlier literary history is not without bearing on the authenticity of *EC*.

On the assumption that *EC* was authentically a document of the mid-eighth century with the provenance that it claimed, Brotanek felt himself under obligation to account for its dissemination to continental centers. He thought that either Boniface or Alcuin might have had a hand in it but preferred to think it was Boniface.[31] On the basis of the address to *reverentissime albine* in the Hague MS., Ker believed that the other hypothesis was "almost certain."[32] We now see that Brotanek's initial assumption is open to question, and hence his further theories may be otiose; but it is, in any case, worth noting that no other MS. of *EC* contains the address, that the Hague MS. dates more than a century later than Alcuin's death, and that "Albinus" is by no means automatically Alcuin: Bede himself wrote a short letter to another Albinus,[33] for example, long before Alcuin was born, and the address may look back to this document or another like it. The exceptional material in the Hague MS. provides nothing whatsoever to support the authenticity of *EC*.

I should like finally to consider the application of these matters to the question of the Bede "signature" in the colophon to Book V of the *HE* in the Leningrad MS.[34] In 1958 Professor E. A. Lowe proposed that the fifth line of the colophon, which reads, *Beda famulus Christi indig[nus]*, was in the hand of Bede himself, because:

1. The first two words clearly are in the nominative, not the usual genitive;
2. The adjective *indignus* could have been applied to Bede only by himself;
3. The normal place for the name of an author in a colophon is before, not, as here, after, the title;
4. The last line is actually in a different hand — a tremulous one — from the first four lines.[35]

After a period of favor, Lowe's theory began to encounter criticism.[36] Point three was weakened by reference to other colophons in Bede MSS., and it was shown that the colophon to a *work* might take one form, and that to the last *book* in a work, as here, another. But points 1, 2 and 4 still stood.

Two obstacles to their acceptance remained. One was a set of notations, calculating how long before the notations certain events in *HE* had taken place, which gave results that in all but one case suggest that the notations were made in 746. If, as some hold, the notations are in the same hand as some earlier parts of the MS., it would probably follow that the MS. could not be earlier than 746. The second obstacle was a number of pen-trials of the letter *a* that appear at the bottom of the last page in a hand which, up to now, no one has dated earlier than the very end of the eighth century; and at least one of these pen-trials overlaps, or is overlapped by, one of the letters in the last line of the colophon. If the colophon is indeed on top of the pen-trial, as some investigators believe, then the colophon too cannot be later than the end of the eighth century, even later than the *terminus non ante quem* given by the chronological notations. All the scholars taking part in this inquiry have assumed as a certainty that Bede died in 735. Since Lowe's points and these obstacles are irreconcilable, the conclusion now generally held is that the "signature" is a forgery.

However, all three assumptions have been challenged. Bévenot has strongly suggested that the "tell-tale dates" were put in by someone other than the scribes who worked on the body of the MS., and although the notations were inserted in 746 they tell us nothing about the date of the MS. as a whole other than by providing a *terminus non post quem*. But Bévenot accepted that the signature was a forgery because of the pen-trials. Meyvaert, on the other hand, who depended on the chronological notations to discredit the signature, was willing to accept that the evidence of the pen-trials is indistinct: they may or may not antedate the signature.[37] And the present paper, for its part, has suggested that we do not know the death date of Bede after all: he cannot have been alive at the very end of the eighth century, of course, but he would not have been older than 76 in 746.

Accepting that the physical arguments for forgery in the signature have not been established, what are the other arguments? Meyvaert says that the signature was forged to enhance the "relic" value of the MS. and adduces examples of other such schemes.[38] Yet all of these examples have two things in common: they *declare* in no uncertain terms that the MS. is *written* by the saint (Augustine of Hippo, Boniface). Here we have something quite different. The signature does *not* declare that the saint wrote the MS. with his own hand, and indeed it makes no predication that he even wrote the last line of the colophon. The "relic" value, as in none of the examples Meyvaert cites, is merely that the saint was associated with the MS. and put his hand to one line of the last page, and even then the hand of the author does not contain any declaration other than what can be inferred from the nominatives and from *indignus*. Reliance on such grammatical and lexical subtleties is surely most unlike a medieval forgery.

If the date 735 has a place in this controversy, then the question is one of conflicting evidence: either the Leningrad signature or *EC* (or both) is a forgery. The value of *EC* to the Bede cult would in any case be far greater than that of the Leningrad signature, and I hope I have shown the *EC* is even more open to question as a document. What is more, it would by its nature do its public relations job better than the colophon because it makes its point openly and repeatedly rather than leaving it to the keen eye of a scholar to pick up the faint hints of a saintly connection. For all three reasons, an either/or juxtaposition between the two is bound to conclude in favor of the signature and against *EC*. But, of course, we are not committed to such a juxtaposition, and even if scholarly opinion hardens against the Leningrad colophon, the proponents of *EC* will have a great deal to explain away.[39]

NOTES

1. On the general topic, see H. Fuhrmann, "Die Fälschungen im Mittelalter," *Historische Zeitschrift*, CXCVII (1963), 529–601. For an illustrative recent defense ("rebunking"?), see Dorothy Whitelock, *The Genuine Asser* (Reading, England, 1968).

2. See, for example, Dorothy Whitelock's refutation of the traditional materials for an *obiit* of Aelfric of Eynsham, "Two Notes on Ælfric and Wulfstan. (i) The Date of Ælfric's Death," *MLR*, XXXVIII (1943), 122–24.

The present paper is an expansion of my remarks in *A History of Anglo-Latin Literature, 597–1066, Vol. I: 597–740* (Princeton, 1967), 104–5. For Bede, see 101–85, 264–87.

3. Ed. Elliott van Kirk Dobbie, *The Manuscripts of Cædmon's Hymn and Bede's Death Song, with a Critical Text of the Epistola Cuthberti de Obitu Bedæ*, Columbia University Studies in English and Comparative Literature, No. 128 (New York, 1937). The literature on the *Epistola* is not extensive, but see also R. Brotanek, "Zur Überlieferung des Sterbegesanges Bedas und der Epistola Cuthberti ad Cuthwinum," *Texte und Untersuchungen zur altenglischen Literatur und Kirchengeschichte* (Halle, 1913), pp. 150–94, 201–2; and *idem*, "Nachlese zu den Handschriften der *Epistola Cuthberti* und des *Sterbespruches Bedas*," *Anglia*, LXIV (1940), 159–90. The present paper normalizes all Latin quotations according to the practice in my *History of Anglo-Latin Literature*.

4. M. L. W. Laistner and H. H. King, *A Handlist of Bede Manuscripts* (Ithaca, 1943), p. 120.

5. See C. E. Whiting, "The Life of the Venerable Bede," *Bede: His Life, Times, and Writings*, ed. A. H. Thompson (Oxford, 1935), p. 35.

6. Whiting, *loc. cit.*

7. Ed. H. Keil, *Grammatici latini*, VII (Leipzig, 1880), 217–60.

8. Laistner-King, pp. 131–32.

9. N. R. Ker, "The Hague Manuscript of the Epistola Cuthberti de Obitu Bedæ with Bede's Song," *Medium Ævum*, VIII (1939), 40–44.

10. F. Wormald, *English Kalendars before* A.D. *1100* (London, 1934), pp. 34, 118, 132, 160, 188, 202, 230.

11. Ed. and trans. B. Colgrave, *Two Lives of St. Cuthbert* (Cambridge, 1940); ed. W. Jaager, "Bedas metrische Vita Sancti Cuthberti," *Palaestra*, CXCVIII (1935; also published separately, Weimar, 1935); ed. C. Plummer, *Venerabilis Baedae opera historica* (Oxford, 1896), *HE*, IV, 25–30.

12. So, for that matter, is the *praefatus puer* Wilberht. See W. G. Searle, *Onomasticon Anglo-Saxonicum* (Cambridge, 1897), s. v. Cuthwine and Wilbeorht.

13. Ed. A. H. Smith, *Three Northumbrian Poems* (London, 1933, 1968). The evidence of this poem cannot be used to provide a date for *EC*; "there is nothing to indicate the date of the extant versions of Bede's Death Song" (Smith, p. 23) in the linguistic data, and in any case such a date would be nothing more than a *terminus non ante quem* for *EC* as a whole.

14. Ed. J. W. Bright, *The Gospels in West-Saxon*, 4 vols. (Boston, 1904–5). The dialect is not Northumbrian and the date is *c.* 1000.

15. Cf. E. A. Lowe, "A Key to Bede's Scriptorium," *Scriptorium*, XII (1958), 182–90. According to M. L. W. Laistner, "The Library of the Venerable Bede," *Bede: His Life, Times, and Writings*, ed. A. H. Thompson (Oxford, 1935), p. 256, "Bede . . . treats Isidore with more freedom and less respect than his other authorities. He names him only three times in all, in each case only to controvert him." Laistner does not deny that Bede knew Isidore's *De natura rerum* (the *libri rotarum*), *Etymologies*, and *Chronicon*, and perhaps the *Quaestiones in vetus Testamentum* as well; but his remarks cast further doubt on the authenticity of the report that Bede actually chose Isidore as the sole patristic writer he wished to translate. See C. W. Jones, "Manuscripts of Bede's *De natura rerum*," *Isis*, XXVII (1937), 430–40, especially 437.

16. F. Wormald, *English Benedictine Kalendars after* A.D. *1100*, I (London, 1939), 38.

17. Ed. C. Plummer (note 11, above), I, 405–23.

18. Because they record fixed, not movable, feasts.

19. One instance of each year can, however, be found as follows: 724, *MGH Scr.*, XXIV, 495 (*Beda . . . cardinalis obiit*); 730, IX, 494; 731, V, 98; 734, XXX.2, 751; 735, III, 116; 736, III, 34; 737, V, 546 (*2 Kal. Ian.*, perhaps miswritten for *7 Kal. Iun.* or *II Kal. Ian* for *VII Kal. Iun.?*); *non post* 742, X, 128.

20. Ed. C. W. Jones, *Bedae opera de temporibus*, Mediaeval Academy of America, Publication No. XLI (Cambridge, Mass., 1943).

21. See *MGH Scr.*, XIII, 41, 77, 700; V, 417, 545. The Chronicles are ed. T. Mommsen, *MGH Auct. Ant.*, XIII.2 (Berlin, 1895), 223 ff.

22. Ed. J.-P. Migne, *PL*, XC, coll. 35–42.

23. Ed. T. Arnold, *Rolls Series*, LXXV.1 (London, 1882), 43–46.

24. Ed. and trans. B. Colgrave, *The Earliest Life of Gregory the Great* (Lawrence, Kansas, 1968).

25. Ed. and trans. B. Colgrave, *The Life of Bishop Wilfrid by Eddius Stephanus* (Cambridge, 1927).

26. Ed. and trans. B. Colgrave (note 11, above).

27. Ed. and trans. B. Colgrave, *Felix's Life of St. Guthlac* (Cambridge, 1956); cf. W. F. Bolton, "The Latin Revisions of Felix's 'Vita Sancti Guthlaci,'" *Mediaeval Studies*, XXI (1959), 36–52, esp. 37, note 7.

28. Ed. Migne, *PL*, LXXIII, coll. 125–70.

29. E.g., the remark in IV attributed to Bede, *cupio dissolvi et esse cum Christo*, from Phil. 1.23.

30. Bede, *ed. cit.*, p. 272; Felix, *ed. cit.*, p. 152.

31. Brotanek, *Texte und Untersuchungen*, p. 192.

32. Ker, "The Hague MS.," p. 40.

33. Ed. C. Plummer (note 11, above), I, 3. Albinus was abbot of St. Augustine's, Canterbury.

34. See O. Dobiache-Rojdestvensky, "Un manuscrit de Bède à Léningrad," *Speculum*, III (1928), 314–21, and ed. O. Arngart, *The Leningrad Bede*, Early English Manuscripts in Facsimile, II (Copenhagen, 1952).

35. E. A. Lowe, "An Autograph of the Venerable Bede?," *Revue Bénédictine*, LXVIII (1958), 200–202; see also note 15, above, and D. Misonne,

" 'Famulus Christi': à propos d'un autographe de Bède le Vénérable," *Revue Bénédictine*, LXIX (1959), 97–99.

36. P. Meyvaert, "Colophons dans des manuscrits de Bède," *Revue Bénédictine*, LXIX (1959), 100–101; *idem*, "The Bede 'Signature' in the Leningrad Colophon," *ibid.*, LXXI (1961), 274–86; D. H. Wright, "The Date of the Leningrad Bede," *tom. cit.*, 265–73; M. Bévenot, "Towards Dating the Leningrad 'Bede,' " *Scriptorium*, XVI (1962), 365–69.

37. The present paper is concerned mainly with *EC* and only in passing with the Leningrad signature, but I should like to say that I do *not* think that the pen-trials antedate the fifth line of the colophon. If those who have scrutinized the MS. cannot reach a clear decision about which writing is on top of which, we shall have to take another approach. Now either the scribe of the pen-trials found a blank below the fourth line, carried out his defacement, and was followed by the forger who used such space as the *a*-scribe left him; or the *a*-scribe in the late eighth century found all five lines already in place and filled in the remaining space barbarically. All five lines are equally spaced; all five are aligned on the left (the right-hand margin has been trimmed with some loss of letters). The pen-trials extend into the left-hand margin and begin in the space between the last line of the text and the first line of the colophon; they continue in the spaces between all the lines except that between the third and fourth. Only one letter *a* touches a letter of the colophon, but others come very close. The question then is this: did a forger find the MS. already defaced but with a space exactly suitable for the fifth line, or did a later scribal hack fill in among the five existing lines and — by chance — overlap one? We have no choice between the villainies of forgery and defacement. Looking at photostats of the page, however, I cannot accept as a likelihood that the scribe of the pen-trials left such a convenient space when he had used up so much else of the blanks on the page, nor that a page thus defaced would strike a forger as a suitable place to carry out his scheme of enhancing the "relic" value of the MS.

38. Meyvaert, 1961, pp. 284–85.

39. Since the completion of this paper (March, 1969) there has appeared A. S. C. Ross, "A Connection between Bede and the Anglo-Saxon Gloss to the Lindisfarne Gospels?" *Journal of Theological Studies*, N.S., XX (1969), 482–94, which takes the *Epistola Cuthberti* as evidence for the possible connection. Ross does not doubt the authenticity of the *Epistola*. Otherwise his remarks are not concerned with the burden of this paper.

The Hussite Revolution and the German Peasants' War

AN HISTORICAL COMPARISON

Frederick G. Heymann

THE GERMAN PEASANTS' WAR, *der deutsche Bauernkrieg*, is the name that has been given to the most violent phase of the great upheaval that was contemporary with an equally prominent phase of the German, specifically the Lutheran, Reformation. The movement was not limited to or universal among the peasantry — there were even parts of northwest Germany where the peasants remained quiet, while there were bloody rebellions in prominent cities such as Cologne. It has sometimes been suggested that the name *Bauernkrieg* should be changed, and in the recent East German literature the expression mostly used is *frühbürgerliche Revolution*,[1] a term difficult to translate. The term *Peasants' War* is old, indeed contemporary with the event, and it is perhaps best to retain it.

There has been general agreement among German historians that the Peasants' War was of quite striking importance for the whole history of Germany. The feeling that this was not just a tragedy for the peasantry but for the nation as a whole has been expressed by several significant writers. "The great mistake," wrote Alexander von Humboldt to Julius Fröbel in 1843, "was that the movement of the Peasants' War did not succeed." Similar utterances abound; for example, Johannes Bühler emphasizes the "tremendous significance of the Peasants' War," mainly because it definitely established the absolute power of the German princes.[2]

With judgments like these, it was bound to be asked why, in contrast to the other great revolutions of the fifteenth, sixteenth, and seventeenth centuries, this German revolution ended in such a dismal failure. There have been many answers to this question; indeed, there cannot be just one answer, since such powerful upheavals are always due to multiple causes. But perhaps more clarity can be gained by comparing the peasant revolution with one or another of the various revolutions with which it had something in common.

141

Among the European revolutions there are three that could possibly be considered as having some aspects which might make a comparison at all feasible: the Hussite Revolution, the revolution of the Netherlands, and the Puritan revolution in England. In all three, as in the Peasants' War, a political revolution took place against the background of a religious reform movement. However, in the two later revolutions the actual role of the religious movement was weaker than in the Peasants' War, and was not autochthonous but imported. Also, in both of these later upheavals the peasantry, with but few exceptions, had not such a prominent part. Finally, both arose out of societal situations in which early modern capitalist developments had already led to rather deep structural changes. In contrast, German society during the Peasants' War was still essentially medieval in nature, even though some of its features, above all the classical form of feudalism, had for some time been undergoing a process of decomposition. The background world of the Hussite Revolution, on the other hand, was structurally much nearer to that of the Peasants' War. The century that separated the two had, of course, brought about considerable changes in Germany, including the beginnings of a vigorous merchant and banking capitalism, not limited to such booming places as Augsburg, home of the Fuggers and Welsers. But this development could only strengthen the class antagonism within the cities, which had been strong in Bohemia for some time before the Hussite period. In the majority of German cities, as in the rural regions, economic and social life was still late-medieval in character, much as it had been a century earlier in Bohemia and Moravia. Thus an analytical sketch comparing the Peasants' War with the Hussite Revolution seems more profitable than any other such comparison.

In order to enter upon such a comparative discussion we should probably begin by looking at similarities. Both revolutions occurred against the background of religious reform movements which in both cases preceded and survived the revolutions by long periods of time. It is difficult to date with any precision the point of departure of the Hussite Reformation, which depends above all on the decision to include or exclude earlier reform movements inside, and perhaps even outside, Bohemia.[3] But there is no question that by 1408/9 the religious movement later called Hussitism had been born, and was about to survive much resistance and gain much strength, even before it received the energizing shock of Hus' martyrdom. As such it served as an important motive force for the actual outbreak of the violent revolution, marked by the First Defenestration of Prague on July 30, 1419. The Lutheran Reformation has always been dated from 1517, and while there had been some peasant rebellions as well as city rebellions even in the fourteenth and much more in the fifteenth and early sixteenth centuries, the actual outbreak of the Peasants' War as a truly widespread (though never fully nationwide) revolution dates from 1524. The Hussite Revolution, with its successes and failures, expired in 1434 with the Battle of Lipany, even though the official burial of the war had to wait till 1436. The Revolution as a violent societal process lasted, then, for fifteen years. The German peasants' revolution, on the other hand, was fully suppressed in 1526, though not too much had survived after the bitter defeats of the summer of 1525. On the whole it lasted barely two years, a rather short period as full-sized revolutions go.

In both cases the reformations which had preceded the revolutions by several years also survived them by long periods: Hussitism continued to exist, in two forms, the Utraquist and Neo-Utraquist churches and the Church of the Brethren, right into the sixteenth and seventeenth centuries, by which time both branches had taken their place within the number of Protestant denominations then existing in Bohemia and Moravia.[4] The Lutheran Reformation, of course, went on far beyond the end of the Peasants' War, though as a result of Luther's turning against the peasants it lost a good deal of its original character as a revolutionary religious mass movement.

In both cases the religious reform movements had already, to a considerable extent, a revolutionary character. In both cases they challenged many aspects of the dominion of the Roman church. As this dominion was far from merely spiritual, but included a large degree of worldly power, the challenge of the reform movements struck economic and political issues as well.[5] In both movements the more radical religious groups argued by contrasting the poverty of Christ and the Apostles with the wealth and luxury of Rome and the Papacy. In both cases the issue of indulgences played an important role, especially in the early phases of the religious struggles that preceded the outbreak of the social revolutions.[6] In both cases sharp attacks directed against the Holy See went so far as to accuse the Pope of being Anti-Christ himself. In both cases the Church, allied with the Emperor, tried to silence the most prominent representatives of the reform, by either making them recant or killing them. And though Hus died while Luther survived, both became not leaders merely, but shining symbols, in the eyes of those who saw in their teachings a new, glowing freedom of religious thinking and preaching and a more direct way of finding God. The waves of both reform movements seemed to overwhelm all resistance.

At the death of Hus, and for quite some time after, no part of Bohemia's lay society was unaffected. Not only peasants, townsmen, and knights, but even many members of the baronial class identified themselves with the teachings of Hus and the masters of Prague University.[7] At the same time, among the lower classes in cities and rural regions, the seeds were growing for a movement that would contain stronger socio-political elements than could be found in the original teachings of Hus and his friends.

In a similar way the Lutheran movement expanded in the years immediately preceding the Peasants' War and was accepted by princes and nobles, burghers and peasants to an extent that made the early resistance of the Catholic establishment ineffective. Socio-political unrest, long present but mostly as an underground development among the lower classes, had in all of upper Germany become a steadily increasing threat to the German form of late feudalism. And again the religious and moralistic rebellion against the ecclesiastical power structures strengthened the movement for a combined religious and social revolt.

There is nothing surprising in the fact that both movements, in their religious as well as in their socio-political aspects, had left and right wings.[8] The ideological and structural religious differences, described by George Williams as those of a magisterial and a radical reformation, did exist in Bohemia and Germany in closely similar forms. There were important similarities between the teachings of Prague's Utraquist church, especially by John Rokycana (d. 1471), and those of Luther.[9] There are similar parallels also between both radical reformations. Thomas Müntzer was surely aware of the ties that connected his ideas and those of early Tábor, with its fanatical chiliasm and iconoclasm.[10] There are even parallels to the extremely radical movement of the Adamites, who indulged in uninhibited orgies because they felt that there was no longer sin in them,[11] and which found a close replica in the movement of the so-called Blutfreunde in Thuringia, though this emerged some twenty years later than the Peasants' War. Common medieval sectarian origins, such as that of the Brethren of the Free Spirit, may have been the main cause of these remarkable parallels, while for the main strands of the two radical reformations the underground survival of Waldensianism had been important. It is from this source, presumably, that we can trace the other, non-violent, indeed deeply pacifist, strand existing in each of the movements. Within the Hussite framework this was the earliest beginning of the Czech Brethren under the influence of Peter Chělcický,[12] and in the sixteenth century the growth of the antimilitarist wing (in the form of Mennonitism, the only wing to survive) of German, Swiss, and Dutch Anabaptism. Many of these sectarians found a temporary asylum in Moravia where they met and exchanged ideas with the much older communities of the Czech Brethren.[13]

If we can find a rather large number of parallels and similarities in the religious trends and movements that triggered the two revolutions, we can also see a corresponding parallel in at least one of the main directions that both revolutions took once they had become open movements. They, and especially their more radical wings, turned with special emotion against the high clergy and even more against the monastic clergy. In Bohemia the Archbishop of Prague, Conrad of Vechta, saved himself and part of his possessions by joining the Hussite side and adhering to its great charter, the Four Articles of Prague. The Bishop of Litomyšl, Aleš of Březí, however, had to flee before the revolutionary conquerors, and his see remained unoccupied until 1443. The Bishop of Olomouc, John "the Iron," was in a better position since Moravia was partly occupied by troops of Duke Albert of Austria, but between him and the Hussites of Moravia there arose a steadily exacerbating struggle.[14] In Germany a century later there were many archbishops and bishops who were subject to a political if not a military attack on the part of the revolutionaries.

Even greater was the similarity in the case of the monasteries. In the Hussite Revolution the many great and rich monastic establishments of Bohemia were almost regularly the first object of attack by the militant brotherhoods of Tábor and Oreb. John Žižka, the captain general of the Taborites (whom sixteenth-century portraits called "the severe avenger of the insolence and avarice of the clerics"),[15] gave his soldiers free play in burning monasteries. Frequently monks not willing to accept what the Hussites called the Law of God were burned as well, on the basically Catholic assumption that it was necessary and meritorious to burn heretics.[16] The German revolutionaries of 1525, peasants as well as city rebels, were not quite as pitiless; indeed most of the monks of those destroyed monasteries were personally spared. But the monasteries were occupied and burned with the same regularity as they had been in Bohemia a century earlier. In both cases the rich stores of victuals were seized, and in both cases, if we can trust reports mostly coming from hostile sources, the peasant-soldiers indulged with special glee in a mass consumption of large quantities of wine in the monastery cellars.[17]

These violent attacks upon the clergy and the monasteries are closely connected with what can be considered the most lasting results of both revolutions: a large step forward, in each case, in the great process of secularization. In both countries this process diminished radically the enormous wealth that the Church had had at its disposal (in Bohemia, for example, the Church was estimated to have owned about half the area of the country).[18] In both countries, however, those profiting were not the revolutionary masses but those who already had dominant positions in society: in Bohemia the high nobility, in Germany the territorial princes.

The ultimate outcomes, however, were different. In Bohemia the high nobility, despite their gains of Church land, were not, on the whole, the only or even the main winners from the socio-structural changes which the Hussite Revolution brought about. The gentry profited even more, at least in relation to its previous status, which had been rather weak, and was able to maintain a strong position into the Habsburg era of the following centuries. For some time even the cities profited, with the zenith of their strength in the period before the Battle of Lipany (1434), and could be considered as an important element of Bohemia's socio-political structure. Only in the later Jagiellon era were the cities forced to retreat before the coalition of barons and knights, and finally deprived of many of their gains by Ferdinand I. In Germany, on the other hand, knights and cities, together with the peasants, were the losers, and the princes the only winners. The lower nobility had already lost out, to a considerable extent, as a consequence of the Sickingen movement that had almost immediately preceded the outbreak of the Peasants' War; and the cities, especially those that had taken the side of the revolutionaries, were frequently punished and emerged in most cases weaker than they had been before the revolution. These developments, however, are intimately connected with the basic fact that the Peasants' War, both in the form of the rural and of the urban revolts, was soon beaten and suppressed, and that — with the single exception of the secularization which was a partial result of the revolution — none of its goals was reached.

But this fact, the early and utter failure of this great movement, so different from the development and outcome of the Hussite Revolution, is just what remains to be explained, and it is the differences of the two revolutionary movements that should help us to understand it.

Among these differences one that seems most obvious is based on political geography. It is true that like Germany the Bohemian realm was not a united and centrally structured political body. The area under the crown of St. Wenceslas included, besides the Kingdom of Bohemia proper, the Margraviate of Moravia, the Duchy of Silesia (consisting of many small principalities), and the Margraviates of Upper and Lower Lusatia. Silesia and Lusatia remained largely untouched by the revolutionary movement. Indeed these territories, which were mainly ruled by Germans and whose Slavic population contained few Czechs but mostly Poles and Lusatian Serbs, came out strongly against Hussitism. But even Moravia, which had been so long and so closely tied to the Bohemian crown, was never, during the whole course of the revolution, firmly in Hussite hands. Such was not even the case in all of Bohemia. Even there, as in those border regions that had a strong German population, but also the ethnically Czech city of Pilsen, the royalists took an early stand against the Revolution, allied themselves with foreign powers against it, and were strong enough to survive. This, then, seems to be not too much different from the situation in Germany, which in the sixteenth century had become a vast hodgepodge of greater and smaller principalities, bishoprics, and free cities.

Nevertheless there was a considerable difference. The Kingdom of Bohemia proper, a good deal larger than any of the German territorial principalities, was yet small enough for a military genius like Jan Žižka, the greatest of the Czech captains, to think and indeed to act in terms of a strategy which took the whole country into consideration.[19] Such a strategy, given the realities of military and political geography, would have been hardly thinkable for the whole of Germany. However, it would almost certainly have been a possibility in the framework of one of the major regions of Germany such as Swabia, Franconia, or Thuringia. Indeed the proof that this would have been possible was delivered by the enemies of the revolution, specifically by George Truchsess of Waldburg, the commander in chief of the Swabian League, whose strategy concerned a large part of southern Germany. If in any of these regions the revolutionaries had achieved a decisive victory, the whole history of the Peasants' War might have taken a different turn.

There is one other difference between the two revolutions that borders on aspects of political geography. This is the presence, in the case of Bohemia, of a great city which had long played the role of a national center, as residence of the king and more recently as seat of a university. Here in Prague the Revolution erupted, and its early development is difficult to imagine without Prague's initial leadership.[20] There was no such center in Germany, and it is difficult to imagine any place that could have played the role of the national center of the revolution.

There is another element that made it easier for the Czech than for the German revolution to achieve a high degree of ideological and political concentration: this is the presence in Bohemia, but the absence in Germany, of a great dominating enemy figure.

The leading enemy throughout the decisive earlier phase of the Hussite Revolution was of course Sigismund, King of Hungary and of the Romans, "natural" successor to his brother King Wenceslas IV and persistent claimant to the Bohemian throne. The antagonism against him was not, for the majority of the Czech people, the expression of an anti-monarchial disposition. Beginnings of republicanism do appear both among the Prague radicals and in Tábor, but the majority of the people of all social strata took monarchy as the normal state of affairs, just as they did in Germany a century later. That Sigismund, in spite of his hereditary rights, was considered unacceptable was due to the feeling that, by allowing Hus to be executed, he had mortally offended the whole Czech nation; this antipathy had become even worse through his general attitude toward the Czech Hussites and especially through his "crusades." Originally it was the high nobility which had paved the way for this revolutionary attitude; this was not too astonishing, as the Czech magnates, as was rather common with feudal barons in the Middle Ages, had tried for centuries to limit the power of the kings. (We may remember that the French Revolution too was mainly started by the high nobility.) The majority of the barons, even including some Catholics, were still willing to cooperate with the other estates in deposing Sigismund at the great diet of Čáslav in June, 1421.[21] Among the knights and burghers, and certainly among the peasants as well, there was no doubt that Sigismund was "the great and cruel enemy of the Czech Kingdom and Nation."[22] We know from the history of the other great revolutions — the Dutch, the English Puritan, the American, and the French — the unifying force of one great royal enemy. Their leaders were very conscious of this, and (as did Jefferson in his presentation of George III in the Declaration of

Independence) went to great lengths to make "the Tyrant" appear in the worst possible light. The Hussite Revolution is the first one in which this feature appears so clearly.

It hardly needs to be proved that no such unifying enemy existed in the German Peasants' War. Emperor Charles V, at the time, was far away. His brother, Archduke Ferdinand, who to some extent operated as his viceroy, was frequently if wrongly considered a friend of the peasants, and whatever influence his generally cautious and clever maneuvering had upon the course of events served to divide rather than unite the revolutionaries.[23] Instead, they had many enemies, and none more hated than the ecclesiastical and temporal princes who tried to expand and fortify their usually small local power. These many regional or local enemies tended to divide the rebels, who would attack the nearest foe. This, in turn, weakened the chance for cooperation among the many revolutionary troops who were peasants and who preferred to remain near their homes.

Among those leaders of the revolution who were of urban or even knightly origin, quite a few tended to look at the revolution as the decisive phase in the long (and always unsuccessful) struggle for imperial reform. This, of course, would mean strengthening the central power of the Emperor against the attempts of the princes to achieve an ever larger measure of sovereignty. The urge to weaken or eliminate the little rulers, especially the ecclesiastical ones, in favor of larger political units emerged quite naturally from the logic of the political history of Germany in the late Middle Ages. But this desire never found support from the usually absent Emperor.

There is still another, even more important element that made for a measure of cooperation and unity among the Hussites but was almost completely lacking in the German revolution: the force of nationalism.[24] Beginnings of nationalism, above all in the negative form of anti-German feelings and utterances, can be found as early as the beginning of the twelfth century.[25] In the Hussite period it was probably stronger and more akin to modern nationalism than in any other European country of this time and even much later periods. To some extent this nationalism had social causes, especially in many of the cities, where frequently the city councils, or at least a considerable part of their seats, were in the hands of German patricians, while the craftsmen, organized in guilds, and the poorer people without guild standing were mostly Czechs. There was also resentment against many German abbots and other monastic clerics dominating monasteries in mainly Czech districts of the country. Once the series of anti-Hussite crusades had begun to invade Bohemia the national hatred from both sides increased markedly, especially since many of the "crusaders," the majority of them Germans, would kill Czech-speaking people without much regard whether they were really "heretics" or not.[26] There were also bitter complaints about the brutality of the Hungarian soldiery. They indulged, so it was claimed, in wantonly destroying Czech villages, burning the men, mutilating the boys, raping the women and girls.[27] To what extent the Hungarians really behaved worse than other soldiers of their time would be hard to determine, but the feeling that our sources present is certainly one of passionate national resentment and hatred in which the nationalist element is stronger than that of religious antagonism.

Together with what we might call the negatively based form of nationalism we also find a positive variant: the messianic, and often chiliastic, conviction that God had given "his faithful Czechs" a very special task, that of showing the whole Christian world "the truth of God and the Law of God," which is often taken as the preparation for the impending coming of Christ.[28] Chiliasm soon exhausted itself, and even the idea of the Czechs as the chosen people did not last with equal vigour through those long fifteen years. Yet the consciousness of being different and special, of being closer to God than any other nation, persisted, especially among the more radical groups of which Tábor was by far the most significant.[29]

How very different was the situation in Germany. Chiliasm did exist, indeed, and with it a feeling of a great mission, especially in one sector of the revolution — the one led by Thomas Müntzer in Thüringen.[30] It is surely not just incidental that Müntzer was the one great figure who had spent some time in Bohemia (in Žatec and Prague) and had, in spite of considerable difficulties, been under the influence of the heirs of the Hussite movement.[31] But if Müntzer told his adherents that they could not possibly lose out because God was on their side, he did not, and could not, claim that this had anything to do with their being Germans. Their adversaries, after all, were just as German as they themselves. There had been national protests in the writings of Hutten — but he had died before the Peasants' War had broken out, and if there were elements of nationalism in Luther's attacks against Rome and the Papacy this was still far apart from the glowing identification of the Czech nation with the religious struggles of the Hussite movement. It was this identification which made the Czech revolutionaries willing to fight in a common front, making sacrifices for a greater, a religious-national cause, while in the German Peasants' War the peasants as well as the cities were moved most of the time by narrow local or at best regional considerations.

This phenomenon of a nationwide as opposed to an essentially local or regional orientation is present not only among the peasants (where it may be more easily understandable), but also in the participation of the cities in the revolution. Here, indeed, is an especially valuable key for the understanding of the difference between the two movements.

For the early phase of the Hussite Revolution the role of Prague is, as mentioned before, of special significance. For here the great city (actually a union of three cities, of which one had been destroyed by the war) had assumed a truly revolutionary role. There was, at this moment, no acknowledged government in the country, and it was the city of Prague that now undertook, at least partially, to function as such. It was Prague which corresponded, in the name of Hussite Bohemia, with foreign powers such as Venice,[32] it was Prague that sent an embassy to the King of Poland with the task of negotiating with him about the possibility of his accepting the crown of Bohemia,[33] and in June, 1421, after nearly two years of revolution, it was Prague that invited the Estates of Bohemia and Moravia to a great diet, a sort of National Assembly, for the purpose of developing a new understanding on an all-national basis and installing a governing regency council.[34] While this leading role was not maintained for much more than this initial phase, the city did manage to dominate, long beyond that early phase, a fairly large number of other royal cities, forming a league which could present a considerable military power.

But there was another league of towns, led by another centre, the newly built fortress-city of Tábor in southern Bohemia. Tábor was, at the same time, the centre of a radical religious movement, going much farther in cutting all ties with Rome and basing its puritanical and iconoclastic teachings on the idea of a church as near as possible to the *Ecclesia Primitiva*. A fighting theocracy, the Taborite brotherhood, for some time led by Žižka, dominated a number of satellite towns. When later Žižka's religious ideas conflicted with those of Tábor, he took over the leadership of a third city league, the Orebites in eastern Bohemia, with Hradec Králové (Königsgrätz) as the leading place. Throughout the greater part of the duration of the Revolution the two brotherhoods and city leagues, though differing on some religious questions, cooperated politically and in their military operations. It was these two brotherhoods, based on the cities that belonged to them, which played the decisive role in destroying the invasion armies sent into the country as "crusades." It was the same city leagues which, by invading in turn their hostile neighbors, especially Germany, eventually forced the other side to agree to negotiate. The outcome was the Compacts by which the Council of Basel gave the Czech people the right to worship, within certain limits, in the Utraquist way.

If the Czech revolution survived fifteen years, largely because of the strength of the city leagues organized in the two great brotherhoods, then we may perhaps wonder why, in the Germany of the early sixteenth century, city leagues could not have played a similar role. Germany, after all, had been the country where city leagues had been a characteristic feature of the later Middle Ages. But in the fifteenth century this was no longer true, since in the long struggle between cities and princes the princes had generally won out. From now on effective city cooperation had become rare.

Actually the potential power of the imperial cities — and only they could easily try to act as free agents — was still respectable, in economic as well as in political terms. In the critical period when the Swabian League, the one great combined organisation of princes and cities, had gained the upper hand against the peasants and their urban allies, the single city of Nürnberg was able to hold her protecting hand over smaller neighbors and prevent radical acts of punishment. Yet the cities rarely acted in close cooperation, not even neighboring cities that were badly in need of such cooperation because they were already engaged in revolutionary activities.

The number of cities that either took the side of the peasants or else engaged in an internal revolution was limited but not insignificant. Frequently the pattern of such social explosions — in many cases provoked or strengthened by religious motives and movements — was rather similar to developments which had occurred during the last few years or the last few decades preceding the great outbreak of 1524–26. In most cases there was a rebellion, sometimes but not always a violent one, against the city council, and in the majority of these cases the council gave in, often by admitting members of the craft guilds into the "outer council," and not infrequently by agreeing to the creation of a special committee which would have the function of supervising the city council and changing its previously conservative political course. When the peasants approached them with suggestions for cooperation — or indeed for acceptance of their great charter, the Twelve

Articles — the next step was often to allow the peasants, or at least their leaders, to enter the city; specific arrangements for political and military cooperation were then made.[35]

Such developments took place with greater ease in the case of smaller towns, partly because they felt that resistance to the peasant troops was hopeless, partly because in the smaller towns there was a relatively greater proportion of *Ackerbürger* (farmer-burghers), whose views and interests were often similar to those of the peasants. Among the larger cities those who took this stand were more frequently minorities. If such groups were well organized, and found strong and skillful leaders, and if the city council happened to be rather weak, local revolutions might nevertheless occur, sometimes with very little direct influence from the peasants, while in other cases acting in a rather parallel way.[36] In the majority of the larger cities, however, the city councils dominated by patricians (and sometimes also by well-to-do craftsmen who had equally much to lose) kept things strictly under control. In these cases there was hardly any chance for the city to join up with the revolution, and they chose the alternatives of strict neutrality or cooperation with the anti-revolutionary forces, notably the Swabian League. The strongest motivation in these cases was fear: fear on the part of the upper layers of society that they would lose their position and their wealth, and fear of even a larger part of the citizens that revolutionary action would result in severe punishment which might be meted out to the whole city by the Swabian League or by individual princes. There was thus, in strong contradistinction to the Hussite developments, no real feeling of a common city front such as had existed in Bohemia, no strong confidence in support being available from other cities, and generally little readiness to give any such support if requests for it were received.

Under these circumstances the cities, which alone, along with the peasantry, might have carried the revolution forward, were inadequate as a militant power. Only in a limited number of cases did individual cities take the side of the revolution and help to support this or that peasant army with supplies, additional manpower, leadership, and moral support; these usually ended by sharing (or trying desperately to escape from) the final fate, *Vae victis.* Some of them switched sides as soon as it became doubtful whether there was any chance for success.

Yet the attitude of the cities, on the whole so disappointing to the protagonists of the revolution, had something also to do with the course of the religious reform movement. Those cities that took any, even a limited, part in the revolution had all undergone an effective — if not in every case lasting — religious reformation, and the same was true for many cities which had done any fence sitting or had maintained, with some difficulty, a precarious neutrality. For all these, the attitude of the spiritual leaders of the Reformation frequently was of considerable importance.

This, of course, was just as true in the Hussite Revolution. There arose, at that time, the question of whether the people of Bohemia, in their desire to follow and protect the truth and the law of God, had the right to fight for it. This question, whether to yield before the authority of Sigismund as the "natural king" or to resist him by force of arms, was presented more than once to the masters of Prague University.[37] These representatives of a magisterial reformation, among them some strongly conservative masters, decided in the affirmative, provided the war was purely defensive.[38] This decision carried enough authority to bar, for seven long years, any move on the part of the Czech revolutionaries which would have carried the war beyond the borders of the kingdom (only in 1426 was this policy changed). But at the same time the fact that this revolution was allowed, by an express ecclesiastical sanction, to use force against force in defending itself, and thus to become and remain a revolution, had an enormous impact upon the people of Bohemia, among whom the towns played such a crucial role. With the one exception of the very small group of extreme pacifists who would rather be victims than kill anyone,[39] the Czech adherents of the Hussite Reformation, for all their internal divisions, could in critical phases close their ranks and fight with extreme devotion for their faith. They felt certain that they were on the side of God, and expected accordingly that God would be on their side.

How different was the situation in the Germany of the early sixteenth century. Luther's actions, so revolutionary in the spiritual field, had led masses of people in town and country to expect that he would also support a fight for liberty in other than purely religious terms. He had criticized in harsh forms the widespread exploitation of the peasantry and had come out in favor of changes which, like the partial elimination of the tithe, stood in the forefront of the rather moderate early demands of the peasants. There was nothing in the famous Twelve Articles that their authors could not expect to be substantially acceptable to Luther. Accordingly the so-called Christian Union, formed by the peasants of Upper Swabia, had as late as March, 1525, demanded at a congress in Memmingen that all the leaders of the

Magisterial Reformation, led by Luther, Melanchthon, and Zwingli, should decide as arbitrators the justice of the peasants' demands.[40] But the Swabian League, with its strict Catholic leadership (especially on account of the Bavarian chancellor Leonhard Eck), refused categorically any appeal to Luther as an acceptable arbitrator.

Both sides were wrong in their expectations. Far from supporting the side of the peasants, the Wittenberg reformer, after a first, more cautious warning, published a pamphlet containing the most extreme, most hate-filled condemnation of the revolution, whose adherents, he proclaimed, were to be killed off like mad dogs. Rarely, in a great rebellion, has a glowing expectation of moral support been answered in bloodier terms. Luther's extraordinary turn against the peasant revolution has become the subject of a fair-sized monographic literature.[41] The motivation and the judgment behind this act does not concern us here, but rather the effect that it had upon the revolutionaries and their revolution. Obviously this effect was extremely damaging.

It cannot be claimed that an endorsement by Luther and the early Lutheran church of the main peasant demands, specifically of the Twelve Articles, would have brought about or have made possible a victory of the revolution. Such a statement would be weakly founded and historiographically irresponsible. We cannot know what a different attitude of Luther and his church would have achieved, and it could probably be argued that the anti-revolutionary forces, and especially the common front of the territorial princes, Catholic as well as Lutheran, would in the end have proved superior in any case. Indeed the question arises whether, at the time that Luther's vicious pamphlet became public, the revolution had not already (or very nearly) passed the phase of its greatest strength. Even so Luther's action was, in relation to the peasants and their leaders and to those cities that had taken their side, eminently confusing and confounding. Nor is there any doubt that Luther's turn against the peasants weakened materially the democratic element in the spread of Lutheranism. The Lutheran church ceased to be a great popular religious movement, and instead, under the vigorous supervision of the princes, became an establishment in its way just as conservative as the Catholic church had been, only less autonomous, more subject to princely pressure and direction. Thus Luther, in contrast to the equally magisterial Utraquist church of Bohemia, notably contributed both to the early defeat of the revolution at a stage when it had achieved almost nothing substantial and to the prolonged strengthening of a highly reactionary and exploitative ruling class.

By referring to Luther we have already based one element in our search for the causes of the failure of the German revolution upon decisions and actions of a single individual. In a rather negative way, this can also be done in relation to the military leaders of the Peasants' War. Here the lack of great figures becomes notable when compared with the Hussite wars. The Czechs had the good luck of finding in John Žižka one of the truly outstanding organizers and leaders of armies among the great generals of history. He was followed by an almost equally gifted successor in the person of the Taborite priest-general Prokop the Great.[42] There was no lack, at any time, of gifted and successful secondary leaders and lieutenants.

In the German Peasants' War, on the other hand, the one remarkably gifted (and highly experienced) military leader was George Truchsess of Waldburg, commander of the armies of the counter-revolutionary Swabian League. None of the actual peasant leaders rose to be a successful and widely recognized military commander, though some of them achieved partial or temporary successes. For the peasants it was, of course, not easy to gain the experience necessary for successful military leadership higher than a subaltern command. It should perhaps be noted that none of the members of the gentry who fought in the ranks of the revolution, people who in terms of social rank were the equivalent of Žižka and several of his lieutenants, rose to real greatness. To some extent this may be due to the debacle which the Knights' Rebellion of 1523 had suffered. Among those that did join the peasants, Goetz of Berlichingen had no real interest in the victory of the revolution and looked only to his personal gain. Florian Geyer, on the contrary, was one of the most idealistic and most attractive of the leaders of the revolution, but he too fell far short of organizational and military eminence. Thomas Müntzer, finally, was a man of great spiritual and even political charisma, but had little if any military understanding, relying more upon the certain help of God than upon rational considerations of the conduct of war.[43] The one and only man in the peasant revolution who rose, for a while, to real prominence and who, in this position, proved to be a really effective organizer and commander of armies was Michael Gaismair, the leading figure of the Tyrolian Peasant War. He, too, was not a peasant but came from a middle-class background. Yet his work started rather late, and his successes were gained at a time when outside the Alpine regions the revolution had already been defeated. So he could be outmaneuvered by his enemies without too much difficulty.[44] It is hard to decide whether the presence of great leaders in the Hussite Revolution, and their absence in the German Peasants' War, was largely accidental or is open to some sort of a sociological explanation. This, indeed, is not the only issue which probably needs much additional investigation in depth.

The present sketch is, of course, far from such an investigation in depth. It rather seems to me that the preliminary discussion of similarities and differences between the two movements might help to develop a sort of program for further research in the history of Germany's first great revolution.

NOTES

1. See, e.g., the volume published by the Deutsche Historiker-Gesellschaft under the title *Die frühbürgerliche Revolution in Deutschland*, ed. G. Brendler (Berlin: Akademie-Verlag, 1961).
2. "Eines der entscheidenden Ereignisse der deutschen Geschichte. . . . Weit mehr noch als zwei Jahre zuvor der Sieg über das Rittertum, ebnete nun der [Sieg] über die Bauern den Fürsten den Weg zum Absolutismus. Eben darauf beruht . . . die ungeheuere Bedeutung des Bauernkrieges. Infolge ihrer Niederlage wurden nicht nur die Bauern selbst, sondern auch die Angehörigen der übrigen Städte mehr und mehr zu Untertanen im Sinne des Absolutismus." See Bühler, *Deutsche Geschichte*, Vol. III, *Das Reformationszeitalter* (Berlin, 1954), pp. 346 ff.
3. See especially the early chapters of H. Kaminsky's *A History of the Hussite Revolution* (Berkeley, 1967).
4. See above all the later volumes of F. Hrejsa's monumental work *Dějiny křesťanství v Československu* (Prague, 1948–50).
5. See, e.g., for the development in Bohemia Vol. I of *Přehled československých dějin* (Prague, 1958), pp. 167–68, and for Germany W. Andreas' *Deutschland vor der Reformation*, 3rd ed. (Stuttgart, 1942), pp. 70 ff.
6. Hus' role in fighting the indulgences is much less known than that of Luther. See, e.g., in the most recent work on him, M. Spinka, *John Hus, a Biography* (Princeton, 1968), pp. 132 ff.
7. See F. M. Bartoš, *Husitská revoluce* (Prague, 1965), Vol. I., pp. 15 ff.
8. The left wings in both phases are treated most authoritatively by George Williams in his work *The Radical Reformation* (Philadelphia, 1962).
9. See my articles "John Rokycana — Church Reformer between Hus and Luther," *Church History*, 28, 1959, pp. 240–80, and "Luther's Impact upon Bohemia," in *Central European History*, Vol. I, No. 2 (1968), pp. 107–30.
10. The best presentation of Müntzer's visit to Bohemia, and of his contacts there, is Václav Husa's book *Tomáš Müntzer a Čechy*, (Rozpravy čsk. akademie věd, No. 67) (Prague, 1957).
11. The significance of the ideology of these radical anarchists is still strongly

disputed. See, e.g., Macek's interpretation in his *Tábor v husitském revolučním hnutí*, Vol. II (Prague, 1955), pp. 321 ff., and Ernst Werner in the combined work *Circumcellionen und Adamiten* (Berlin, 1959), pp. 73–92, 129–34, and on the other hand, most recently, Kaminský, *op. cit.*, pp. 429 ff., and my *John Žižka and the Hussite Revolution* (Princeton, 1955), pp. 212 ff., 261–64.

12. See Kaminský, *op. cit.*, pp. 391–94.

13. The meeting of these two generations of reforming movements is the subject of a new work by J. Zeman, *The Anabaptists and the Czech Brethren in Moravia, 1526–1628* (The Hague, 1969).

14. See Bretholz, "Die Übergabe Mährens an Herzog Albrecht V. von Oesterreich i. J. 1423," *Archiv für oesterreichische Geschichte*, Vol. LXXX (Vienna, 1894).

15. See R. Urbánek, ed., *Sborník Žižkův 1424–1924* (Prague, 1924), Illustrations 18 and 19, Appendix p. ix.

16. See my *Žižka*, pp. 68 ff.

17. There are, of course, innumerable examples. See, e.g., M. U. Chrisman, *Strasbourg and the Reform* (New Haven, 1967), pp. 141 ff., and my *Žižka*, p. 168.

18. See J. V. Šimák, *Hus a doba před ním* (Prague, 1915), p. 29.

19. See my *Žižka*, pp. 451 ff.

20. *Ibid.*, pp. 164 ff.

21. For the diet, see my article "The National Assembly of Čáslav," in *Medievalia et Humanistica*, Fasc. VIII (Boulder, 1954).

22. For examples see my *Žižka*, pp. 114 ff., 179 ff.

23. Ferdinand's clever tactics are shown repeatedly and in some detail by J. Macek in his *Tyrolská selská válka a Michal Gaismair* (Prague, 1960), e.g., pp. 216 ff. (now also in German translation).

24. The problem of Czech nationalism in the Middle Ages, and especially in connection with Hussitism, is not a simple one and has been under strong dispute from the Czech as well as the German sides. Hans Kohn has treated it in his *The Idea of Nationalism* (see the recent edition of Collier Books, New York, 1967, pp. 109 ff.). In a more detailed way Eugen Lemberg has shown the origin as well as the limitations of this nationalism in *Die Geschichte des Nationalismus in Europa* (Stuttgart, 1950), mainly pp. 135 ff. Finally, and perhaps most clearly, the issue is treated by Ferdinand Seibt in his *HUSSITICA, Zur Struktur einer Revolution* (Köln-Graz, 1965), in the third chapter, "*Jazyk-Linguagium*," where, among other arguments against a simple identification of the participants in Hussite struggle with the two nations we find also a fully documented reference to the activities of German Hussites. Much has been done in the same direction by the east German scholar H. Köpstein.

25. See the *Chronica Boemorum* of Cosmas of Prague (d. 1125), ed. B. Bretholz, *Monumenta Germ. histor., Scriptores rer. Germ.* Nova Ser. II (Berlin, 1955), pp. 73, 75, 177: all references to the negative qualities of the Germans and their regrettably arrogant attitude toward the Bohemians. (It is, however, of interest that a good deal of nationalistic aversion is directed by Cosmas also against the Poles. See *ibid.*, pp. xvii and xviii. The feeling of a common Slavic heritage is of much later date.) The same was true in the

later rhyme chronicle (early fourteenth century) of the so-called Dalimil. See the Cambridge MS., ed. V. E. Mourek, 2d edition (Prague, 1910), pp. 79 ff.

26. See the report of Nürnberg's city council to Ulm of Sept. 1, 1421, on the order given by the crusading German electoral princes that everyone, men and women, in Bohemia be killed except small children "die ir vernunft nicht haben," in Palacký's *Urkundliche Beiträge zur Geschichte des Hussitenkrieges* (Prague, 1873; reprinted Osnabrück, 1966), Vol. I, p. 144.

27. See, e.g., my *Žižka*, pp. 288, 291, with sources.

28. The most thorough treatment of Hussite chiliasm is given in Kaminský, *op. cit.*, 339–60.

29. Some valuable remarks in this connection are given in F. Seibt, *op. cit.*, pp. 100–102.

30. See, e.g., E. Bloch, *Thomas Münzer*, new edition (Frankfurt, 1962), pp. 56 ff.

31. *Ibid.*, 20 ff., and Václav Husa, *Tomáš Müntzer a Čechy*, passim.

32. An impressive example is the long letter sent by the Prague city council on July 10, 1420, printed by Palacký in his *Urkundliche Beiträge*, Vol. I, pp. 39–43.

33. See Lawrence of Březová's "Kronika Husitská," ed. J. Goll, in *Fontes rerum bohemicarum*, Vol. V (Prague, 1893), p. 447.

34. See my article, cited in n. 21.

35. See, for the characteristic example of Rothenburg o.d.T., G. Franz, *Quellen zur Geschichte des Bauernkrieges* (Munich, 1963), pp. 321–30.

36. See, e.g., the development in Frankfurt and the 45 (or 46) Articles of The Frankfurt Commune, in *Quellen und Forschungen zur Frankfurter Geschichte*, Vol. II (Frankfurt, 1888), pp. 184–91; also in Franz, *op. cit.*, pp. 455 ff.

37. The most thorough and up-to-date treatment of this question is to be found in the second chapter of Seibt, *op. cit.*, "Bellum iustum," pp. 16–57.

38. See especially the role of Master John Příbram, discussed very carefully by Seibt, *op. cit.*, 38 ff.

39. See the discussion of Chelčický's background and role in Kaminsky, *op. cit.* above, in n. 11.

40. See G. Franz, *Der deutsche Bauernkrieg*, 4th ed. (Darmstadt, 1956), p. 130.

41. See *ibid.*, p. 283, n. 4.

42. For Žižka see my book mentioned above (n. 16) and the large literature quoted therein. On Prokop the Great the most up-to-date works are R. Urbánek, *Lipany a konec polních vojsk* (Prague, 1934) and J. Macek, *Prokop Veliký* (Prague, 1953).

43. The best military evaluation of the different phases of the history of the Peasants' War, as well as (to a lesser extent) of its leaders, is contained in the concise and well-organized book by M. Bensing and S. Hoyer, *Der Deutsche Bauernkrieg 1524–1526* (Leipzig, 1965). However, as in other recent treatments of the Peasants' War and of Thomas Müntzer, there is a tendency to overrate the capacities of Müntzer as an organizer and military leader.

44. See Macek's book quoted above in n. 23.

Number Symbolism and Medieval Literature

Edmund Reiss

WHILE AN AWARENESS of the symbolic significance of numbers was hardly peculiar to the Middle Ages, it was doubtless then more pervasive and acute than at any other time in Western civilization. Stemming from the Pythagorean belief that the elements of number were the elements of all things, and that numbers could give man the key to cosmic secrets, numerology came to influence practically every area of medieval thought.[1] From astrology and medicine to church ritual, music, architecture, and scriptural exegesis, an understanding of number was basic to an understanding of order, harmony, and existence.

Coming to patristic thought by means of its place in the writings of such Neoplatonists as Plutarch, Plotinus, Iamblichus, Proclus, and Macrobius,[2] number symbolism soon became a significant part of Christian theology and methodology. First, Philo Judaeus, in the first century A.D., having combined Pythagorean principles with those of astrology, showed how numbers in Genesis represented principles of divine authority;[3] and it was Philo's method of explication that became the model for later Christian biblical commentary. Second, such theological developments as the formulation of the concept of Trinity by Clement of Alexandria and his pupils, Origen and Hippolytus, with its mystical relationship of three in one, allowed for a mystical sense of number in orthodox Christian doctrine. And third, number symbolism was seen having a basis in scriptural and apocryphal statements, such as that in the Book of Wisdom which says that God arranged all things in terms of number, measure, and weight.[4] Such developments and authorities as these gave number symbolism philosophical and theological relevance and made it increasingly respectable in the Christian world.

Much of the research for this paper was done with the assistance of a study fellowship from the American Council of Learned Societies. A shorter version was read at the Fourth Conference on Medieval Studies at Western Michigan University in March, 1968.

The new interest in numbers may clearly be seen in the writings of such Fathers as Irenaeus, Tertullian, Justin Martyr, Origen, and Jerome;[5] but it was St. Augustine, more so than anyone, who made it necessary for Christian man to have an awareness of the significance, as well as the general science, of number. Augustine developed fully the idea that number was a basic principle of God's creation and that the created world could — indeed should — be understood through number. Throughout his writings he emphasized the divine nature of numbers, showing various ways of interpreting them and bringing out the particularly Christian significances inherent in them.[6]

Augustine's influence contributed to the popularity in the Middle Ages of the *Introduction to Arithmetic* by Nicomachus of Gerasa (*c.* 100), a work representing in effect a guide to the nature and uses of numbers. Versions of this work were essential in the developing quadrivium, specifically in its subjects of arithmetic and music; and also, through being reproduced by Martianus Capella and Boethius, for instance, versions began to include commentary that brought out the mystical significance of the numbers.[7] By the time of Isidore of Seville, the encyclopedia of numbers had developed sufficiently so as to be standard in and necessary to medieval thought and expression. In the following centuries collections of numbers were written by such eminent compilers as Cassiodorus, Bede, Alcuin, Raban Maur, Gerbert (Pope Sylvester II), and Hugh of Saint Victor,[8] representing a tradition culminating in the Renaissance compendia of such writers as Pietro Bongo and Cornelius Agrippa.[9]

At the same time, even more thinkers gave full accounts of numbers while explicating a particular text or theological subject. For example, Cassiodorus explored the Psalms in terms of the particular number assigned to each; Gregory the Great brought out their meanings in his treatise on Job, Raban Maur in his examination of the symbolism of the cross, and Hincmar of Rheims in his analysis of the structure of Solomon's temple; even Albert the Great was concerned with numbers in such works as his commentary on Matthew, as was Thomas Aquinas in his exegesis of the Apocalypse.[10] All these represent explications especially useful in understanding the Christian uses and meanings of numbers.

In what is still the best modern introduction to number symbolism, Vincent Hopper rightly insists on the pervasiveness of this symbolism in the Middle Ages and rightly cautions us about misreading numbers found in the writing of the period: "Although symbolic numbers are profusely scattered through the pages of nearly all medieval writings, it is necessary to distinguish, especially in secular and unscientific literature, between the philosophical or scientific use of number, the symbolic, the imitative, and the merely naïve preference for certain commonly used numbers."[11] As "the language of Eternal Verities," number symbolism was, in Hopper's view, different from "the more objective medieval symbols" — that is, it would seem, from such symbols as animals, plants, precious stones, clothes, and colors — for "the abstraction of number was itself shrouded in mystery, to which only a complete metaphysical erudition could provide the key."[12]

Such a distinction between number symbolism and the other kinds of symbolism that likewise permeated medieval thought and expression is misleading, in that it fails to take sufficiently into account how in the medieval Augustinian view of life everything in this world was seen as a reflection of a greater reality. While number may have been the basic expression of existence, and while its symbolism may have been, in one sense, qualitatively different from that of animals, plants, etc., number is still to be viewed, as indeed it was, as a parallel way of expressing and comprehending the meaning of existence. It provided, in other words, a detail that in medieval expression could be as concrete as, say, a rabbit, an oak tree, or an emerald. In a text referring, for instance, to six brown rabbits, the number six might function as symbolically as the color brown or as the animal rabbit. On the other hand, it could, of course, be just a number chosen at random — perhaps to indicate a plurality of rabbits or perhaps for the quality of its sound — just as the rabbit might represent no more than a rabbit. But the compilers and audience of Latin and vernacular bestiaries were well aware of the possible symbolic associations of rabbits, and so, through the several medieval "numeraries," were people aware of the possible symbolic significance of numbers. In any statement of number the context or what followed would show the relevant possibilities.

Hopper does not want to be too encouraging about recognizing number symbolism in secular or popular literature, although he does acknowledge some of the possibilities, especially in Dante's *Commedia* — though he most likely would not consider this to be secular. But while number symbolism has been mishandled and misunderstood by some modern scholars, the subject itself should not therefore be viewed as a silly topic of inquiry or as something unworthy of serious discussion.[13] In studies of classical literature, for instance, some quite perceptive work has been done on number symbolism;[14] and even though the numerical studies of medieval literature have traditionally focused on Dante and on explicitly Christian writing, scholars have long realized that numbers were both pervasive and widespread in medieval secular works, even though they have not always known what to do with these numbers.[15]

But increasingly over the past twenty years scholars of medieval literature have been using number symbolism to reveal aspects of imagery and artistic structure that had never before been seen. The main approach has been in terms of numerical composition (*Zahlenkomposition*), or, more accurately, understanding literary composition in terms of numerical principles of symmetry that go back to Pythagorean thought. Contrary to the practices of earlier exponents of number criticism, however, the more recent trend has been to focus on numerical structure at the expense of numerical signification. Earlier scholars, Hopper and E. R. Curtius among them, realized that medieval writers organized their material in terms of certain numbers because these numbers possessed particular symbolic values. Augustine, for instance, constructed the *De civitate Dei* in 22 books, thereby having it parallel the Old Testament as well as the Hebrew alphabet. He also divided it in terms of "2 groups of 5, devoted to refutation, suggestive perhaps of the 20 prohibitions of the Old Law, and 3 groups of 4, imitative of apostolic evangelization, to positive argument and exposition."[16] Hopper also recognized that the encyclopedias of Bartholomew the Englishman, Thomas of Cantimpré, and Robert Grosseteste "are each composed of 19 books, doubtless symbolic of the 12 signs and the 7 planets, and therefore universal."[17] Also writers on Dante have long realized that the structure of the *Commedia* is in terms of numbers (e.g., 1 + 33 + 33 + 33) that are symbolically meaningful according to Christian concepts and values.[18]

But the recent exponents of *Zahlenkomposition* have been concerned more with the formal aspects of numbers than with their meanings, particularly the traditional Christian meanings they had in the Middle Ages. In their view what is of most significance is seeing the symmetry found through counting and relating the number of chapters, stanzas, lines, or syllables in a given work. Most of these critics would probably go along with Michael S. Batts' preference to speak of the "non-numerical," rather than the "symbolic," significance of numbers, and perhaps would even agree with his unfortunate conclusion that "the planned arithmetical form of medieval *secular* literature may have in fact no symbolic meaning," that it may be primarily based not on "the tradition of Christian numerical exegesis which infuses much of the religious writing of the period," but on "a fundamentally secular tradition drawing directly from Roman poetry of the immediately pre-Christian era."[19]

Without denying the value of using principles of *Zahlenkomposition* as a way of understanding medieval literature, one may still object to the excesses, inadequacies, and false principles seen in some particular applications of this approach. Granted, there has been some quite good work, mainly — aside from Dante studies — in criticism of medieval German poetry,[20] though also in some articles on Provençal and Old French poetry,[21] and, to a lesser degree, in some studies of Middle English literature.[22] But too much of the existing criticism suffers from an inability to be convincing, to make its conclusions appear believable and relevant; and too often the approach seems to be more trouble than it is worth, or even much ado about nothing.

Should one accept a critic's demonstration that a work is constructed in terms of, say, the number 5, he still wants to know the point of such construction and the justification for this particular number. The Middle English lyric "I syng of a mayden," for instance, is composed of five stanzas of two lines each with five stresses per line.[23] The "mayden" who is the subject of this poem is the Virgin Mary, but this fact is brought out only indirectly as the poem develops. Nevertheless, the numerical structure of the lyric makes this identification clear since the number 5 is most associated with the Virgin. It is the number of letters in the Latin form of her name, Maria; it is the number of her Joys; and, among other things, it was generally seen as the number signifying True Faith. In this lyric the symbolic significance of 5 clearly gives point to the structural and metrical uses of this number. The other main structural number of the poem is 10, representing the total number of lines and the total number of stresses per stanza — with the grand total of stresses being 100. These numbers traditionally signify totality, wholeness, and the return to unity — that is, the perfection resulting from the birth of Mary's son, Jesus. The critic studying *Zahlenkomposition* could easily recognize the prevalence of 5 (and its multiple of 10) in this poem, but should he neglect the symbolic significance of the number, he would be inadequately viewing the work.

Along with not sufficiently showing the significance and relevance of the numbers they find structuring a piece of literature, the form-through-number critics have frequently made too artificial a distinction between the secular and the religious literature of the Middle Ages and have unnecessarily limited the range of their exploration as well as the significance of their work. First, in emphasizing number as structure, they have too often neglected number as meaning; and, second, in searching for inherent number, they have tended to overlook stated number — that is, the numbers appearing in the text of a given work. The rest of this paper will be concerned with showing the need for, and ways of, understanding these numbers, especially as they appear in medieval "secular" literature.

To begin with, it should be obvious that not every number appearing in a medieval text has symbolic significance. Some, like 10, 50, and 100, are "round" numbers, which, while possibly having additional signification, possess mainly, as Curtius says, "aesthetic significance." [24] Should a writer speak of, say, 1000 warriors, the chances are good that he means merely a large number of warriors, unless the context indicates that he may have something more in mind. But should he speak of, say, 37 warriors, the chances are good that he has chosen that particular number with an eye to its symbolic significances, which are, most frequently, Christian in nature. The particular number, the context, and an author's habits in other works may act as indicators of how we should view the stated number in the work at hand.

At times a writer will himself give an explication of a number. This is what Dante does in several places, as in the *Vita Nuova* (XXX) when he pauses over the number 9, which he had often mentioned in terms of Beatrice, and states explicitly how it functions as a mystical number and how he is using it to reveal the essential nature of Beatrice. It is also what the author of *Sir Gawain and the Green Knight* does when he pauses over the pentangle on Gawain's shield and gives its significance.[25] Such a method is operative in religious poetry where the poet shows a numerical sense and a clear awareness of traditional values, even though he may not give a detailed explication, as, for instance, in Otfrid von Weissenburg's *Evangelienbuch*.[26] It functions too in some lyrics where the numbers act as the organizing principle of a developing allegory, and where the statement of significance represents the poem proper. Such may be seen in the Middle English lyric "The Lily with Five Leaves,"[27] which progresses by stating the significance of each leaf: the first signifying charity, the second brotherly love, and so on. The cataloguing here is designed to instruct the audience, and the lily itself is forgotten for the instruction; it functions merely as the means to take us to the didacticism.

But in most poetry, where there is little occasion for such explication, we are not quite sure how to proceed with an interpretation of the stated number, even when we feel certain that it is to be read symbolically. Unfortunately, lists detailing various approaches to number symbolism, such as the useful one by Hugh of Saint Victor,[28] are only lists of possibilities: they are certainly not prescriptive and do not pretend to advise which approach should be used for different occasions. Still, it is necessary to realize that some numbers mean far more than their stated value would indicate: some, to be fully meaningful, need to be broken into their component parts or, conversely, to be seen as part of a larger sum. The latter is the case in the familiar early English song "The Twelve Days of Christmas," where the total number of gifts actually given by the lover over the twelve-day period is 364; the 365th gift, completing the year, would obviously be the divine one of Christ, given on Christmas Day.[29]

Sometimes numbers act as verbal puzzles in that they stand for equivalent letters in the alphabet, but these numbers are not so much symbols as elements in a code. They do not stand for concepts but rather for parallel terms in a more familiar language of communication. The audience is asked, in effect, to solve a riddle, albeit one that is fairly obvious, as may be seen in a Middle English number maxim:

> In 8 is alle my loue
> & 9 be y-sette byfore
> So 8 be y-closyd aboue
> Thanne 3 is good therefore.[30]

Here 8, or its alphabetical equivalent, the letter H with a tilde over it ("y-closyd aboue"), is the central letter; it is preceded ("y-sette byfore") by 9, or I, and followed by 3, or C. The answer, IHC, is an abbreviation of Ihesu Crist, who is here all the narrator's love. At other times the numbers represent real puzzles, as in John Skelton's *Ware the Hawk* and *Garland of Laurel*, where they appear to be determined by means of a private code and designed to mystify all but the initiated.[31] A related kind of number maxim may be seen in the following couplet, where the numbers refer not to letters but to Christian commonplaces:

> Kepe well X and fle fro VII;
> Rule well V and come to hevyn.[32]

There is still a one-for-one correspondence, and the numbers, referring, of course, to the Ten Commandments, the Seven Deadly Sins, and the

Five Senses, function as a device similar to that of rhetorical synecdoche, where the parts stand for the whole.

In real number symbolism, however, the number exists to take the audience to a concept or value that will both deepen their understanding of the whole work and increase the significance and relevance of the work itself. Sometimes these numbers appear in terms of a pattern, and sometimes these patterns exist in literature that is considered secular. At the beginning of his *Canterbury Tales* Geoffrey Chaucer refers to "nyne and twenty" pilgrims who set off for Canterbury (A 24), even though there turn out to be more than this number; and at the end of the whole work, in the prologue to the last tale, he refers again to "nyne and twenty" (I 4), this time in terms of the position of the sun. The repetition of the number "nyne and twenty" is not accidental, nor is the choice of the particular number itself. As I have shown elsewhere, 29, or "nyne and twenty," signifies the approach to perfection and is clearly relevant as the encompassing number for Chaucer's pilgrimage narrative.[33]

Sometimes a number appears in conjunction with or through a name. This is the case in Chaucer's *Book of the Duchess*, where the dreamer comes upon a hunt led by the emperor Octovyen (368). Without even considering the other implications of the emperor's name, we may notice in it a suggestion of the number 8 (*octo* or *octavus*) — a number repeatedly indicating in medieval numerology resurrection or rebirth, and one pertinent to the recall to life that is, as it were, the final condition in this poem. But this finding of the number 8 in the name Octovyen may seem farfetched and doubtless would be were it not for the fact that it is prepared for earlier in the poem: at the beginning the narrator complains that his spirit has been deadened for "this eight yeer" (37). The number here suggests that the time for coming back to life is at hand, and thus calls up early the major theme of the poem. A pattern of eights is created, and the number 8 may be said to function in the *Book of the Duchess* as did 29 in the *Canterbury Tales*, as the encompassing number, suggesting a thematic context that allows for a wider and deeper understanding of what follows in the narrative.

Chaucer not only uses number symbolism but in fact comments on numbers, and implicitly on the symbolism itself, when, also in the *Book of the Duchess*, he refers to the significant Arab mathematician Al-Kwārizm, here called Argus, and says that he was one who "rekened with his figures ten" (437).[34] These are the figures, writes Chaucer, that all who are "crafty" are able to know ("mowe al ken," 438) and thereby "telle of every thing the noumbre" (440). To tell the number of everything was in the Middle Ages apparently to get at the essential reality and the full meaning of life. Even a vernacular writer as "secular" and as "popular" as Chaucer knew this and, moreover, throughout his many writings put into practice the dictum he gave in this early work.

Hopefully these examples of number symbolism, which are but a few chosen from a great many possibilities, have demonstrated something of how it may work; hopefully they have also shown the need for medievalists to be concerned with number symbolism, as well as with numerical structure. They may also serve to make us re-examine the secular-religious dichotomy held up to deny Christian signification to numbers found in literature not explicitly Christian on its surface. We must be concerned with and knowledgeable in this symbolism if we want to understand fully the nature and accomplishment of all medieval literature.

NOTES

1. See Aristotle's words on Pythagoras in *Metaphysica*, I. 5. On Pythagorean influence, see, e.g., F. E. Robbins, "The Tradition of Greek Arithmology," *Classical Philology*, XVI (1921); F. M. Cornford, "Mysticism and Science in the Pythagorean Tradition," *Classical Quarterly*, XVI (1922), 137–50; XVII (1923), 1–12; Matila C. Ghyka, *Le nombre d'or. Rites et rythmes pythagoriciens dans le développement de la civilisation occidentale. I, Les rythmes* (Paris, 1931); Paul-Henri Michel, *De Pythagore à Euclide* (Paris, 1950); and Gottfried Martin, *Klassische Ontologie der Zahl. Kantstudien.* Ergänzungsheft 70 (Cologne, 1956), esp. pp. 11–71.

2. On the Neoplatonic use of numbers, see L. Robin, *La théorie platonicienne des idées et des nombres après Aristote* (Paris, 1908); Julius Stenzel, *Zahl und Gestalt bei Platon und Aristoteles* (Leipzig, 1924); A. E. Taylor, "Forms and Numbers: A Study in Platonic Metaphysics," *Mind*, XXXV (1926), 419–40; XXXVI (1927), 12–33 (rewritten in condensed form in *Plato, the Man and His Work*, 6th ed. [London, 1952], pp. 503–16); F. S. C. Northrop, "The Mathematical Background and Content of Greek Philosophy," in *Philosophical Essays for Alfred North Whitehead* (London, 1936), pp. 1–40; and Gottfried Martin, "Platons Lehre von der Zahl und ihre Darstellung durch Aristoteles," *Zeitschrift für philosophische Forschung*, VII (1953), 191–203.

3. Philo, *De opificio mundi*, XV–XVI, XXX–XXXVII (Loeb, I, 36–40, 72–90); *Legum allegoriarum*, I. ii, iv–v (Loeb, I, 146–48, 150–54); *Quaestiones et solutiones in Genesim*, II, 12–14, 31–33; III, 49 (Loeb, Supp. I, 84–92, 109–12, 247–51).

4. Wisdom 11:20; see also Isaiah 11:26 and Matthew 10:30. On number symbolism in the Bible, see J. Sauer, "Zahlensymbolik," *Lexikon für Theologie und Kirche*, X, 1025–30; William W. Westcott, *Numbers: Their Occult Powers and Mystic Virtues* (London, 1890); Ethelbert W. Bullinger, *Number in Scripture, Its Supernatural Design and Spiritual Significance* (London, 1894); Reginald T. Naish, *Spiritual Arithmetic*, 3d ed. (London, 1926); A. Kenney-Herbert, *Number in the Bible* (London, 1934); and Leo Stalnaker, *Mystic Symbolism in Bible Numerals* (New York, 1951).

5. Irenaeus, *Aduersus haereses*, II. xxiv. 4 (Migne, *PG*, VII, 793–97); Tertullian, *Aduersus Marcionem*, IV. xiii (Migne, *PL*, II, 416–17); Justin Martyr, *Cohoratio ad Graecos*, XIX (*PG*, VI, 275–76); Origen, *De principiis*, II. ix. 1 (*PG*, XI, 225–26); Jerome, *Epistola*, XLVIII. 19–20 (*PL*, XXII, 508–9). In citing authorities for the symbolic value of the number 2, Jerome lists Clement, Hippolytus, Origen, Dionysius, Eusebius, Didymus, Tertullian, Cyprian, Victorinus, Lactantius, and Hilarius, thereby giving an indication of both how widespread number symbolism was among the Fathers and how conscious they were of previous work on the subject. On the early Christian use of number symbolism, see Ursula Grossmann, "Studien zur Zahlensymbolik des Frühmittelalters," *Zeitschrift für katholische Theologie*, LXXVI (1954), 19–54.

6. See esp. *De doctrina Christiana*. II. xvi. 25; II. 25; II. xxxviii. 56; II. xxxix. 58; III. xxxv. 51 (*PL*, XXXIV, 48, 61, 62, 86); and *De civitate Dei*, XI. 30, 31; XV. 20; XVIII. 44 (*PL*, XLI, 343–45, 462–65, 605); also *De ordine*, II. 39 ff. (*PL*, XXXII, 1013 ff.); *De libero arbitrio*, II. viii. 21; II. xi. 31 (*PL*, XXXII, 1251–52, 1258); *De Genesi ad Litteram*, IV. iii. 7–8; V. vii. 20 (*PL*, XXXIV, 299–300, 328); *Evangelium tractatus in Johannes*, XXV. vi (*PL*, XXXV, 1599); *Contra Faustum*, XII. 14–21 (*PL*, XLII, 262–65); and *De Trinitate*, III. ix. 16; IV. iv. 7; IV. vi. 10 (*PL*, XLII, 878, 892–95). See also A. Knappitsch, "St. Augustins Zahlensymbolik," in *Jahresbericht des Fürstbischöflichen Gymnasiums* (Graz, 1905); A. Schmitt, "Mathematik und Zahlenmystik," in Aurelius Augustinus, *Festschrift der Görres-Gesellschaft zum 1500* (Cologne, 1930), pp. 353–66; Pierre Charles, "L'élément populaire dans les sermons de saint Augustin," *Nouvelle Revue Théologique*, LXXIX (1947), 619 ff.; and William G. Most, "The Scriptural Basis of St. Augustine's Arithmology," *Catholic Biblical Quarterly*, XIII (1951), 284–95.

7. Nicomachus, *Introductionis arithmeticae*, ed. R. Hoche (Leipzig, 1866), esp. I. vi. 1–2; vi. 3; Martianus, *De nuptiis Philologiae et Mercurii*, II, VII, ed. A. Dick (Leipzig, 1925); and Boethius, *De arithmetica* (*PL*, LXIII, 1079 ff.). See also Augustine, *De musica* (*PL*, XXXII, 1081 ff.); and Boethius, *De musica* (*PL*, LXIII, 1167 ff.); along with H. Krings, "Das Sein und die Ordnung. Eine Skizze zur Ontologie des Mittelalters," *Deutsche Vierteljahresschrift für Literaturwissenschaft und Geistesgeschichte*, XVIII (1940), 233–49; Leo Spitzer, "Classical and Christian Ideas of World Harmony," *Traditio*, II (1944), 409–64; III (1945), 307–64; and Edgar de Bruyne, *Etudes d'esthétique médiévale* (Bruges, 1946), 3 vols.

8. Isidore, *Etymologiae*, III. iii–ix (*PL*, LXXII, 155–61); and the attributed *Liber numerorum qui in sanctis scripturis occurrunt* (*PL*, LXXXIII, 179–

200); Cassiodorus, *De artibus ac disciplinis liberalium litterarum*, IV, "De arithmetica" (*PL*, LXX, 1204–8); Bede, *De temporum ratione*, I (*PL*, XC, 295–98); *De arithmeticis numeris* (*Ibid.*, 641–48); and *De computo* (*Ibid.*, 647–52); Alcuin, *Epistola*, CCIII, "Ad Gallicellulam" (*PL*, C, 476–78); Raban Maur, *De clericorum institutione*, III. xxii (*PL*, CVII, 399–400); *Liber de computo*, I (*Ibid.*, 671 ff.); and *De universo*, XVIII. iii, "De numero" (*PL*, CXI, 489–95; Gerbert, *De numerorum divisione* (*PL*, CXXXIX, 85–92); and Hugh of Saint Victor, *De scripturis et scriptoribus sacris*, VI, XV (*PL*, CLXXV, 15, 22–23). See also Guy Beaujouan, "Le symbolisme des nombres à l'époque romane," *Cahiers de civilisation médiévale*, IV (1961), 159–69.

9. Pietro Bongo, *Numerorum mysteria* (Bergamo, 1591); Cornelius Agrippa, *De occulta philosophica*, II (Cologne, 1533); along with, e.g., Athenasius Kircher, *Arithmologia, sive De abditis numerorum mysteriis* (Rome, 1665); and Josse Clichtove, *De mystica numerorum significatione opusculum* (Paris, 1513). See also C. A. Patrides, "The Numerological Approach to Cosmic Order during the English Renaissance," *Isis*, XLIX (1958), 391–97; and S. K. Henninger, Jr., "Some Renaissance Versions of the Pythagorean Tetrad," *Studies in the Renaissance*, VIII (1961), 1–33.

10. Cassiodorus, *Expositio in Psalterum* (*PL*, LXX, 9 ff.); Gregory, *Moralium in Job*, XXXV. xvi. 42 (*PL*, LXXVI, 772–74); Raban, *De laudibus sanctae crucis* (*PL*, CVII, 133 ff.); Hincmar, *Explanatio in ferculum Salomonis* (*PL*, CXXV, 817–32); Albert, *Expositio Matthei*, XIII. 8; and Thomas, *Expositio II in Apocalypsem*, VIII.

11. V. H. Hopper, *Medieval Number Symbolism, Its Sources, Meaning, and Influence on Thought and Expression* (New York, 1938), p. 127. See also S. Rubin, *Die Symbolik der Zahlen in der Philosophie und dem Mysticismus aller Voelker* (Vienna, 1896); Roy Melton, *Metaphysics of Numerology, I, Number Ontology* (Boston, 1934); Franz C. Endres, *Die Zahl in Mystik und Glauben der Kulturvölken* (Zurich and Leipzig, 1935); and Ernest Bindel, *Les elements spirituels des nombres* (Paris, 1960).

12. Hopper, p. 135.

13. On this point, see Michael S. Batts, "Numbers and Number Symbolism in Medieval German Poetry," *Modern Language Quarterly*, XXIV (1963), 343.

14. On Greek literature, see, e.g., Gabriel Germain, *Homère et la mystique des nombres* (Paris, 1954); and Cedric Whitman, *Homer and the Homeric Tradition* (Cambridge, Mass., 1958). On Roman literature, see esp. G. E. Duckworth, "Mathematical Symmetry in Virgil's *Aeneid*," *Transactions of the American Philological Association*, XCI (1960), 184–220; and *Structural Patterns and Proportions in Vergil's Aeneid, A Study in Mathematical Composition* (Ann Arbor, 1962). Cf. also the study of early Norse literature in Sigurd Agrell, *Runornas Talmystik och des antika Förebild* (Lund, 1927).

15. A good example of not knowing what to do with numbers may be found in B. Q. Morgan, "On the Use of Numbers in the *Nibelungenlied*," *Journal of English and Germanic Philology*, XXXVI (1937), 10–20. After noting the numbers found in *Nibelungenlied*, *Beowulf*, *Edda* (Poetic?), Gottfried's

Tristan, Gudrun, Aeneid, Iliad, and the Bible, noting specifically the numbers 10 and 12, Morgan concludes that certain works favor certain numbers, and that the "passionate fondness" of *Nibelungenlied* and *Gudrun* for 12 must be regarded as "a personal foible" of its authors, and perhaps as support for the claim that the two works are by the same author. Notwithstanding such conclusions, Morgan's collection of numbers is at least worth noting. Another study likewise not going far enough is William Rose, "El número en el 'Romancero del Cid,' " *Hispania,* XLIV (1961), 454–56. Much better is Lewis E. Nicholson, "The Literal Meaning and Symbolic Structure of *Beowulf,*" *Classica et Mediaevalia,* XXV (1964), esp. 175–79, 194–95.

16. Hopper, p. 87. Cf. Ernst Robert Curtius, "Numerical Composition, Excursus XV," in *European Literature and the Latin Middle Ages,* tr. W. R. Trask (New York, 1953), pp. 501–9. Raban Maur's *De universo* is likewise in 22 books, even though its source, Isidore's *Etymologiae,* had only 20 books.

17. Hopper, p. 88.

18. P. Petrocchi, "Del numero nel poema dantesco," *Rivista d'Italia,* III (1901); Howard Candler, "On the Symbolic Use of Number in the 'Divina Comedia' and Elsewhere," *Transactions of the Royal Society of Literature,* ser. 2, XXX (1910), 1–29; Ferdinand Koenen, "Dantes Zahlen-symbolik," *Deutsche Dante-Gesellschaft,* VIII (1924), 26–46; H. D. Austin, "Number and Geometrical Design in the *Divine Comedy,*" *Personalist,* XVI (1925), 310–30; H. Flanders Dunbar, *Symbolism in Medieval Thought and Its Consummation in the Divine Comedy* (New Haven, 1929), *passim*; Vincent Hopper, "The Beauty of Order — Dante," in *Medieval Number Symbolism,* pp. 136–201; and, for a more recent analysis, Charles S. Singleton, "The Poet's Number at the Center," *Modern Language Notes,* LXXX (1965), 1–10.

19. Batts, "The Origins of Numerical Symbolism and Numerical Patterns in Medieval German Literature," *Traditio,* XX (1964), 462, 470. Batts may be following Curtius' lead, but, far from stating that these numbers are not symbolic, Curtius goes on to point to the elaborate numerical structure of the *Commedia* and to say, "Here number is no longer an outer framework, but a symbol of the cosmic *ordo*" (p. 509). To say that the *Commedia* is not "secular" is only to show the inadequacy of the secular-religious distinction. Moreover, number as an expression of proportion and harmony was very much a part of late medieval aesthetics, as may be seen in the writings of such twelfth-century thinkers as William of Conches, Alan of Lille, and Hugh of Saint Victor. See also De Bruyne, *Etudes d'esthétique médiévale,* esp. II, 272 ff., 292 ff.

20. Of the many studies approaching German literature in terms of numerical principles, see esp., along with Batts' articles, the following more general studies: J. A. Huisman, *Neue Wege zur dichterischen und musikalischen Technik Walthers von der Vogelweide. Mit einem Exkurs über die symmetrische Zahlenkomposition im Mittelalter* (Utrecht, 1950); A. T. Hatto and R. J. Taylor, "Recent Work on the Arithmetical Principles in Medieval Poetry," *Modern Language Review,* XLVI (1951), 396–403; Fritz Tschirch, "Schlüsselzahlen. Studie zur geistigen Durchdringung der Form in der deutschen Dichtung des Mittelalters," in *Beiträge zur deutschen und nor-*

dischen Literatur. *Festgabe für Leopold Magon* (Berlin, 1958), pp. 30–35; and "Zum symbolbestimmten Umfang mittelalterlicher Dichtungen," in *Stil- und Formprobleme in der Literatur.* Vorträge des VII. Kongresses der internationalen Vereinigung für moderne Sprachen und Literaturen in Heidelberg (Heidelberg, 1959), pp. 148–56; and Heinz Rupp, "Neue Forschung zur Form und Bau mittelalterlicher Dichtung," *Deutschunterricht,* XI. 2 (1959), 117–24. For studies of lyrical poetry, see also Karl-Heinz Schirmer, *Die Strophik Walther von der Vogelweide. Ein Beitrag zur den Aufbauprinzipien in der lyrischen Dichtung des Hochmittelalters* (Halle, 1956); and "Zur Aufbau des hochmittelalterlichen deutschen Strophenliedes," *Deutschunterricht,* XI. 2 (1959), 35–59; Heinz Rupp, *Deutsche religiöse Dichtungen des 11. and 12. Jahrhunderts* (Freiburg/Br., 1958); as well as several studies of the *Annolied,* most recently, M. S. Batts, "On the Form of the 'Annolied,'" *Monatshefte,* LII (1960), 179–82; and Werner Betts, "Zur Zahlensymbolik im Aufbau des Annoliedes," in *Mediaeval German Studies Presented to Frederick Norman* (London, 1965), pp. 39–45. For narrative poetry, see esp. Hans Eggers, *Symmetrie und Proportion epischen Erzählens. Studien sur Kunstform Hartmanns von Aue* (Stuttgart, 1956); "Vom Formenbau mittelhochdeutscher Epen," *Deutschunterricht,* XI. 2 (1959), 81–97; and "Der goldene Schnitt im Aufbau alt- und mittelhochdeutscher Epen," *Wirkendes Wort,* X (1960), 193–203; and several studies of the *Nibelungenlied,* most recently, M. S. Batts, *Die Form der Aventiuren im Nibelungenlied,* Beiträge zur deutschen Philologie 29 (Giessen, 1961); Sister Mary Frances, "Architectonic Symmetry as a Principle of Structure in the *Niebelungenlied,*" *German Review,* XLI (1966), 157–69; and Peter Wiehl, "Über den Aufbau des Nibelungenliedes," *Wirkendes Wort,* XVI (1966), 309–23. Of related interest are Johannes Rathofer, *Der Heliand, Theologischer Sinn als tektonische Form* (Cologne, 1962); and "Zur Aufbau des Heiland," *Zeitschrift für deutsches Altertum und deutsche Literatur,* CXCIII (1964), 239–72.

21. See esp. Carl Appel, "Zur Formenlehre des provenzalischen Minnesangs," *Zeitschrift für romanische Philologie,* LIII (1933), 151–71; C. A. Robson, "The Technique of Symmetrical Composition in Medieval Narrative Poetry," in *Studies in Medieval French Presented to Albert Ewert* (Oxford, 1961), pp. 26–75; along with recent studies of various saints' lives: of the *Vie de Saint Alexis,* see Anna G. Hatcher, "The Old-French Poem St. Alexis: A Mathematical Demonstration," *Traditio,* VIII (1952), 112–58; and Eleanor W. Bulatkin, "The Arithmetic Structure of the Old French *Vie de Saint Alexis,*" *PMLA,* LXXIV (1959), 495–502; of the *Vie de Saint Thibaut, Confesseur,* see Robert Lucas, "The Golden Section in the Structure of an Old French Poem," *Romance Notes,* VIII (1967), 1–9. See also Gerald F. Carr, "The Prologue to Wace's *Vie de Saint Nicholas*: A Structural Analysis," *Philological Quarterly,* XLVII (1968), 1–7.

22. Though these have been few and minor, see, e.g., Coolidge O. Chapman, "Numerical Symbolism in Dante and *The Pearl,*" *Modern Language Notes,* LIV (1939), 256–59; P. M. Kean, "Numerical Composition in *Pearl,*" *Notes & Queries,* XII (1965), 49–51; Linda L. Lattin, "Some Aspects of Number Symbolism in Langland's *Piers Plowman,* A Text," *Emporia State Research*

Studies, XIV (1965), 5–13; and Russell A. Peck, "Number Symbolism in the Prologue to Chaucer's *Parson's Tale*," *English Studies*, XLVIII (1967), 205–15. There have been several important studies recently of Renaissance English literature: e.g., A. Kent Hieatt, *Short Time's Endless Monument: The Symbolism of the Numbers in Edmund Spenser's Epithalamion* (New York, 1960); Maren-Sofie Röstvig, "The Hidden Sense: Milton and the Neoplatonic Method of Numerical Composition," in *The Hidden Sense and Other Essays*, Norwegian Studies in English 9 (Oslo and London, 1963), pp. 1–112; and Alastair Fowler, *Spenser and the Numbers of Time* (London, 1964).

23. Some editors print this poem in five stanzas of four short lines each; I follow the transcription in *Religious Lyrics of the Fifteenth Century*, ed. Carleton Brown (Oxford, 1938), no. 81, p. 119. See also the discussion in Stephen Manning, *Wisdom and Number. Toward a Critical Appraisal of the Middle English Religious Lyric* (Lincoln, Neb., 1962), p. 167.

24. Curtius, p. 505.

25. Ll. 623 ff. See also Richard H. Green, "Gawain's Shield and the Quest for Perfection," *ELH*, XXIX (1962), 127–39.

26. See esp. Hilda Swinburne, "Numbers in Otfried's *Evangelienharmonie*," *Modern Language Review*, LII (1957), 195–202; and Heinz Rupp, "Otfrid von Weissenburg und die Zahlen," *Archiv*, CCI (1964), 262–65.

27. No. 19 in *English Lyrics of the XIIIth Century*, ed. Carleton Brown (Oxford, 1932), pp. 29–30; the same method is found in various songs of the Five Joys of Mary (e.g., in *Religious Lyrics of the Fourteenth Century*, ed. C. Brown, 2d ed. [Oxford, 1957], no. 11, pp. 13–14; no. 31, pp. 44–46), as well as in "The Bird with Four Feathers" (*Ibid.*, no. 101, pp. 208–15), where the feathers symbolize youth, beauty, strength, and riches, and act as a focal point for the subsequent narrative.

28. Hugh, *De scripturis et scriptoribus sacris*, XV (*PL*, CLXXV, 22–23).

29. See William H. Riker, "A Note on Numerology in 'The Twelve Days of Christmas,'" *Journal of American Folklore*, LXXII (1959), 348.

30. No. 82 in *Secular Lyrics of the XIV and XV Centuries*, ed. R. H. Robbins (Oxford, 1952), p. 80; cf. variations, p. 253.

31. *Ware the Hawk*, l. 240; *Garland of Laurel*, after l. 752 (*The Poetical Works of John Skelton*, ed. Alexander Dyce [London, 1843], I, 163, 391); see Hopper, pp. 66–67. On a number-letter puzzle in Gottfried's *Tristan*, see Jean Fourquet, "Le cryptogramme du *Tristan* et la composition du poème," *Etudes Germaniques*, XVIII (1963), 271–76.

32. No. 83 in *Secular Lyrics*, ed. Robbins, p. 80.

33. "The Pilgrimage Narrative and the *Canterbury Tales*," forthcoming in *Studies in Philology* (1970).

34. Al-Kwārizm or Abū 'Abdallāh Muhammad ibn Musa. The form *Argus* or, more commonly, *Algus*, is an Old French adaptation of the Arabic. See *The Works of Geoffrey Chaucer*, ed. F. N. Robinson, 2d ed. (Boston, 1957), pp. 775n., 684n.; and Florence A. Yeldham, *The Story of Reckoning in the Middle Ages* (London, 1926), esp. pp. 61 ff.

Some Common Features of Italian Urban Experience (c. 1200-1500)

Marvin B. Becker

LEONARDO BRUNI ARETINO and Niccolò Machiavelli were quite correct in their assessment of the significance of the shift from citizen military service to an army of mercenaries.[1] Although their judgments must be modified to indicate that hired troops were in evidence long before the period they deemed crucial, still their stress on this point was not misplaced.[2] This thesis can be readily extended to include the effects of warfare in general upon the rise of late medieval and Renaissance territorial states as well as the decline of the commune in north and central Italy. Monumental studies such as P. Pieri's *Il Rinascimento e la crisi militare italiana* (Turin, 1952) are devoted to a consideration of the social, economic, and political structures influencing the conduct of war. Military activity is viewed as a function of the underlying civil society.[3] Critics have suggested, without disvaluing Pieri's contribution, that his military history is really a generalized description of "culture."[4] Moreover, the debacle of Italian arms in the first part of the sixteenth century led Pieri, like so many of his confreres, to draw particular moral conclusions.[5] While profiting so substantially from these works, I would like to venture a different perspective, hoping that in so doing certain pragmatic definitions applicable to the experience of several Italian states may emerge.

I

Perhaps there is something of a liberal bias in the fact that modern scholars have discounted the obvious and primary activity of both late

---

This paper was presented to the Columbia Renaissance Seminar in March of 1969. The present version is slightly expanded but represents only a summary of ideas to be developed in a monograph on "War and Society in the Italian Renaissance."

medieval and Renaissance city states — warfare — in order to concentrate upon questions of ideology and problems of class conflict. Similarly, scholarly concern with the rise and decline of private economies has led to a substantial neglect of public financing for war.[6] Surely, an interest in ideology, class conflict, or business activity needs no justification, but those involved in causal investigations may have to inquire into martial affairs. A hypothesis of the present study can be stated thus: It was warfare and the attendant accumulation of indebtedness that undermined older political structures and styles of rule, while at the same time prompting the development of new political institutions and forms. Therefore, I shall concentrate upon the emergence of a new political matrix — a superstructure, if you will — that housed a variety of city-state societies, each with rather distinctive qualities.[7] Yet another way of indicating my purpose is to suggest that the superstructure in Venice evolved as a resultant of forces comparable to those acting to generate similar structures in Florence or Genoa or Pisa or Milan. The possible advantage of this approach is twofold: first, hypotheses can be offered as to the nature of the causes at work undermining the older commune; secondly, certain of the characteristics of these emerging superstructures may be shared by several of the cities. Possibly we shall find that Renaissance political problems, whether Florentine, Venetian, or Genoese, were not so disparate. If this be so, then the possibility of formulating pragmatic definitions articulating features of these medieval and Renaissance political structures shall be enhanced. In any case, we can always plead in the name of methodological modesty, like the novelist Henry James, that all we are doing is seeking to put together what goes together.

The medieval commune that developed in north and central Italy was a configuration of economic, social, religious, and political organisms coexisting in a pluralistic, civic environment. The commune itself was at first only a sworn association of men devoted to keeping the urban peace, and this clearly implied making war.[8] There were sworn associations of knights (*commune militum*) and sworn associations of foot soldiers (*commune peditum*). On the façades of cathedrals we would find the foot soldiers on the left hand of the Redeemer and the knights appropriately on His right. Guilds, religious confraternities, philopapal and philoimperial organizations were an essential part of this manifold political universe. Indeed, the medieval city-state can be likened to a body possessed of no political center of gravity.[9] Fundamental to an appreciation of the political texture of this type of community is a comprehension of the abundant number of immunities, privileges, and ecclesiastical liberties. The city in medieval Italy was primarily an aristocratic foundation; likewise, the commune of the eleventh and twelfth centuries was chiefly a patrician construct.[10] Moreover, where political development was most precocious, such as in Milan, the archbishops and other prelates played a decisive role in encouraging the formation of political associations. Two factors worth a brief glance are the persistence of urban forms of association throughout the early history of medieval Italy and the intense involvement of large segments of the population in the work of religious reform in cities such as Milan and Florence in the eleventh and twelfth centuries.[11] The conglomerate character of the *civitas* can be observed if we realize that great feudatories and prelates, and even guilds, retained control of areas of life that today would be considered public. A guild might collect the wine tax or oversee the use of weights and measures; a great feudatory might hold the customs toll as a fief or exercise his jurisdiction over a market. The prelate held ecclesiastical court, claimed exemption from communal imposts, and denied the right of secular jurisdiction over his clergy.[12]

By the twelfth century we note a peculiar mix of social classes and quasi-political bodies. While popular participation in the polis increased as a result of the revolutionary movement accompanying the Gregorian reforms in the latter half of the eleventh century, and was accelerated by struggles against the Holy Roman Emperors, still most urban regimes remained firmly in the hands of consular aristocracies.[13] Indeed, these great families, often feudal in origin, had achieved a remarkable preeminence as a consequence of substantial victories over imperial armies. Their leadership over town militia and cavalry also proved essential for securing trade routes and commercial advantage. In Milan the *capitanei* and *valvassori* dominated the military and juridical life of the community, replacing the ancient authority of the archbishop. In Pisa and Genoa their aristocratic counterparts were likewise preeminent, leading the grand naval expeditions that rolled back Mohammedan occupation of Mediterranean islands, giving their townsmen rich possibilities for trade and investment.[14]

The late twelfth and early thirteenth centuries can be seen as the golden age of the upper and middling north Italian nobility. Already, half a century before, the German chronicler Otto of Freising had complained that few nobles placed fidelity to the Empire over loyalty to their natal *patria*. By an ancient Milanese custom the vassal of a lord did not forfeit his fief if he failed to join his *dominus* in war against the city. Again, Otto noted that the consulate of Milan was staffed by men from the high and middling nobility. When imperial authority receded and civil strife became intolerable, efforts were made to install more impartial magistrates. The institution of the podestà — a complex phenomenon at the least — was at first the exclusive preserve of urban nobility. While the paucity of evidence does not allow us to reconstruct in depth the effects of extensive participation by these nobles in the bureaucratic and juridical life of the polis, still, service in high magistracies worked to discourage old loyalties and habits. It is clear from the histories of Pisa, Pistoia, and Genoa that important sectors of the nobility were themselves sponsors of basic reforms, and even leaders of popular regimes. Certainly, a part of this can be attributed to demagoguery, but much more is explicable in terms of the high degree of military and juridical involvement in government of these aristocrats. Yet another more obvious force stemmed from extensive participation by Venetian patricians, Pisan feudatories, and Genoese consular nobility in the thriving commercial activities of the Dugento. That portion of the well-born most readily assimilated into business and government were as anxious to promote urban peace through law as were many of the haute bourgeoisie.[15]

The early thirteenth century is the locus for a political amalgamation that was most firm in Genoa, Venice, Milan, Pisa, and other towns. Yet there were disruptive forces at work that would transform the basic qualities of this aristocratic synthesis. As we have seen, the political society of the towns in north and central Italy was intrapluralistic, characterized by an abundance of immunities, privileges, and liberties. At mid-twelfth century the chronicler Otto had commented in disgust that all manner of men bore arms in the Italian city; even lowly artisans and vile mechanics were enrolled in the communal militia. (These were the *iuvenes inferioris* considered so pestiferous by the chronicler.)[16] Citizen military service had a most significant effect upon the Italian town chroniclers, who now depicted *il popolo* as the protagonists of the narrative — not the kings, princes, and bishops of yore. It was the urban militia that gained the victories on the plains of Lombardy who would now be called upon to assist in keeping civic peace.[17]

Even at the moment of its greatest success citizen military service was proving inadequate to the demands of war and peace. Already, during the 1160's in Milan, the 1170's in Venice and Genoa, and the final decades in Siena and Pisa, it was clear that revision of military finances was vital. In Milan, during its struggle against imperial power over the second half of the twelfth century, the hire of substantial contingents of cavalry at high wages was required to supplement the citizen militia. This practice, endemic throughout north and central Italy, paralleled the discontinuance of gratuitous or meagerly paid citizen military service. By 1228 the Milanese citizen cavalry was being indemnified, and hired troops were bearing the brunt of warfare in the Piedmont.[18] Economic interests in each of the major cities encouraged policies of conquest and firm control of territories so that trade might be secure and free from obstruction.[19]

In Florence we note that contemporary chroniclers began the history of their own times with the Arno city's decisive victory over its neighboring rival Fiesole in 1125. Indeed, there is ample reason to believe that it was the circumstances of twelfth-century Florentine imperialism that contributed the essential ingredient to the new civic historical consciousness.[20] The theme of urban expansion was foremost in the minds of contemporary commentators, generating as it did both pride and anxiety. Clearly, such bloodshed and violence contradicted fundamental Christian teachings. The minds of such citizen-patriots as the poet Dante and the chronicler Giovanni Villani were disquieted as well as entranced. Only with the fifteenth century and civic humanism did imperialism find its justification, in the writings of Bruni and Machiavelli. For Florence the two centuries after the conquest of Fiesole were an era in which energies and revenues were committed to expansion, in part through citizen service and in part by mercenaries; even in 1125 hired troops had been utilized.[21]

Genoa offers a telling example of the new problems and pressures; her great naval expeditions in the eleventh and twelfth centuries had been mainly privately financed.[22] Communal government tended to be lackluster in this pluralistic world of medieval politics. Influential nobility captained the forces, advanced monies, and shared the booty; later, the families of the consular aristocrats even held the conquered territories of the commune as fiefs. In the thirteenth century much of this underwent deep alteration: the navy was now financed by the communal treasury, and war became a public prerogative.

Communal administrative machinery was profoundly influenced by the experiences of the hundred years after 1150. Persistent experimentation led to the erection of bureaucratic and juridical systems that would prove effective in making warfare a public prerogative. Two vexing issues were to be confronted: first, how this shift might be adequately financed; and second, how to release the commune from military dependence on the consular aristocracy. Each of course was closely connected with the other. Perhaps, so that we may better see the connection, the word violence may be employed for the moment in place of the word war. Again, to illustrate from Genoese history, we find that the family of Folco di Castello, commanders of the Genoese contingent on the Third Crusade, attacked the communal magistrates in an attempt to seize power. In Pisa, Ubaldo Visconti tried to dominate the city, just as he controlled the island of Sardinia, that prize of the republic's wars. Against him stood the clan of Gherardesca. We could easily duplicate the circumstances for virtually each Italian town. The exercise of violence by the *milites* of the city was surely inflamed by chivalric codes placing primacy on the vendetta and blood feud. The contemporary word used to describe violence among noble *consorterie* was *guerra*.[23] To repress this *guerra* the right to bear arms would have to be limited and the *potentes* be compelled to use force only in ways commensurate with public order. The phrase appearing with monotonous regularity in documents of the period, "the peaceful and tranquil state of the city," expressed that ethos aiming to make the *buono stato* prevail. In thirteenth-century Florence, where guild organization was particularly vigorous, the effort to displace the association for citizen cavalry (*societas militum*) was an energetic blow against forces that might disrupt public order. While this *societas* continued as an aristocratic social organization, its military function was curtailed. Cavalry responsibility was no longer a personal duty. Instead, a charge was placed on landowners; they were required to furnish horses and knights, which were to be inspected periodically by a town official. Subject territories paid imposts in terms of an assessment designating the numbers of troops to be provided. This technique of taxation lasted well into the fourteenth century.

Earlier, many cities had assigned public revenues to the *societas militum* or to other organizations performing a variety of military and defense duties. In the late twelfth and early thirteenth centuries, as the commune assumed these responsibilities, attempts were made to recover these sources of revenue.[24] The general thrust over the Dugento was to correct a persistent imbalance between communal income and expenditures for war. A series of devices were tried to help defray costs: in Florence payment was made in lieu of military service; in Venice a consortium of financiers advanced large sums to the treasury; while at Genoa the entrepreneurs organized private expeditions to rout the Saracens from their Mediterranean stronghold. Still the imbalance between communal income and outlays for war grew more threatening; in fact, if there is a single enduring socioeconomic feature of the Italian urban experience from the thirteenth through the sixteenth centuries, it is just this disequilibrium. While costs of city administration increased over this period, the increment was trifling when compared with expenditures for war.[25]

At the onset of the thirteenth century disaffection among the newer citizens was pervasive concerning inequities in the communal tax system. Citizen services (military and others) and the utilization of the public patrimony to finance armies and navies were inadequate. Moreover, collections from indirect levies (the gabelles) were insufficient to bridge this gap. The press for a more impartial government to mobilize statal resources more effectively was no simple class phenomenon. The thrust in this direction was evident in Florence, Pisa, Siena, Bologna, and virtually every other sizable town at this time.[26]

Crucial benefits were to be gained by both the nobility and affluent commoners from a surcease of the *guerrae* between contending factions. In many a city substantial elements of the older nobility were the very capstones of a thriving business and commercial world. Intermarriage, joint partnerships, membership in aristocratic societies did the work of amalgamation. The very magistracy — the podestà — employed to implement more general fiscal and juridical norms was almost always occupied by a noble with training in the law; the prerequisite was precisely that the podestà be a *miles*. In Milan, where evidence for the early tenures of these officials abounds, the first of a line of foreigners imported for this post was the Bolognese noble Uberto da Vialta.[27] It was he who promulgated the celebrated statutes of December, 1214. Already, in 1211, feudal jurisdiction had been suppressed by Milanese law; the high clergy agreed not to create new fiefs without consent of the commune. The jurisdiction of the commune was elevated so that disposition of cases between *signori* and *villani* was remanded to Milanese courts. Rural inhabitants and clerics alike were made liable for contributing to the maintenance of public fortifications and castles. The novel features of Da Vialta's tenure can first be discerned in his efforts to systematize that welter of legal accretions regulating relationships between the commune and the many quasi-political bodies coexisting in the urban milieu. Further, we note a concerted challenge against the medieval preoccupation with status and fiscal exemption; in its stead we find the assertion of the claims of territorial law and tributary equality. To enforce these demands a bureaucracy was lent further structure; under Da Vialta's administration new and more secret voting procedures were installed.

The epitomization of programs was realized, at least in theory, when Da Vialta and his subordinates attempted to draw up a general estimate of the value of all citizen property for the purpose of achieving greater equality in taxation. Special attention was focused on the troublesome question of greater parity between urban and rural imposts. The commune asserted the right to impose customs and hearth taxes; the former had frequently been retained by the nobility as a fief, while the latter were recognized as a regalian right, i.e., belonging to the Emperor. Finally, the effort to achieve equity was continued in levies upon noble and commoner, and even in those falling on the various grades of nobility. The difficulties confronting such a formidable enterprise were attested to by the halting, long-term endeavors to complete this type of estimate of wealth. The advantages to a militarily beleaguered community were obvious: taxes and loans could be assessed in proportion to citizen wealth. If the total were known, then the commune could assess that percent which would yield it the requisite sum.[28]

Still, the press for further fiscal reorganization persisted; tensions between custom and innovation were strong and practical difficulties always baffling. Minor accomplishments of successive podestàs, who displaced ancient feudatories (the Visconti) from their role as collectors of taxes on tradesmen, contributed toward the gradual formation of a more unitary political structure. But the monies realized for the commune proved insignificant in meeting the escalating costs of warfare. In 1233 control of communal finances was centralized, and again the bureaucratic structure was renovated. This at precisely the moment when we observe the beginnings of the existence of a permanent mercenary army. The terrible years of hostilities with the Emperor demanded extreme citizen sacrifice. *Il popolo* claimed that they were assuming "the whole weight" (*totum pondus*) of military expenditures. In 1240 their leader, Pagano della Torre (*caput credentiae*), gained control of the communal government. With the support of other nobles (the Da Soresina, Crivelli, Pirovana) and the papal legate, he was able to put into effective operation the first extensive tax on fixed and movable properties. The difficult business of achieving an estimate of citizen holdings had been accomplished ("Tempore istius Pagani, primum inventarium institutum fuit"). Until that decade nobles and clergy had effectively resisted its thorough implementation; the problem of medieval tax liability was always thorny. Should allodial tenures be liable for imposts or only benefices? What about land that had been exempted by imperial diploma? What of the clergy? (At this time they did not resist the levy because Milan was warring against the archheretic Frederick II.) What of the confraternities? (The question of status was particularly vexing, and again the Milanese clergy acknowledged communal rights only because of the exigencies of war.) The need for revenue again assumed primacy: war and the carrying charges on the public debt had prompted reforms that strengthened the fiscal authority of the commune.

During these years, Milan anticipated special problems with the communal credit system that were to confront Florence almost a century later. The issue of whether full value should be accorded titles to the public debt was resolved in favor of the creditors. Efforts to amortize the principal, however, were continually frustrated by warfare, hire of additional mercenaries, and chronic budgetary deficits. Decrees prohibiting the treasury from contracting new debts proved as ineffectual in Milan as they were in many other cities. Substitution of mercenaries for the old militia was simply too costly. Moreover, forced and voluntary loans were easier to garner (much less time-consuming than other tributary measures) and added to the sum total of public indebtedness.

Popular forces routed from the guilds were not strong enough to promote reorganization of the state and its finances. The path of the despot was presaged by the roles of such strong men as Gregorio da Montelongo and Beno de' Gozzandi, who responded to military needs by sponsoring administrative and fiscal reorganization of the commune during the middle years of the thirteenth century. These men were both foreigners and were expected to stand above factional interests, while Milanese families, with their followings would soon enter a deadly contest for political control. While there were to be significant differences in political styles among the Della Torre, Visconti, and Sforza, still the march toward centralization and bureaucratization proceeded quite steadily. No matter who the ruling elite might be, deficit financing and warfare remained the essential problems. Without minimizing the differences between republics and despotisms, both were generating political superstructures with comparable features. The daily intrusion of political power into citizen life and the high degree of economic supervision by a centralized government were encouraged by identical sets of factors — budgetary and military considerations. Integration of territories and bureaucratic development maximized opportunities for citizen participation in diplomacy and civil service. While there was a substantial difference between the active citizen of a republic and his more docile Milanese counterpart, yet both political orders were staffed by numerous functionaries whose dedication to administrative problems was uncritical and lifelong. Such a reorganization was prompted largely by old familiar considerations. There was, however, an added incentive for the despot. He felt more secure with a standing army at his side. So, the citizen army was to undergo further eclipse.[29]

II

Throughout north and central Italy we observe the creation of a creditor class as a consequence of expansion through diplomacy and warfare. Venice borrowed from a consortium to raise a subvention for the league organized against Frederick I.[30] Two "new citizens," Sebastiano Ziani and Orio Mastropiero, each contributed one-sixth of the total, with the government pledging income from market rights for restitution. While this instance is early and somewhat isolated (at least so far as surviving evidence suggests), examples will multiply over the thirteenth and fourteenth centuries. Indeed, if there is a corollary to our single enduring socioeconomic fact that warfare and deficit financing were decisive for late medieval Italian urban experience, it might run thus: in Genoa and Venice in the thirteenth century, and Florence in the fourteenth, entry into the communal creditor class was the surest passport to political influence. By mid-fourteenth century those Florentine nobles who were no longer large-scale communal creditors lost much of their political standing, while "new citizens" who advanced capital to the government were playing crucial roles in public life.

In Genoa the *Maona* was inaugurated in 1235 to finance naval expeditions against the Emir of Ceuta. These were loans made to the state not in money but in the form of galleys and armed men, with the government guaranteeing both interest and capital to the shipowners.[31] In addition to this novel type of communal credit, there was always that hardy perennial, the forced loan. In 1259 debts contracted in this manner were consolidated and declared interest-bearing without directly committing the public treasury to the restitution of capital within a fixed period of time. The popular regime that accomplished this funding was unable to install an effective system of direct taxation, since resistance on the part of the populace to the *estimo* proved too formidable. Subsequent regimes, popular and oligarchical, continued to impose forced loans in order to meet the carrying charges of the debt. This would only swell the total; in the case of Genoa, the debt became unmanageable, and the creditors came to play an increasingly crucial role in the political decision-making process. Genoa's costly victory over Pisa at the end of the thirteenth century and her still more costly defeat by Venice in 1381 were but the beginning and end of a century of escalating warfare. Carrying charges on the public debt were so high that the government was compelled to assign her colonies and even her territories in Liguria to the ministrations of the creditor class. In 1407 the creditor's organization, the Casa di San Giorgio, was frankly acknowledged as the vital center of communal politics. Sometimes referred to as "a state within a state," the Casa prospered and flourished while the husk of the commune withered.[32]

In Venice forced loans were being collected in 1207 to underwrite extensive naval activities connected with crusading and the conquest of Constantinople only a few years before.[33] In 1207, Pietro Ziani introduced a series of reforms designed to prevent a monopoly of power by a very few patricians. New councils were created and magistracies were increased as the authority of the commune was asserted over the regal power of the doge. Articulation of the Venetian constitution, with its growing reliance on revived Roman law, accompanied this shift from the widespread exaction of personal service to the steady levying of imposts and forced loans. By mid-thirteenth century (1252?) a bureaucracy was in process of being formed to manage the administration of this debt and to provide for interest payments to citizen creditors. After 1262 direct taxation in the city was abandoned (only revived briefly during the War of Chioggia) in favor of compulsory loans. In that year outstanding claims were consolidated into a funded debt with shares paying 5 per cent and declared negotiable.

For one hundred years the government set aside large sums during times of peace and prosperity for amortization of the principal. In 1363 a new technique was introduced when the government decided to employ public revenues to purchase shares of the debt; in this way the market price of these public stocks was to be shored up. It is not with the success of these policies or the fluctuations in the value of these shares that we are concerned; even the fact that the patrician ruling families were its principal shareholders is not central to the argument. That the parvenus benefited from certain aspects of tributary policies and were able to acquire sizable blocks of shares adds dimension to the observation that these centuries witnessed a tightening of the nexus between citizen and polis. What stands as most germane, however, is the astronomical leap in the total debt: in 1255 it was at the trifling figure of 15,000 *lire a grossi*; in 1279 it was 400,000; and by 1313 it totaled almost 2,800,000. There was a substantial reduction in the 1330's and 40's, but again the climb proved irrepressible; in 1353 it stood at 3,100,000, only to reach 12,300,000 at the conclusion of the War of Chioggia in 1381.[34]

The costs of equipping war galleys, staffing them with mariners and troops, and maintaining the great Venetian arsenal served to prompt stricter enforcement of statal norms.[35] To meet the carrying charges on this aggregate of indebtedness required the application of highly rationalized fiscal techniques. Chronic warfare allowed no surcease, and in time of stress the Venetian naval forces could boast of 36,000 sailors.[36] Words attributed to doge Andrea Contarini, in 1381, make explicit that awareness which made the "buon stato" preeminent: "It is a manifest thing that the Republic can easily tolerate the adversity of private citizens, but that they are not sufficient unto themselves to sustain the adversity of all the realm." The state commenced to elevate itself above society with its central organs, the Senate and Council of Ten, exercising influence over the farthest reaches of civic life. The powerful bureaucracy, like capillaries, extended throughout the body politic. Soon Venetian humanists of the early fifteenth century celebrated the *Principatus Venetus,* as did Lorenzo Monacis in his *Chronicon de rebus Venetis,* as being that city where law prevailed and the doge ruled like a king.[37] Gladly would the citizen sacrifice his life for this *Principatus.* Chroniclers maintained that any who opposed the Republic were in blasphemous contest, "contra divinam potentiam," for "divina providentia" herself ruled and ordered the city. Bernardo Guistinian, in his eulogy of the doge Francesco Foscari, set forth the sacrifices of the ancient Athenians, who won a maritime empire, as well as those of the Romans, who brought Carthage to heel and gained the expanses of the Mediterranean for the Eternal City.

Again, at Pisa we observe the pressure of population and escalating costs of war as challenges to the continued existence of a pluralistic urban community.[38] In the eleventh century the leading naval entrepreneurs were for the most part scions of landed nobility; these patricians, with their own organizations headed by consuls, armed and equipped the Pisan fleet for crusading service. Their private associations assumed public roles, rendering justice on shipboard and making war and peace. Peasants of the countryside were frequently their tenants; later they became workers in their shipyards and sailors on their galleys. This patriciate dominated the port's carrying trade and industrial development; it was their gifts that contributed to the building of the spectacular cathedral. This *duomo* was the first *Palazzo del Popolo*, where the consular government was to assemble. On excellent terms with the archbishop, this patriciate held fiefs from his Eminence in vassalage and sat in his feudal curia. Here again we observe feudal forms thriving alongside the newer institutions. Generally, the archbishop was chosen from the ranks of these very families (the Upezzinghi, the Lanfranchi, and the Gaetani). It was the archbishop, with his jurisdiction over Corsica and its prelates, who opened the island to Pisan economic penetration. It was the prestige of the archbishop and the pontifical legate in the Holy Land that assured Pisan merchants commercial rights over the ports of Syria. This explosive blend of civic pride and Christianity, a byproduct of the crusading wars, generated one of the first sustained outpourings of twelfth-century communal historiography, rivaled only by the chronicles written when the Lombard cities were contesting the power of the German emperors.

Among the consular families the tradition of command persisted and added to the popular respect won by patrician naval commanders; this preeminence was buttressed by favorable electoral procedures. The years in which the German emperors attempted to assert their claims over north Italy were a time when this nobility gained further recognition by securing (however belatedly) an autonomous status for the city. Meanwhile, the archbishop lost much of his political authority, and the consular government assumed additional juridical and fiscal powers.

During the early tenure of the podestà, at the close of the thirteenth century, the maritime and military aristocrats from the Visconti and Gherardesca families regularly occupied or dominated this magistracy. Yet the anatomy of the administration and bureaucracy was ever more discernible, and increasing participation by judges and notaries had become a fact of civic life. Pisa appears to have been the first of the Italian towns to apply the norms of Roman law to everyday political life. Written law vied with custom with the appearance of the *Breve populi*, first noted in 1171. Duties of new officials were defined with greater precision, and they were required to take an oath to observe the new rudimentary legal codes. In 1162 one of the consuls was himself a legal specialist, and soon this type of appointment became a commonplace with the creation of the *consul justiciae*. By the end of the century there were several of these magistrates, and their courts were exceedingly active. Gradually, then, there was a displacement of much judicial business from ecclesiastical and feudal courts into the tribunals of the commune.

Even under this canopy of law and increasing legal sensibility the familiar pluralism of communal life prospered, with guild courts (*Curia Maris*) collecting customs receipts and the military nobility retaining their own organization with *capitanei militum*. But again warfare, deficit financing, and population increase worked to tip the balance toward more impartial and unitary regimes. Participation by the new citizens, first in the urban militia, then in the *societates armorum*, and finally as administrators and government creditors, was a relevant aspect of this transformation. Military service and then financial contribution brought greater equality to the ruling and bureaucratic cadres of the society. As in Arezzo, Ravenna, and Treviso, the formation of *il popolo* at Pisa was not exclusive nor were its leaders unmindful of the traditional claims of the nobility for status. Great nobles such as the Donoratico, who had rendered valuable service to the commune, took the sacred oath to the Pisan people ("sacramentum Pisani Populi").

The need for revenue proved difficult to resist; there was a general administrative reform of fiscal and institutional procedures: between 1230 and 1288 communal income increased from 2,400 lire to 40,000 lire. Even taking into account coin devaluation and inflation, this was a sizable accomplishment. Still, it was not possible for the city to meet its military commitments. Efforts at the beginning of the century by foreign podestàs to install a revenue system based upon the imposition of direct taxes proved no more successful at Pisa than at many another Italian town. Chronic war with Genoa, culminating with the crushing defeat of Meloria in August of 1284, did not dissuade the Pisans from continuing an overly ambitious foreign policy. Contemporary chroniclers may have exaggerated the sums that the ill-fated expedition of Henry VII ("exercitus felicissimus Domini Imperatoris") cost his Pisan ally, but the bankruptcy of the public treasury attested to the barren fiscal facts. Failure to collect sufficient monies from direct taxes and the preference for interest-bearing loans caused an escalating debt. These risky imperialistic policies were underwritten by new and old citizens who advanced capital to the communal treasury. In a single register for the year 1304 (few survive for this period), we find that measures taken by the government concern almost exclusively militia activity, armaments, higher taxes, and the imposition of interest-bearing loans. Increasingly, members of the executive branch of the communal government (the *anziani*) were to be the principal creditors. These citizens formed companies (*societas*) to advance capital to the government. Less than two generations later their creditor organizations would be well represented in the regime, and management of the public debt would become a central concern of all Pisan regimes.

In Florence, conquest and expansion characterized the city's history from the eleventh through the fourteenth centuries.[39] Indeed, as we have seen, the conquest of neighboring Fiesole in 1125 marked the beginnings of a new historical consciousness among Florentine chroniclers. The memory of this victory was ritualized when on St. John's Day former tenants of the bishop of Fiesole proceeded to the Florentine cathedral and rendered homage to their new lord. Later, Florence's subject cities were to bring wax candles of enormous size to the cathedral to be lit in homage to the city's patron saint on his name day. War against the counts Alberti, Adimari, Buondelmonti, and Foraboschi secured communications throughout Tuscany, and later, after innumerable additional campaigns, Florentine banking and business interests were also firmly ensconced.[40] At first, the work of conquest was achieved by a communal army with a sprinkling of mercenaries who joined the forces of the bishop and his vassals. The great nobles (*cives maiores*), the counts Guidi, Alberti, Firidolfi, Pazzi, and Ricasoli, served personally in the armies of the commune and therefore were exempt from many imposts. By the end of the eleventh century levies for defense were being imposed regularly on the countryside, and by the start of the thirteenth century the lands of the nobility were declared liable for imposition of taxes. Meanwhile, over the twelfth century, the commune appropriated authority to impose the hearth tax; this was a prerogative belonging to the Empire. As a consequence of the war for Semifonte in 1201, the first direct taxes were placed upon citizen property at a rate fixed on a percentage basis in terms of the total evaluation.

Even before the establishment of *il primo popolo* in 1250, the guilds, stronger in Florence than in most Italian cities, had organized their own effective militia. These troops were able to replace the *societas militum* after 1282. Required cavalry were no longer furnished through personal service, but principally by means of a tax charge on landowners. The guilds attempted to concentrate effective military police power in the hands of their own armed companies. By the late thirteenth century the might of the greater guilds was such that the bankers and industrialists could successfully finance great military expeditions. Even as far back as 1265–66, Florentine cameral merchants had accepted the risks and reaped the benefits by underwriting the campaigns of Charles of Anjou. In fact, the bankers who had been banished from their *patria* by their Ghibelline adversaries in 1260 were little short of a government in exile. With the victories of Charles of Anjou over the imperial armies, the bankers were restored to their city and granted vital commercial privileges in the Italian holdings of the Angevin line. Further loans, perhaps more than a hundred thousand florins, gained Florence control over Poggibonsi and other Tuscan centers, as well as trading concessions in the kingdom of Sicily. It is well to remember that since Florence was required to import at least two-thirds of her wheat from abroad, favorable connections with Sicily and south Italy were essential. The wealth of the pro-papal Guelf party from confiscated Ghibelline properties was so substantial that she held current accounts with ten of the leading banking and commercial companies in the city. These same financial institutions were now assuming the bulk of banking activity for the papacy. Increasingly, the leaders of the greater guilds (members of the *calimala, cambio,* and *lana*) placed their capital at the disposal of the commune for the purpose of carrying out a very successful foreign policy. So triumphant was this program that by the decade of the 1280's Florence through her armies, diplomacy, coinage, and exchange came to exercise dominion over Tuscany.

The difference between the Florentine constitutional system and that of so many of her neighbors stemmed in part from the city's diversified banking, commercial, and industrial economy — exceptional for Tuscany. So well endowed and resolute were the greater guilds that a regime could be founded upon the effective rule of leading members of the *arti*. What emerged at the early fourteenth century was a system of guild rule characterized by extensive immunities and privileges for the membership. This system of exemptions coexisted with a tendency toward relaxed rule of the countryside and an easy entente with the nobility. After 1315, direct taxation was abandoned; except in moments of emergency or under military despotism, it was not resorted to. While Florence's military objectives were at least as ambitious as those of other towns, she did not yet run the sizable budgetary deficits of her neighbors and rivals. In 1315, communal obligations totaled a trifling figure — somewhat less than 50,000 florins. Loans from bankers, the Guelf party, and wealthy guilds were of incomparable assistance to the treasury. But this casual regimen was soon to be undone: escalating wars and exaggerated imperial ambition promoted even larger deficits. Within a period of thirty years communal indebtedness increased more than tenfold.

It was to be the great work of the regimes after 1343, culminating in the formation of the territorial state of the late Trecento, that repressed recalcitrant patricians, obdurate magnates, and overly expansive corporate bodies. In the course of this process traditional forms of government intimately associated with the era of the medieval commune dissolved, while successive regimes replaced private immunities with public law.

Out of this experience emerged a cohesive aristocracy quite different from the patriciate of the communal age. They were concerned with the procedures of communal finance, the techniques of diplomatic maneuver, and the conduct of the interminable wars of the early Quattrocento. Sedition and violence were more sporadic than formerly, and the disputes between *optimates* centered around the management of the funded communal debt or the extent to which the signory should sponsor mercantilistic programs. The ties of *consorteria* and even of guild slackened, and an intimate nexus developed among the great oligarchs, who were now virtually stockholders in a giant corporation called the state. They were joined in this partnership by the most affluent of the *novi cives*. Less and less was the signory forced to play its great medieval role of peacemaker. The canopy of law, bureaucracy, and public power spread increasingly over private lives. Swarms of treasury officers and judicial officials entered state service during the mid-Trecento, so that within a generation Florentine bureaucracy had increased threefold, with a corresponding increase in power. Further, the same men tended to continue in office throughout their adult lives. Regularization of political procedure contributed to the efficiency of law enforcement. Judicial dispensation and annulment of sentences eventually became rarities in the less permissive world of the new polis.

Under this stricter regimen the polis exercised tight controls over the countryside during the late Trecento so that additional revenues might be extracted. In the early 1380's "extraordinary" imposts were levied on rural property which very soon became a regular feature of the Florentine tributary system. Tax rates that in the early Trecento averaged only ten soldi per lira now doubled and tripled, while the communal intake even quadrupled. What had been a light burden was well on the way to becoming a rugged, persistent program. Originally, such imposts had accounted for only about 10 per cent of the communal intake, but by the early fifteenth century the figure veered between 40 and 50 per cent of total tax revenue. Comparable patterns of rigor can be discerned in the rule of subject cities and allied territories, where communal policy was dictated increasingly by budgetary deficits and the pressing need to underwrite the inflated credit structure; within only a few years taxes in these areas doubled.

Persistent and expanding costs of warfare, as well as the inordinate pressure of trying to meet escalating carrying charges on a burgeoning public debt, had a relentless effect upon the style of politics and the tone of public life. As we have seen, in the first decade and a half of the fourteenth century, when the income of the republic was about 300,000 florins, the public debt (*Monte*) was between 47,500 and 50,000 florins. Carrying charges were a few thousand florins. By the late fourteenth century the public debt stood at 3,000,000 florins, and carrying charges approached 200,000 florins; the treasury was in arrears some 300,000 florins a year. Thus, in addition to warfare, the maintenance of citizen confidence in the fiscal reliability of the polis was a monumental problem for Florentine rulers. Moreover, during these years the increase in forced citizen loans (*prestanze*) was staggering. The annual figure sometimes exceeded 1,000,000 florins. Such an assumption of fiscal liability on the part of the government was revolutionary and awesome.

The problem of finding fiscal support for this inflated credit structure compelled those in power not to overlook any potential source of revenue. That their quest met with some degree of success is attested to by the fact that the value of shares in the public debt did not decline appreciably between the 1380's and the 1430's. This search for revenue led to the integration of Florentine territory, the rise of empire, and a strenuous program of mercantilism. Indeed, growth of the public debt and large-scale warfare did much to destroy the communal regime.

After the first part of the fifteenth century fiscal innovation tended to be exceptional. Ties between the public and private economies did not slacken in Venice, Florence, Milan, or Genoa. When confidence in the public debt floundered late in the fifteenth century, leading Venetian bankers were compelled to close their doors — so tight was their dependency on the state. In Florence, during the first part of the fifteenth century, the *Monte delle doti* was established, allowing families to purchase state credits that later could be collected in the form of a marriage dowry when their daughters came of age. Again, in the late fifteenth century, when the strain on the public fisc was particularly intense, there was a serious decline in the number of marriages, so close were the bonds between families and state finances. Milan has been described as the first modern state, and judging from its expanded bureaucracy, extensive control over morals and commerce, as well as its sponsorship of mercantilistic policies, this characterization appears most apt. Here again, citizen dependence upon the public world of bureaucracy and finance was deepened. Genoa's reliance on the management of the public debt was so marked that by the fifteenth century the history of the commune became the record of the activities of the directors of the Casa di S. Giorgio.[41]

Renaissance political structures were characterized by the emergence of a public economy generated largely from war, population growth, and deficit financing. Opportunities for the citizen bureaucrat and capitalist increased as the public sector assumed a more unitary form. Despite differences in the social structures and conditions of political participation in the several Italian Renaissance states, a tighter nexus was forged between public and private worlds. Opportunities for civic participation at the bureaucratic and administrative levels multiplied despite differences in constitutional systems. Neither despots nor republican governments could afford the luxury of ineffectual management of resources and state finances at a time when pressures from the public debt were relentless.

In patrician Venice, public office, with the exception of the chancellory, was the preserve of the bourgeoisie. At Milan the despots regularly balanced the claims of the various orders to public preferment and honor; commoners could readily purchase high office and even patents of nobility. Again, at Venice, during the time of the League of Cambrai and another time in 1510, venality was practiced on a large scale. The bourgeoisie made payments to the state; the monies were employed to hire troops, and the offices were declared hereditary. Interestingly enough, these were fiscal posts and not magistracies as they were in contemporary France.[42] Florence was the most open of the political societies; the problem in the late fourteenth and early fifteenth century was one of staffing a burgeoning administration. Provincials were particularly valuable to the polis, and they had profitable and honorable careers in the bureaucracy. It was not by happenstance that so many of the civic humanists, who extolled the authority of the state and found justification for private wealth largely in terms of public power, came from the provinces. It was members of the Florentine administrative cadre who came to view warfare as natural to the human condition and who sought to provide theoretical justification for the republic's claims to empire. Bruni's celebrated *History* championed not only Florentine *libertas* but also conquest of a Tuscan empire. Some like Machiavelli, who argued that states must either expand or die, did not have to turn to antiquity for examples. Warfare and arms were central to civic humanism, and three generations of Renaissance historians rightly stressed the shift from citizen militia to mercenary army as the hallmark of the grandeur and decay of their times.[43]

III

It remains only to suggest a preliminary context in which this evidence on the fiscal experience of Italian cities may be placed. In the case of Florence, Venice, and Genoa, military and naval expenditures consistently outstripped state income. If we compare the experiences of north Europe, the pattern appears markedly different.[44] English and French military budgets tended to escalate in times of protracted warfare, with only one-third of state revenue being utilized to this end. Even under Louis XVI this percentage was not exceeded. England barely surpassed this fraction on the eve of the Napoleonic Wars. In poorer countries such as eighteenth-century Poland the figure might reach one-half. Even today France and England expend only a third of their revenues on war, while the smaller European countries budget themselves at approximately one-fifteenth. Such percentages are minuscule when compared with outlays in the major Italian cities of the Renaissance. Consequently, the differential between Italian city-state public debts and those of north Europe will also prove dramatic. In France and England, at the end of the Hundred Years' War, the sum total of obligations was not substantially in excess of annual royal revenues. To compare this figure with the Florentine public debt, which stood at a total of more than twenty times the annual state income, is again to confront an overwhelming disparity. Comparable statistics could be cited for Venice and Genoa, where evidence is also firm. Even Spain in the 1560's, under Philip II, had a state debt exceeding yearly revenues twofold. Only with the advent of early modern Europe do we find carrying charges on the public debt approaching those of the

Renaissance city-state. In France in 1789 interest on the debt consumed one-half of the total budget.

It would appear, then, that Italian public finance and the conduct of war were among the primary socioeconomic factors that promoted many of the startling political changes we associate with Renaissance statal structures. The system of immunities, privileges, and liberties in medieval Italian communes could not endure this protracted budgetary pressure. Moreover, the pluralistic communal world was an economic luxury that state treasuries could not abide. What emerged finally was a more unitary state economy, with wealth flowing from the private into the public sector.

IV

Perhaps it would not be overzealous to make a few suggestions as to the possible general import of some of the economic data presented in this study. The exceptional ease with which Italian city-states could borrow large quantities of capital from their economically precocious citizenry permitted the region of north Italy to play a forceful political role on the European scene over the fourteenth and fifteenth centuries. With arms, mercenaries, money, and diplomacy they were able to endure, survive, overcome, and buy off invaders such as Henry VII, Lewis the Bavarian, Charles of Bohemia, and the many companies of freebooters. The contest continued, and it was no bloodless charade, as Jacob Burckhardt would lead his readers to believe. Contrary to the mythic vision of Machiavelli, the Italian professionals waged harsh war. The victory of Visconti cavalry led by Facino Cane and other *condottieri* over German forces near Brescia in 1401, the victory of Carmagnola over Swiss troops at the battle of Arbedo were but early examples of the capacity of Italians to succeed against foreign adversaries. The *condottieri* rendered value to their employers, the city-states. Machiavelli's overly celebrated description of the battle of Anghiari, where he tells us that one man was killed because he was trampled after tumbling from his horse, is a travesty in the best comic mode.[45] Casualties in Italian battles of the period were comparable to those suffered in other European theaters.

Expansion of public credit permitted these states to achieve extraordinary eminence in the fourteenth and fifteenth centuries. Any judgment concerning the inability of north Italy to retain this prominence in the sixteenth century must reckon with the peculiar economic cir-

195

cumstances that promoted the earlier flourishing of public credit. The ability of Spain and France to command greater resources to make warfare a statal activity and to provision large standing armies was manifested at a time when the credit structure of north Italy could least sustain a comparable effort. For two centuries the Italian cities had incurred budgetary deficits truly exceptional in pre-modern history. Their military role as powers in Europe had been aggrandized, but except for Venice, whose resources were substantial, none possessed revenues ample enough to underwrite continued large-scale military operations.

If I suggest that the credit system in the fourteenth and fifteenth centuries did not favor impulses toward unification, then the thread of my generalizations may be stretched to the limit. Yet, without a secular ruler of inordinate prestige the likely road to unification in north Italy would be dominance by a single state. Milan was, of course, the logical contender for the role. Commanding more resources than her neighbors, she was to be checked by the ability of a smaller state (Florence) to expand its credit and thereby to wage war on equal terms. Indeed, governmental borrowing is exceedingly relevant when attempting to explain the parity of military capacity obtaining among the several states. In the fifteenth century, this encouraged an equilibrium that forestalled the dominance of one over the others. Ironically, this was the era most favorable to unification, since with massive intervention by foreign powers after 1494 it was less likely. Once military and tax reforms were installed in France and a standing army established, the propitious days had passed. The unification of Spain also darkened the hour for sixteenth-century Italy.

Lastly, it remains to repeat a disclaimer: My search was for factors common to the experience of several Italian city-states. Had my interest been in making distinctions as to differences in social and institutional forms, I would have stressed such features as the incidence of social mobility, transformations in clan structures, alterations in private modes of economic organization, and so on. Instead, an attempt has been made to construct pragmatic definitions applicable to the experience of several Italian states and to place them within a general matrix.

NOTES

1. For an ample treatment of the literary aspects of this theme, see C. C. Bayley, *War and Society in Renaissance Florence* (Toronto, 1961).

2. A full discussion of this vexing topic relevant to Florence is D. Waley's "The Army of the Florentine Republic from the Twelfth to the Fourteenth Century, *Florentine Studies*, ed. N. Rubinstein (London, 1968), pp. 70–108. Probably from the first, modest sums were disbursed so that the militia was composed in part of paid conscripts. For a revision of thinking on this question as it pertains to other sections of Europe, see J. Prestwich, "War and Finance in the Anglo-Norman State," *Transactions of the Royal Historical Society*, 5th series, IV (1954), 19–43.

3. Cf. Guido Gigli's review in the *Rivista Storica Italiana*, LXV (1953), 590–600, with comments and bibliography.

4. N. Valeri, *Signorie e Principati* (Milan, 1950), p. 831.

5. Among the most influential writers was B. Croce. Cf. especially his *Storia del Regno di Napoli* (Bari, 1931), pp. 95–98, as well as his "La crisis Italiana del Cinquecento e il legame del Rinascimento," *La Critica*, XXXVII (1939), 441–44. Cf. also F. Chabod, *Del "Principe" di Machiavelli* (Milan, 1926).

6. Works on these topics are legion. For an excellent bibliography, see A. Sapori, *Le marchand italien au moyen âge* (Paris, 1952) and his *Studi di storia economica (secoli XIII–XIV–XV)* (3rd ed.; Florence, 1956), Vol. II, pp. 1115–86.

7. In the interest of searching out common factors that might have promoted change, forms of the regimes and styles of rule have been little studied. Moreover, the effects of socioeconomic mobility have been dealt with only in the most perfunctory fashion. The unattractive term "superstructure" has been used to suggest exactly those political characteristics that appear to transcend regional differences and local variations.

   While the effects of socioeconomic mobility are not stressed because the quest has been for common features, mention will be made of population increase, since it was a general phenomenon throughout north and central Italy, probably beginning in the late eleventh century and certainly continuing through the first part of the fourteenth. No serious effort will be made to furnish extensive bibliography. For those interested, see M. Becker, *Florence in Transition* (Baltimore, 1967–68), 2 vols. Finally, it should be noted that only limited attention will be paid to the need for urban peace as a causal factor. Only when it influenced military and budgetary decisions will it be regarded as a determinant.

8. The commune is difficult to define, for it was a sworn association or league (a *coniuratio*), one of many formed for the maintenance of peace and the common advantage of its membership. As early as the tenth century this *coniuratio* coalesced with the *arengo*, or town assembly, to form the commune. When the assembly met to swear collectively to such an association, we can be more secure in speaking of the commune. Gradually it assumed a political personality distinct from comital or episcopal authority.

   It would be well to recall that the city did not subvert the feudal nexus or the feudal order, but instead sought to insert itself into it. Further, it would be a gross error to believe that the commune scotched feudalism. Many of the feudal institutions were included as a part of the commune, with the norms of feudal law encompassed in communal statutes. We have the coexistence and copenetration of two juridical systems. Cf. E. Sestan, "L'Italia nell'età feudale," *Questioni di storia medievale*, ed. E. Rota (Milan, 1948), pp. 78 ff.

9. On the agrarian developments preceding intense urban activity, see P. J. Jones, "Per la storia agraria italiana nel medio evo: lineamenti e problemi," *Rivista Storica Italiana*, LXXVI (1964), 300–301. C. Violante's *La società milanese nell'età precomunale* (Bari, 1953) is indispensable for an analysis of the early communal milieu. Cf. R. Lopez's review of this work in *Speculum*, XXX (1955), 619 ff. and his "Il ritorno all'oro nell'occidente duecentesco," *Rivista Storica Italiana*, LXV (1953), 172 ff.

10. Cf. E. Sestan, "Siena avanti Montaperti," *Bullettino Senese di Storia Patria*, LXVIII (1961), 55–64; D. Herlihy, "Direct and Indirect Taxation in Tuscan Urban Finance c. 1200–1400," *Finances et comptabilites urbaines* (Brussels, 1964), pp. 385–405.

11. C. Violante, *La pataria milanese e la riforma ecclesiastica* (Rome, 1955); G. Barni, "Dal governo del vescovo a quello dei cittadini," *Storia di Milano* (Milan, 1954), Vol. II, pp. 124 ff.

12. On this general theme, see F. Carli, *Il mercato nell'alto medioevo* (Padua, 1934).

13. E. Sestan, "Richerche intorno ai primi podestà toscani," *Archivio Storico Italiano*, LXXXII (1924), 178–82; V. Vitale, *Il Comune del Podestà a Genova* (Naples, 1951), pp. 41 ff.

14. Still useful is A. Schaube's *Storia del commercio dei popoli latini alla fine delle crociate*, trans. F. Bonfante (Turin, 1915). Cf. also G. Rossi-Sabatini, *L'espansione di Pisa nel Mediterraneo fino alla Meloria* (Florence, 1935); R. Lopez, *Genova marinara nel duecento. Benedetto Zaccaria, ammiraglio e Mercante* (Messina-Milan, 1933).

15. See Gina Fasoli's lengthy, comparative study, "Richerche sulla legislazione antimagnatizia nei comuni dell'alta e media Italia," *Rivista di Storia del Diritto Italiano*, XII (1939), 86–133. For Otto's comments, see his *Ottonis gesta Friderici imperatoris*, M. G. H., SS., XX (Hanover, 1912), II, 13.

16. *Ibid.*, p. 116.

17. E. Raimondi, "L'Ecerinis di Albertino Mussato," in *Studi ezzeliniani* (Rome, 1963), 192 ff.

18. P. Vayra, "Cavalieri lombardi in Piedmonte nelle guerre del 1229–1230," *Archivio Storico Lombardo*, X (1883), 413–22.

19. It should also be noted that religious values served to promote the tenacity of Italian city-states, since any diminution of the integrity of the diocese was considered to be an offense to the patron saint. The diocese almost inevitably coincided with the geographic limits of the old Roman *provincia*. Cf. H. Peyer, *Stadt und Stadtpatron im mittelalterlichen Italien* (Zurich, 1955), pp. 47–48. Also see his *Zur Getreide politik oberitalischer Städte in 13. Jahrhundert* (Vienna, 1950) for a discussion of policies framed to further city-state autarchy.

20. Cf. N. Rubinstein, "The Beginnings of Political Thought in Florence," *Journal of the Warburg and Courtauld Institutes*, V (1942), 198–225, for a model study of the origins of an historical awareness that can be characterized as communal.

21. D. Waley, *op. cit.*, 72–75; J. Plesner, "Una rivoluzione stradale del Dugento," *Acta Jutlandica*, X (1938), 12–17.

22. H. Sieveking, "Studio sulle finanze genovesi nel medioevo e in particolare sulla Casa di S. Giorgio," *Atti della Società Ligure di Storia Patria*, XXXV (1905), 43 ff. For additional bibliography, see V. Vitale, *op. cit.*, pp. 121–82.

23. E. Cristiani, *Nobiltà e Popolo nel Comune di Pisa* (Naples, 1962), p. 85. This work presents the intricacies of relations among the several orders of communal society, furnishing valuable cautionary notes to the overzealous generalizer. It should be recalled that town burghers were not immune to the pleasures of the vendetta.

24. For a discussion of the centrality of taxation and the rise of *il popolo*, see U. Mondolfo, *Il populus a Siena* (Genoa, 1911), pp. 53 ff. For the tendency of the podestà to attempt initiation of taxes on movable property, see L. Zdekauer, *Constituto di Siena dell'anno 1262* (Milan, 1897), pp. xxxvii ff.

25. On the hire of German mercenaries, see K. Schafer, *Deutsche Ritter und Edelknechte in Italien wahrend des 14. Jahrhunderts* (Paderborn, 1911), I, 75–79. For assessments of the costs of war for the principal cities, see P. Pieri's *Il Rinascimento e la crisi militare italiana* (Turin, 1952), *passim*.

26. Similar pressures were exerted upon the papacy; during the pontificate of John XXII, 63.7 per cent of papal income was expended for warfare, with only 7.16 per cent dedicated to charity and .17 per cent to works of art. Cf. G. Mollat, "The Popes of Avignon and the Great Schism," in *The Cambridge Medieval History* (Cambridge, England, 1932), VII, 281. For a comparable breakdown of papal income in the fifteenth century, see A. Gottlob, *Aus der Camera Apostolica des 15. Jahrhunderts* (Innsbruck, 1889), pp. 253–55.

27. Cf. Gino Franceschini's third chapter, "Il governo monarchio del podestà," in Vol. IV of *Storia di Milano (Dalle lotte contro il Barbarosa al primo signore, 1152–1310)* (Milan, 1954), pp. 179–212. For earlier developments, see G. Zanetti, "Il Comune di Milan dalla genesi del Consolato fino all'inizio del periodo podestarile, *Archivio Storico Lombardo*, LXII (1936), 238 ff.

28. G. Biscaro, "Gli estimi del comune di Milan nel secolo XIII," *Archivio Storico Lombardo*, LV (1928), especially pages 360–67.

29. The history of Milan offers complexities and dimensions that cannot be touched upon in my brief survey. Concentrating upon trends has minimized counter tendencies not contributing toward centralization. Also, limited space prevents a discussion of efforts to establish a standing army. Yet the direction of budgetary deficits, expenditures for war, and the rise of the state debt are readily observable in Milanese territories. For the founding of the Banco di S. Ambrogio, see A. Cova, "Il Banco di S. Ambrogio e le sovvenzioni all città di Milano," *Archivio Storico Lombardo*, XCI–XCII (1964–65), 69–70. By 1660 the debt of the city with the bank totalled the grand sum of 23,033,163 lire, or approximately fifteen times the annual budget. On the question of the great expansion of credit in north Italy from 1550 to 1650, see F. Braudel, *La Mediterranée et le monde mediterranéen à l'epoque de Philippe II* (Paris, 1949), pp. 394–97; C. Cipolla, *Mouvements monetaires dans l'État de Milan (1580–1700)* (Paris, 1952).

30. On the Venetian public debt, see G. Luzzatto, "Il debito pubblico nel sistema

finanziario veneziano dei secoli XII–XV," *Nuova Rivista Storica*, XIII (1929), 625 ff. A more ample discussion of this theme is found in his recent work, *Il debito pubblico della repubblica di Venezia* (Milan, 1963). Especially valuable are the appendix and tables by F. C. Lane; the totals from pages 275–92 are utilized in my study. On the subject of twelfth-century governmental policy, see R. Cessi, "Dal Comune al Principato," in *Storia di Venezia* (Venice, 1958), pp. 390–467, with an extensive bibliography on pages 468–476. Other new names appearing in Venetian political documents during the second half of the twelfth century are given by Cessi in his survey.

31. H. Sieveking, "Studio sulle finanze genovesi nel medioevo e in particolare sulla Casa di S. Giorgio," *Atti della Società Ligure di Storia Patria*, XXXV, Parts I and II, but particularly pages 5–223. This is a pioneer study and also contains useful observations on public debts in Florence and Venice as well as lesser towns like Pisa and Siena. This is an Italian translation of his *Genueser Finanzwesen* (Tübingen, 1900), 2 vols. From 1258 to 1408 the debt climbed from approximately 300,000 lire genovesi to 2,938,000 lire genovesi. By 1454 it was close to 8,000,000, while in 1470 it exceeded 12,000,000. At the middle of the following century it stood at 47,000,000. (The figures presented throughout this paper indicate such substantial increases that fluctuations in the value of coinage can be discounted.)

32. In 1417 the commune confirmed the Casa's military and civil jurisdiction. In 1499, when France gained control over the city, she agreed to respect the rights of the Casa. Machiavelli, in Book VII of his *Istorie Fiorentine*, spoke of two Genoese states, one, the city, turbulent and tyrannical, the other, the Casa, orderly and well administered. Cf. P. Pieri, *op. cit.*, pp. 123–25.

33. R. Cessi, "Venezia e la quarta crociata," *Archivio Veneto*, XLVIII–XLIX (1951), 152 ff.

34. Cf. G. Luzzatto, *op. cit.*, pp. 275–92; R. Mousnier, *La Renaissance en Italie au XVI*e *siècle* (Paris, 1956), pp. 83 ff.

35. A provision of 1509 spoke of the arsenal as the "cuore dello stato." Only a few years before, the Florentine funded debt had been described in equally florid terms as "the blood and body of the state." Cf. R. Romano, "Aspetti economici degli armamenti navali veneziani," *Rivista Storica Italiana*, LXVI (1954), 38. See also the quotation cited from Marin Sanuto's *Cronachetta*.

36. For the paternalistic attitude of the state toward workers, see A. Fanfani, *Storia del lavoro in Italia* (Milan, 1943), pp. 236, 289–93.

37. These quotations are taken from Giorgio Cracco's *Società e stato nel medioevo veneziano* (*secoli xii–xiv*) (Florence, 1967), pp. 449–50.

38. D. Herlihy, *Pisa in the Early Renaissance* (New Haven, 1958); cf. also note 23.

39. For an excellent survey of early Florentine history, see Yves Renouard's *Les villes d'Italie de la fin du X*e *siècle au debut XIV*e *siècle* (Paris, 1963); M. Becker, *Florence in Transition*, Vol. I; C. Paoli, "Le cavallate fiorentine nei secoli XIII e XIV," *Archivio Storico Italiano*, ser. III (1865), 73 ff.

40. J. Plesner, *op. cit.*, 76–91; John Day, "En toscane la circulation monétaire en 1296," *Annales*, XXIII (1968), 1054–66.

41. Cf. note 31 and L. Marks, "La crisi finanzieria a Firenze dal 1494 al 1502," *Archivio Storico Italiano*, CXII (1954), 40–72.

42. M. Valeri, *La Corte di Lodovico il Moro* (Milan, 1913), Vol. I; C. Santoro, *Gli uffici del dominio Sforzesco*, 1450–1500 (Milan, 1948).

43. The reasons proffered by Bruni, Machiavelli, and other Renaissance commentators tended to be moral and psychological. The present study would concur with their judgment as to the centrality of war as a causal factor in promoting change on the urban scene, but would stress increased public expenditures as the primary mechanism for altering the political character of the Renaissance city-state. The tendency of Bruni, Machiavelli, and others to look back to Rome for validation of civic and military virtues only served to strengthen their proclivity for ethical assessments. It should be stressed that Machiavelli's very influential treatment of the military lapses of the *condottieri* and his accounts of mock battles can no longer be viewed seriously. Cf. the extensive bibliography provided by P. Pieri in his *Il Rinascimento*, pp. 642–53.

44. M. A. Arnould, "L'impôt dans l'histoire des peuples," *Collection Histoire,* XIII (1966), 13–26. This article contains a collection of exceedingly valuable statistical data as well as bibliography on northern European public finances.

45. W. Block, *Die Condottieri. Studien uber die sogennanten "unblutigen Schlachten"* (Berlin, 1913), pp. 176 ff.; P. Pieri, *Scritti vari* (Turin, 1966), pp. 99–119.

Flavio Biondo's Roma Instaurata

Dorothy M. Robathan

A DISTINGUISHED SCHOLAR recently observed that "Flavio Biondo stands at the threshold of a world, when for the first time, history could be presented as art or science."[1] Although it is as a historiographer that Biondo is best known, his contribution to the study of the topography of ancient Rome has long been recognized.[2] As a pioneer in this field Biondo has justly been praised for having had the discrimination to abandon the mediaeval treatises, with their emphasis upon Christian monuments and their practical purpose in serving as guide-books for pilgrims, and instead to correlate the relevant material in the ancient authors with first-hand information of existing monuments, some of which were destroyed in the Sack of Rome in 1527.[3]

In dedicating the *Roma Instaurata* to Pope Eugene IV, to whom he had been appointed Papal Secretary in 1434,[4] Biondo states in his preface that he has been impelled to write it

> quod tanta fuit praeteritorum diu saeculorum hominibus studiorum humanitatis ignoratio, ut cum pauca singulis in urbis ipsius aedificiorum partibus quae olim fuerint, non ab imperita solum multitudine, sed ab his etiam qui doctrina cultiores sunt, sciantur, tum multa ac paene omnia falsis et barbaris appellationibus inquinata vel potius infamata cernamus.

The work, which was completed in 1446, consists of three books, which even Biondo's most ardent admirers could not describe as well-organized. A source of vexation to modern readers are the frequent lengthy quotations from ancient authors. To Biondo's contemporaries, however, who did not always have complete manuscripts of the works cited, this feature may have been a reason for gratitude.

In this paper I shall consider some specific examples that illustrate Biondo's use of ancient sources and his acumen in correlating them with the monuments of antiquity that were visible in his time. Of the twenty-five classical authors from whose works excerpts are included, Livy has by far the largest number of citations; Varro, Suetonius, and Pliny the Elder are runners-up, while at the other end of the scale are

Cato and Lucan, who are each quoted just once. Christian writers include Jerome, Gregory the Great, Bede, Boethius, and Cassiodorus. Frequently cited is one "Sextus Rufus," under whose name a manuscript of the *Regiones Romae* was found by Biondo in Monte Cassino.[5] This pre-Constantinian description of the Urbs Biondo shows the good judgment to prefer to the later mediaeval, interpolated, versions. In general, however, his main sources were classical authors and his own keen powers of observation. Only when these failed him did he fall back upon mediaeval works.

Biondo's painstaking method of piecing together the jigsaw puzzle from literary sources may be illustrated from his discussion of the Flavian Amphitheater (III. 1–2). First he refutes a statement from Cassiodorus (*Variae*, V. 42),[6] to the effect that Titus had constructed the first building of this type in Rome. In Tacitus (*Ann.* XIII. 31), he had found reference to an amphitheater built in the Campus Martius in the time of Augustus. From Suetonius (*Aug.* 29), he learned that Statilius Taurus had erected a building of this kind. This structure Biondo incorrectly locates on the Caelian Hill, evidently confusing it with the Amphitheatrum Castrense, of which remains may still be seen near the church of Santa Croce in Gerusalemme. A well-known epigram of Martial (*Spect.* II. 1) contributes the fact that the Flavian Colosseum was built on the "stagna Neronis." On the authority of Suetonius (*Vesp.* 9), he rightly gives credit to Vespasian for having had a share in its construction, but he is uncertain whether it was completed by him or by his son (*Tit.* 7). Biondo notes that the Roman emperors seemed to group their buildings in one area and that the Flavian Amphitheater was near the Temple of Peace, the Arch of Titus, and the Baths of Titus, which, however, he confuses with the Temple of Venus and Rome (III.3).

It is perhaps more interesting to follow Biondo's mental processes where he used his literary sources conscientiously, but came up with the wrong answer! One of his incorrectly identified monuments is the little round temple by the Tiber (II. 56), which even today is erroneously labelled the Temple of Vesta on some Roman postcards, although the partial restoration of the Temple of Vesta in the Forum has been a conspicuous landmark since the Fascist era. A recent archeological study of the monument by the Tiber affirms that "the identification is quite uncertain."[7] It is not surprising that in the Renaissance, before the circular core in the Forum had been uncovered, an error was made in identifying it with representations of the Temple of Vesta on coins and in sculpture. Biondo, however, before accepting the contemporary ascription, goes over the literary evidence. From Ovid (*Fasti* III. 11–14), he deduces that the temple stood by the Tiber, since the Vestal Virgin Rhea Silvia had sat on its banks when she went to get water for lustral purposes. This hypothesis seemed confirmed by Horace (*Ode* I. 2, 13–20), where the Tiber, having overflowed its banks, had reached the Temple of Vesta. (Biondo does not take into account the fact that even in modern times the Tiber had inundated the low-lying area of the Roman Forum.) Turning to his primary source, Biondo comments that, although Livy describes the establishment of the cult of Vesta, so far as the location of her temple is concerned, "locum non indicat." Taken, however, in conjunction with a passage from Varro (*L. L.* V. 146–47), Biondo succeeds in adding Livy to his list of authorities. His argument runs thus: Livy, in describing a destructive fire, mentions its effect on the Forum Piscarium and adds that the Temple of Vesta had barely been saved (XXVI. 27). Varro places the Forum Piscarium between the Temple of Janus (or Portunus) [8] and the Tiber. Modern scholars locate it on the north side of the Forum Romanum, in the opposite direction from the river.[9] This is a case where Biondo's wrong conclusion results from one weak link in his chain of reasoning.

Accustomed as we are today to this same kind of searching in classical authors for clues to the ancient sites, perhaps more intriguing are Biondo's comments on the vestiges of antiquity that were still extant in his time. As he went between his duties at the Vatican and his home just off the Via Flaminia,[10] he kept his eyes open for glimpses of ancient Rome. Very close to his dwelling, specifically between San Silvestro and San Lorenzo in Lucina, he noted an arch "paene integer. . . . Viam amplexus Flaminiam" (II. 14). This is the monument that was later known as the Arco di Portogallo, from the fact that the Portuguese ambassador once lived in the neighboring Palazzo Fiano.[11] Its date has been variously assigned to the periods of Hadrian, Marcus Aurelius, or even later, depending on whether the reliefs (now in the Museo dei Conservatori) were contemporary with the monument itself or were a later addition.[12] In the Renaissance too, it was ascribed to a variety of emperors, among them Octavian, Domitian, and Marcus Aurelius.[13] The reliefs, which some modern scholars interpret as representing the apotheosis of Sabina, the wife of Hadrian,[14] Biondo assigns to the period of Domitian, on the authority of a passage in Suetonius (*Dom.* 15), which describes a dream in which the emperor saw his patron goddess, Minerva, issuing from a shrine after being disarmed by Jupiter.

It seems likely that this interpretation suggested itself because Biondo believed that other ancient remains in that neighborhood were Flavian. In the vicinity of San Silvestro and its convent (now the Central Post Office of Rome), he says he had seen being dug up some blocks with the words "Domitiana maior pars Domitiana minor pars" impressed upon them (II. 12). This evidence seemingly bore out a statement in the *Liber Pontificalis* that San Silvestro had constructed a church on the site of the Baths of Domitian.[15] Later research, however, has shown that this reference was not to San Silvestro in Capite, but to another church of San Silvestro, which was later incorporated into the church of San Martino ai Monti on the Esquiline, and that the neighboring baths were those of Trajan.[16] As recently as 1894, however, Lanciani believed that the buildings in the area of San Silvestro were Domitianic; they are now assigned to Aurelian's Temple of the Sun.[17]

Biondo fails to identify the Stadium of Domitian, the modern Piazza Navona (or Circo Agonale) correctly (III. 30), having adopted the contemporary theory that it was the Circus Flaminius, the exact location of which has just recently been established.[18] For years this monument was identified with remains in the Piazza Paganica, near the Via delle Botteghe Oscure. Now, however, by a new arrangement of the *Forma Urbis*, it seems to fit neatly between the Porticus of Octavia and the Tiber, a site that confirms a reference to it in the twelfth-century *Mirabilia* as "ad pontem Iudeorum" (i.e., the Pons Fabricius).[19] This piece of evidence had previously been discounted as resulting from a confusion between the Circus and the Theater of Marcellus. It now seems likely that the arches previously thought to belong to the Circus Flaminius were part of the Theater of Balbus.[20]

Biondo's acceptance of the current identification (III. 33–34) was not a casual one, for he tests it as follows: In the fifteenth century there was, as there is today, in the Campus Martius a church of Santa Maria in Aquiro,[21] an epithet that Biondo confuses with *Equuria* or *Eccuria*, which he found defined by Varro as "ab equorum cursu, eo die enim ludis currunt in Martio campo" (*L.L.* VI. 13). He goes further astray when he misinterprets a passage in Cassiodorus (*Variae* III. 51), that describes, not the Circus Flaminius, but the Circus Maximus as rebuilt by Augustus. In Cassiodorus this structure is referred to merely as "fabricam in Valle Murcia." Biondo includes the passage verbatim, substituting for *Murcia* the word *Martia*, a simple palaeographical error, but one that led him to assign the facts to the Mausoleum in the Campus Martius, rather than to the Circus Maximus.[22] He clinches his argument thus:

> Nam si aliquis, quod nos aliquando fecimus, postreman nontis citatorum partem conscenderit et oculis metietur, profecto intelliget ab Augusti sepulchro rectam fuisse viam, aedificiis nunc confectam, in Circum Flaminium, nunc Agonem, recta brevis et usu expeditissima nunc est via.

Unfortunately for us, the view from Montecitorio today does not afford a glimpse of the Mausoleum of Augustus, though on a map we can trace the route that to Biondo seemed conclusive evidence.

For another set of buildings that has been a source of topographical interest for years, the complex of Pompey's structures, Biondo also combines literary material with his own observation (II. 108–12). For the theater itself he quotes Tacitus (*Ann.* XIV. 20), Pliny (*N.H.* XXXIII. 54), Suetonius (*Cal.* 21), and Cassiodorus (*Variae* IV. 51), the last-named as evidence that the building must have stood for four hundred years, since Theodoric ordered some restoration. The *cavea* of the theater he identifies with the curve of the walls of the Theater of Balbus;[23] adjoining the theater he places the *curia* or *atrium* where Julius Caesar was murdered (Suet. *Caes.* 80–81) and the porticus. He concludes that the ensemble extended to the church of San Lorenzo in Damaso (which adjoins the Cancelleria Palace). A few days ago, says Biondo (II. 109), Angelo Pontano was digging beneath his palace to enlarge his wine-cellar:

> fundamenta reperit in saxo quadrato ingenti structura, in quorum uno, quod cementarii extraxerant, litterae essent cubitales GENIUM THEATRI POMPEIANI dicentes, ut coniicere liceat genium ibi proiacti primo fundamenti theatralis initio; in ceteris si educerentur litteris ostendi.

The current view of topographers does not include an extension so far to the north.[24] Huelsen, in accepting as genuine Biondo's report, suggested that instead of GENIUM these letters might have been the end of PROSCENIUM.[25] The dwelling of Pontano, beneath which the inscription was found, has been placed in the Via dei Chiavari, on the southwest side of the Piazza di Grottapinta, where the inner curve of the *scaena* has been visible for years.[26]

The *atrium* or *curia* Biondo identifies with a porticus of twelve columns, an area designated in his time as *satrum*: "atrium vero Pompei credere debemus fuisse ubi nunc corrupte Satrum vulgo appellant et porticus etiam nunc semiintegra cernitur" (II. 112). It is interesting to note that at one time scholars derived the name of the nearby Piazza dei Satiri from two statues of satyrs that were found there in the fourteenth century. The current view rejects this derivation and links the piazza instead with *satro*, "a word of unknown origin," by which this whole region was known.[27] The *curia* is now thought to be indicated by a podium behind Temple B of the Largo Argentina.[28] Pompey's dwelling, which he built after the theater was erected, is perhaps to be identified with an atrium and peristyle behind Temples C and D of the same site.[29] Biondo, in referring to it, says "ubi fuerit nulla possumus assequi coniectura."

In locating the houses of some other ancient Romans, our author evidently felt on surer ground. He had no hesitation in placing the *domus Corneliorum* on the Quirinal near Monte Cavallo (I. 97), as the nearby Vicus Corneliorum was still called by its ancient name, and nearby ruins (probably those of the Temple of Serapis in the Colonna Gardens) were designated in the fifteenth century as *Thermae Cornelianae.*[30] It is fortunate that Biondo's topographical judgment was in general superior to his artistic acumen, since he accepts as genuine the attribution to Phidias and Praxiteles of the statues of the Dioscuri nearby. He affirms that they are "tantis opificibus digna" and that no other sculptor would have been capable of carving or of casting horses of that size (I. 99).

Among dwellings of other ancient Romans Biondo locates that of Virgil on the Esquiline (I. 101), "iuxta hortos Maecenatis" on the authority of Donatus (*Vita Verg.* 13). In Pliny (*N.H.* XVII. 2), he finds in one passage a reference to the homes of Marcus Crassus, Quintus Catulus, and C. Aquilius Gallus. Although Pliny specifically locates two of them correctly on the Palatine, Biondo puts all three on the Quirinal (II. 27), where his source describes that of Aquilius as the most beautiful private home in Rome. Perhaps Biondo's manuscript was garbled! But he merits censure when, in an uncharacteristic attempt to assign an exact location, he points to traces of these houses near the church of Santa Susanna. In the next sentence he locates "in Viminali an in Quirinali an in utroque" the *Horti Sallustiani*. It is now believed that the ruins near Santa Susanna were part of the hippodrome in the Gardens of Sallust.[31] These gardens extended from the northern slope of the Quirinal to the Pincian,[32] which Biondo elsewhere refers to as the Quirinal (I. 91). He realizes, however, that the boundaries of these two hills were "inter se alicubi continuatos" and could not be differentiated just by looking at them (I. 93)! Also from Pliny (*N.H.* XIX. 23), Biondo had learned that arrangements for gladiatorial games involved covering with awnings the Forum Romanum from the house of Julius Caesar to the Capitoline (III. 61).

The Roman Forum, to which much space is devoted in modern guidebooks, comes in for no detailed description in the *Roma Instaurata*, though certain of its monuments are introduced in a discussion of other topics. The Lacus Curtius is mentioned under matters "ad religionem pertinentia" (II. 45); in a section "ad rem publicam pertinentia" (II. 63) the Rostra is incorrectly located; the Comitium is wrongly placed among the Lacus Curtius, the *radices Palatini*, and the Temple of Antoninus and Faustina, then as now incorporated into the church of San Lorenzo in Miranda (II. 67). At this point, Biondo, speaking sorrowfully (*doloris impetu*), has a word for us today: "futurorum saeculorum hominibus notum fore volumus, porcos nunc ex publico aetatis nostrae instituto ibi, et nullo alio in loco, quod saepe vidimus venundari."

Other sites whose desecration Biondo mourns include the Mausoleum of Augustus. Following the demolition of its exterior walls during the Fascist regime, its present condition seems to have reverted to that of the fifteenth century, when it is described as "ita herbidus ut numquam destitutis in pascua animalibus careat" (II. 74). Of the Circus Maximus too, the outlines of which were for years concealed beneath the graves of a Hebrew cemetery and the drums of the municipal gasworks, it is interesting to learn "Circi Maximi locus, etsi omni aedificiorum ornatu ammodo denudatus est et in hortos mutatus, opimis abundatur oleribus, tamen retinet nomen sub rivis Palatii maioris" (III. 26).

Sidelight on another aspect of contemporary life occurs in connection with Biondo's misunderstanding of the site of the *Asylum Romuli* (II. 57), which Livy, in a well-known passage (I. 8), locates "inter duos lucos," the spot that since Michelangelo's time has been occupied by the Palazzo Senatorio. On the basis of a reference in Ovid's *Fasti* (III. 431) to the Asylum as being "sub rupis Tarpeiae," Biondo puts it on the wrong side of the Capitoline, where, he says, a large chunk of rock the size of a spacious house had within recent days collapsed, killing five people at a neighboring inn (II. 58). He also errs in including a temple within its precincts (II. 59). Since he visualizes the Asylum as being between the Tiber and the Capitoline, what was more natural than to assume that the rectangular temple, known variously as Mater

Matuta, Fortuna Virilis, or perhaps more accurately as that of Portunus,[33] was its temple? This area, he tells us, is now occupied by prostitutes, chiefly women who fled from their homes and their husbands ("alterum nunc asylum institutum").

In this same neighborhood, the Velabrum, near the church of Santa Maria in Cosmedin, Biondo informs us: "ubi nunc vetustissimos arcus marmoreos ut in calcem decoquerentur, dolentes vidimus a fundamentis excidi" (I. 20). In his time these pieces were thought to have belonged to a monument to Horatius Cocles in memory of his feat at the nearby bridge. They may perhaps have supported a branch of the Aqua Appia that ran to the nearby Porta Trigemina.[34]

Of the three hills that overlooked the Velabrum, Biondo comments: "multo autem pauciora habet integra Palatinus mons quam Capitolinus aut Aventinus. Qualis autem et quanta olim fuerit ea aedificiorum moles, indicant ruinae inter ceteras urbis conspiciendae" (I. 76). Literary sources informed him that the Palatine was not only the Cradle of Rome but that among its monuments had been temples to Magna Mater, to Apollo, and to Sol Invictus. He does not try to locate them, for he tells us that wherever the high arches are not covered with hanging vines, there is pastureland where horses, sheep, cattle, and goats are continually grazing. On the part of the hill overlooking the Arch of Constantine, he does venture an identification that is of some interest in the light of recent archaeological discussion. Here he says was the *locus Palladii*: "cuius insignes extant ruinae, binas habentes paene integras ex marmore portas, facile superantes aedificii pulchritudine ceteras, quas vetusti ac novi operis Roma nunc habet." Within its walls is the church of San Andrea de Pallara, which Biondo takes to be a corruption of Palladium. Other remains of the monument are to be seen in the vineyard of the Capranica estate.[35] A current discussion of this area[36] may be summed up as follows: On the site of the sanctuary which was erected by Livia to Augustus, afterwards that of the cult of worship of the deified emperors (the *aedes Caesarum*), Elagabalus erected a temple to Sol Invictus, to which he is said to have transferred the Palladium from the Temple of Vesta. An inscription of late antiquity shows that the site was then called Palladium Palatini,[37] and that the name was transferred in the Middle Ages to the church of Santa Maria in Pallara, and then to the church of San Andrea de Pallara, as Biondo conjectured. Recently reported was the discovery of a head of Athena from a Greek statue, apparently of workmanship of the sixth century B.C. It was found "among the refuse in a workroom of the Antiquarium Museum on the Palatine," and the suggestion is made that it perhaps came from the Palladium Palatinum.[38]

On the southwest corner of the Palatine, looking toward the Porta Capena, where Septimius Severus erected his structures, stood a monument that artists in the Renaissance found very attractive. Known as the Septizonium, its three tiers of columns, then intact, seemed to refute the obvious derivation that would suggest seven.[39] Following a reference that he found in the *Scriptores Historiae Augustae* (*Sev.* 19), Biondo makes his own suggestion that Septizonium was a scribe's error for Septizodium, a word which he derived from Greek ὁδός, emphasizing its situation at the place where the Via Appia came into the Piazza di Porta Capena (III. 57). This derivation may have been suggested by a statement in the *Liber Pontificalis* that records the monument as being "in septem vias."[40] Biondo notes, however, that adjoining the remains of the Septizonium was a small church known as Santa Lucia in Septa Solis, and he is led to hazard the opinion that the Severan structure may have been ornamented with a statue to the Sun. Modern scholars too have abandoned the idea of seven tiers. A new arrangement of the Forma Urbis makes it appear likely that the official name was Septizodium, a reference to the Seven Spheres, with one of which Biondo had happened to connect it.[41] Of the Palatine as a whole he concludes: "nunc si absint ruinae, videmus paene ad eam. . . . aedificiorum nuditatem, quam Roma nondum condita habuit" (I. 76).

For those of us who have within our reach the latest topographical and archaeological publications, not to mention scholarly editions of ancient authors with adequate indices, it is difficult to imagine how handicapped we should be if we were pioneering in this field of research in ancient Rome. With some feeling of frustration we should doubtless find ourselves writing, as does Biondo at one point (II. 19): "apud nullum veterum scriptorem invenimus Constantini thermarum mentionem factam esse praeter apud Ammianum Marcellinum" (XXVII. 8). Again, in connection with the Colosseum, he bemoans: "harena quare is locus sit dictus nullo in loco invenimus. Tamen coniicimus ex actu vocabulum habuisse. . . . eratque sparsum solo sabulum, in quod certantes sine laesione caderent" (III. 14). And, in discussing a topic that has been much in the news in recent years, the location of the tomb of St. Peter, we find Biondo saying unequivocally "quis sit is locus omnino ignoratur" (I. 45), and he proceeds to refute a current legend that it was on the Janiculum: "nec desunt qui Ianiculum falso ea gloria ornare quaeritant."[42]

If we were dealing with such problems as these while living near the modern Via del Corso in 1446, our next recourse, as was Biondo's, would be to study epigraphical and numismatic evidence. Having found in the *SHA* (*Alex. Sev.* 28) a reference to the Forum of Nerva, Biondo locates it correctly, placing it in a district known as Arca Noe, which he rightly takes to be a corruption of Nervae, and where he tells us "litterae etiam extant cubitales, Nervae titulos perferentes" (III. 52).

In discussing the baffling question of the various temples to Janus, Biondo remarks (II. 47) that just a few days earlier he had come across an ancient coin with a representation of the Velabrum temple. It was, however, that of the fourth-century A.D. arch, still known colloquially as Janus Quadrifrons. The Temple of Janus in the Forum Holitorium is now identified with remains to the east of the Temple of Apollo Sosianus "ad theatrum Marcelli."[43] Numismatic evidence is also adduced in connection with a description of the Colossus of Nero (III. 46). From the *Life of Commodus* (*SHA* 17), Biondo quotes: "Colossi autem caput depressit quod erat Neronis, ac suum imposuit." He therefore concludes that a comparison of the large bronze head of Commodus (then standing near the Lateran Palace), with representations of that emperor on coins, confirms the statement of the ancient biographer (III. 47).

Since Biondo's project for the *instauratio Romae* depended upon the identification and preservation of ancient sites, he does not conceal his distress at the current destruction of this material. In his discussion of the Colosseum (III. 6), he introduces from Cassiodorus part of a letter from Theodoric, granting, he says, permission to Roman citizens to use material from their amphitheater to repair the city walls. Although brick stamps bearing the name of Theodoric have been found in the Aurelian Wall, nothing is known of the use of material from the Colosseum for this purpose.[44] My efforts to trace this reference failed until I came across the passage which Biondo quotes verbatim (III. 1) from a letter of Cassiodorus (*Variae* III. 49) addressed, however, to the citizens of Catania in Sicily. In the text itself there is nothing to indicate that the *amphitheatrum* was not the one in Rome, and Biondo did not have the use of Mommsen's edition, in which the salutation includes the words "civitatis Catinensis." The point I am making, however, is Biondo's reaction to the practice described: "cuius rei tanta per singulos dies videmus exempla, ut ea solummodo causa nos aliquando Romae fastidiat habitatio. Multis enim in locis vineas videmus, ubi superbissima vidimus aedificia, quorum quadrati lapides tiburtini in calcem sunt concocti" (III. 7).

Comment upon another extract from the *Variae* (VII. 6) throws light upon the deplorable condition of the aqueducts in Biondo's time (II. 99). In seeking to assign the blame for their dilapidation, he absolves Theodoric of the charge, asserting that so far from destroying the water supply of the Urbs, the emperor had taken pains to repair the aqueducts and had even imported a dowser (*aquilegus*) from Africa, whose experience with drought conditions in his own country had made him an expert in detecting hidden streams (*Variae* III. 53). Since Rome abounds in subterranean springs, it was desirable to enlist the aid of someone who also knew the mechanics of bringing this water to the surface. If Theodoric was not responsible for the destruction of the aqueducts, neither was length of years (*vetustas*). Biondo points out (II. 101) that substantial remains of ancient constructions are still standing where they have been for thousands of years. "Solae igitur incusandae ac detestandae sunt manus improbae illorum qui, ut privata et quidem sordidissima erigerent aedificia, lapides aut in calcem de-coquendos aut casarum muris adhibendos, ab illa moenium maiestate non sunt veriti asportare." Although Biondo feels that in many cases *vetustas* has been the enemy of preservation, in this instance it was human beings whose "cura formarum cessavit."

On this theme, the decline of the City, Biondo asserts that though his affection for Rome is so strong that it is second only to that be-stowed upon his religion (III. 83), his passion does not blind him to the realization that the Rome of his day falls short of the prestige of ancient Rome. Still he does not believe that its glory has vanished com-pletely: "Sed contra non sumus ex illis quos videmus praesentem Romanae rei statum haud secus spernere et pro nihilo ducere, ac si omnis memoria simul cum legionibus, consulibus, senatu, Capitolii Palatinique ornamentis penitus interiisset, Viget certe viget adhuc . . . urbis Romae gloria maiestate" (III. 84).[45]

To this expression of faith in Rome's immortality, let me append Biondo's apology for his own shortcomings in attempting to present a true picture of the city in antiquity:

> Si quis enim urbis Romae aetatis nostrae partes singulas vel
> mente vel oculis lustrando pervagabitur, ea quae populo nunc
> et domibus frequentata sunt, a nobis paene intacta intelliget,
> quod quidem nulla a nobis negligentia aut inadvertentia magis

factum est, quam ne ignota imprudenter asserere aut impossi-
bilia vane et leviter conari compelleremur [III. 77].

He adds "Sunt etiam alia per urbem tunc speciosa, sed simul vetustatis
suae ignoratione obscura, quae illis relinquimus describenda, quibus
fortassis curae erit hance describere quam nostrum saeculum habet
Romam" (III. 84).

In the past thirty years our knowledge of the topography of ancient
Rome has been greatly enriched by systematic excavation and scholarly
research. Among the literary tools of this investigation are the works
of such Renaissance scholars as Pomponio Leto, Poggio Bracciolini,
Maffeo Vegio, and Flavio Biondo. The few examples that I have chosen
as illustrative of Biondo's methods of workmanship reveal not only
his diligence in searching the texts of ancient authors, but his intelligent
assessment of archaeological and numismatic evidence, combined with
keen enthusiasm for his project, which he describes as "amplum et
vastum . . . campum dispersa per urbem loca describendi" (III. 77).[45]

NOTES

1. Denys Hay, "Flavio Biondo and the Middle Ages," *Proceedings of the British Academy*, XLV (1959), 97.
2. Over forty years ago B. Nogara referred to the *Roma Instaurata* as "una delle pietre miliari della storia della topografia di Roma." "Scritti inediti e rari di Biondo Flavio," *Studi e Testi*, 48, p. 101.
3. For the *Mirabilia Romae* (twelfth century) and the *Graphia Aureae Urbis* (thirteenth century) cf. R. Valentini-G. Zucchetti, *Codice Topografico della Città di Roma* (Fonti per la Storia di Roma, 90 [1946]), III, 3–110.
4. The most recent bibliography and survey of the life and works of Flavio Biondo (or Biondo Flavio) is found in the *Dizionario Biografico degli Italiani* (Rome, 1966), pp. 3–25, ascribed to R. Fubini. See also M. E. Cosenza, *Italian Humanists and the World of Classical Scholarship in Italy* (Boston, 1962), I, 618–22. References in this paper are to the 1527 (Turin, Bernardinus Sylva) edition of the *Roma Instaurata*. Extracts from the work, with valuable topographical commentary, have been published by Valentini-Zucchetti (see note 3), IV (1954), 207–55. References to this volume and to the preceding three (I, 81 [1940]; II, 88 [1942]; III, 90 [1946]) are hereafter abbreviated as V-Z.
5. Biondo's discovery must have antedated 1455, the year ascribed to it by R. Sabbadini, *Le Scorperte dei Codici Latini e Greci*, II (1914), 248. The Monte Cassino codex is perhaps to be identified as Vat. lat. 3227 (V-Z, I, 75).
6. References to the *Variae* are to Mommsen's edition (*Mon. Germ. Hist., Auct. Antiq.*) XII (1894).

7. D. E. Strong and W. Perkins, in *Papers of the British School in Rome,* XV, 28 New Series (1960), 7.

8. Varro, *De Lingua Latina,* Book V, ed. Jean Collert (Paris, 1954). See apparatus, *loc. cit.*

9. G. Lugli, *Monumenti antichi di Roma e Suburbio,* III (Rome, 1938), 394.

10. "Forum Livii nos genuit aluitque et forte nunc ab eadem in urbe Roma sub citatorum monte Flaminiam incoluimus Viam" (III. 371).

11. Lugli, *op. cit.,* pp. 267–70.

12. E. Nash, *A Pictorial Dictionary of Ancient Rome* (2 vols.) (New York, 1961), I, 83. See also Inez Scott Ryberg, *Panel Reliefs of Marcus Aurelius* (New York, 1968).

13. Lugli, *op. cit.,* p. 267.

14. Nash, *op. cit.,* I, 86.

15. Lib. Pont., ed. L. Duchesne (Paris, 1886), I, 170; V-Z, II, 192; 230, note 4.

16. Nash, *op. cit.,* II, 472; V-Z, IV, 292, note 1.

17. Lugli, *op. cit.,* p. 279.

18. *Ibid.,* pp. 14–23.

19. Nash, *op. cit.,* I, 232.

20. *Ibid.,* II, 414; Lugli, *op. cit.,* pp. 85–90.

21. See M. Armellini, *Le Chiese di Roma* (Rome, 1942), I, 381–83.

22. The form *Martia* is cited in Mommsen's apparatus as being found in the Editio Accursiana (1533).

23. See above, note 20.

24. Nash, *op. cit.,* II, 424.

25. *C. I. L.,* VI, 1193; C. Huelsen, "Miscellanea Epigrafica," *Röm. Mitt.,* XIV (1899), 25.

26. V-Z, IV, 239, note 3; Nash, *op. cit.,* II, 423.

27. Lugli, *op. cit.,* p. 76.

28. Nash, *op. cit.,* I, 136.

29. Lugli, *op. cit.,* p. 82.

30. Nash, *op. cit.,* II, 376; V-Z, IV, 282.

31. Nash, *op. cit.,* II, 145.

32. *Ibid.,* I, 491–99.

33. *Ibid.,* I, 411.

34. V-Z, IV, 265, note 1.

35. See Fubini, *op. cit.,* p. 6, for Biondo's friendship with D. Capranica.

36. Nash, *op. cit.,* I, 537; V-Z, II, 337, note 2.

37. *C. I. L.,* X, 6441 (*praepositus Palladii Palatini*).

38. A. Van Buren, "Notes from Rome," *American Journal of Archaeology,* LXIX (1965), p. 260.

39. Lugli, *Roma Antica: Il Centro Monumentale* (Rome, 1946), pp. 519–20.

40. Duchesne, II (1892), 21, 79; V-Z, II, 174, note 3.

41. Nash, *op. cit.,* II, 302.

42. See M. Escobar, "La Roma di Pietro," *Capitolium,* XLII (1968), 16: "Vale la pena di insistere sull' absurdità dell' ultimo romanzo della letteratura apocrifa su San Pietro: quello sottoscritto da un umanista lodigiano, Maffeo Vegio, sostenitore della tesi della crocifissione dell' Apostolo sul Gianicolo."

43. Nash, *op. cit.*, I, 500.
44. V-Z, IV, 310, note 3: "si ignora la concessione fatta ai Romani di adoperare per il restauro le pietre cadute dal Colosseo."
45. My interest in the Italian humanists as well as in the topography of ancient Rome has prompted me to undertake a critical edition of the *Roma Instaurata*.

The Kambriae Descriptio *of*
Gerald *the* Welshman

Urban T. Holmes

THOSE INTERESTED in the life and work of Gerald owe much
to J. Conway Davies, the founder of the *Journal of the Historical Society of the Church in Wales*. His detailed biography of Gerald which
appeared in *Archaeologia Cambrensis* for 1947 (pp. 85–108, 256–
75) is most valuable. It is regrettable that the *Archaeologia Cambrensis* and his *Journal of the Historical Society* are not available in many
of our larger libraries.[1]

Gerald's principal writings are polemical and autobiographical
works, letters, and saints' lives, but a different key is struck in his
Topographia Hibernica and his *Kambriae Descriptio* (closely associated with his *Itinerarium Kambriae*). They demonstrate keen originality in the observation of geographic, social, and scientific details.
We should like to know how and why he broke with the customary
bestiary lore and generalisations of his age. He knew that he was
being different, and he hints at his trust in direct observation throughout his works. We are gathering some of these statements together,
and then following this with some observations on the material in his
Kambriae Descriptio. It is well known that his *Topographia* was read
in a newer, approved version, three days running, at Oxford (see below). It is not well known that the *Descriptio* was completed at a time
when he probably had taken up residence in his benefice at Chesterton (Oxon) on Akeman Street. This is ten miles from Oxford. We
know from a dispute with Bishop Hugh of Lincoln that he was there
by 1194 (M. A. Lobell in the *Victoria County Histories, Oxon*, Vol.
VII). His death was certified from there in 1223. Perhaps there is
some influence from the *studia generalia* of Oxford in the perfecting
of his faith in direct observation.

In the catalogue of his works which Gerald himself made, he lists
three titles pertaining to the description of Wales: his *Kambriae
Descriptio*, the *Kambriae Itinerarium*, and a *Kambriae Mappa*.[2] The
Itinerarium we have reason to believe was completed by 1191, and

the *Descriptio* in 1194. From an item in Gerald's *Symbolum Electo-rum* [3] it is evident that Gerald made a special presentation of the *Descriptio* to Bishop Hugh of Lincoln, probably in 1197–98; the *Itinerarium* had been given to him shortly before. Henry Wharton saw this manuscript which belonged to Bishop Hugh, and noted that it had at the beginning a fine map of Wales, drawn, it is believed, by Gerald. Centuries later this particular manuscript was evidently removed to Westminster Abbey by John Williams, Bishop of Lincoln and Dean of Westminster. This was in about 1641. In 1691 a fire destroyed this codex. Samuel Pepys probably saw it, and we wish he had described it. Gerald's *Mappa* is gone forever, and Davies does not believe there is even an approximate copy of it among the earliest surviving maps of Wales.[4] Let us quote what Gerald himself said about his *Mappa*:

> So, in order to illustrate our native land more fully and to sharpen my mind with various studies, and avoid idleness, I have displayed clearly a map of all Wales, compressed on one leaf — in small space — showing the high mountains, savage woods, rivers, tall castles, cathedrals, and even churches, and many monasteries especially those of the Cistercian Order, constructed with richness and skill.[5]

and again,

> Also, about the time that we penned the *Kambriae Descriptio* we made public, not without much labor, a map of the same, arranging it clearly and distinctly, not only in writing but with certain drawings and various pictures so that our work would be expressed perfectly — on a restricted page — including very many places.[6]

The loss of a map of Wales drawn by Geraldus is quite tragic. His enthusiasm for it and the fact, verified elsewhere, that he had special genius and skill in portraying the reality of things around him make us suspect that this was something very superior for its time. As it is, we can only repeat this dictum of J. K. Wright:

> In surveying the extant maps of our period as a whole [1100–1250], and in comparing them with one another, it is impossible to detect any appreciable development from worse cartography to better. To be sure, Matthew Paris' three maps of Britain made at the very end of our century and a half, are probably the best. In their relative accuracy and fullness of detail as well as in their freedom from servile dependence on

acknowledged authorities, Matthew Paris' three maps of Britain occupy a place by themselves in medieval cartography.[7]

After examining the "best" of these maps of Britain it is difficult to believe that even Gerald, despite his genius, could have come anywhere near the completeness which he claimed in his own words.

This map of Wales was associated with the *Itinerarium Kambriae* which described Gerald's journey around the coast of Wales. This tour began on March 2, 1188 (Ash Wednesday), when Archbishop Baldwin of Canterbury met with Welsh chieftains at New Radnor and preached a sermon on the Crusade. Gerald was the first to take the Cross at this point and then joined the Archbishop's party in their preaching around Wales. This ended at Chester at the close of the Easter Octave on April 24. (Easter was on April 17.) The Archbishop had set foot on Welsh territory soon after leaving Hereford. As Gerald himself states, one of the reasons that the Archbishop undertook this journey was in order to assert his metropolitan authority over the Welsh Church by celebrating Mass in each of the cathedral churches. It is a little strange that Gerald, with his supposed feelings about the autonomy of the Welsh Church, could have taken part in this. The Archbishop even joked openly about his mission: "The nightingale followed wise counsel and never came to Wales, but we, unwise counsel, who have penetrated and gone through it." [8]

They continued through (Old) Radnor, Hay, Llandduw (where Gerald's own residence as archdeacon was placed), Brecon, Abergavenny, Caerleon, Newport, and Cardiff, Llandaff, Margam, River Neath (which is just as muddy today as Gerald found it), Swansea, Kidwelly, Carmarthen, Haverford (West), Camrose, Newgale, and Saint David's. They passed through Nevern, St. Dogmells, crossing the River Teifi (in which there were still beavers), and turning slightly inland through Newcastle-Emlyn, to Lampeter. Out from Lampeter they sought the Cistercian Abbey of Strata Florida (which was to be prominent in Gerald's life), and then on to St. Padarn (which is now on the outskirts of Aberystwyth). They crossed the Devi River, which divided South from North Wales. They then proceeded along the coast — to Llanfair (near Harlech) — through what is now Criccieth, on the Lleyn Promontory, to Nefyn where, Gerald says, he traced with much labor the works of Merlin Silvester. Thence on to Caernarvon they went, to Bangor, to Conway, to Rhuddlan, Saint-Asaph, the Cistercian Cell of Basingwerk, and then to Chester. Some three thousand young Welshmen — most of whom perished miserably several years later before Acre in the Holy Land — were persuaded to take the Cross.

In this account Gerald has space for digressions. He describes the glorious valley and Augustinian abbey of Llantoni (in the Black mountains near Abergavenny), and he speaks of his native manor of Manorbier. It is this interspersed narrative and commentary which interests us most.

Early in this journey, when he had stopped near Llandduw, Gerald presented to the Archbishop a copy of the first edition of his *Topographia Hibernica*. Baldwin soon praised it highly and had sections read to him almost every day.[9] He was asked who could compose the history of the coming Crusade, and he replied that the account in prose should be by Gerald.[10] Obviously he was much impressed by Gerald's ability as a descriptive narrator. An interest in the manners and customs of "strange" people was at the root of all Gerald's topographic descriptions. He had spent nearly a year in Ireland in 1183–84, accompanied by his oldest brother, Philip (*Opera*, V, 351–52). When Prince John went there in 1185, conducted by the justiciar Ranulph of Glanville, Gerald was designated as one of the party. He comments as follows:

> Seeing that the Count [John] accomplished nothing and that by his coming the state of the land was growing worse, day by day, Gerald reflected that he might make some gain by a little labor, since there were many strange things there, unknown in other kingdoms. He took care to collect by diligent study and inquiry material for his *Topographia Hibernica* and for his *Expugnatio*. . . . When John had remained, uselessly, through the whole summer and a part of the winter the prince then crossed the water back to Wales and England. Gerald stayed with Bertran de Verdun, the seneschal, in order to do the study mentioned, gathering and digesting until the following Easter [April 13, 1186].[11]

In 1188–89 Gerald made a somewhat revised edition of this *Topographia Hibernica*, after his return from the Welsh journey.[12] We have just suggested that association with Oxford may have prompted his revision. The Archbishop was again present when he read this new version before three different audiences at Oxford. Gerald says that the Archbishop

> listened diligently to that part which concerned the birds, their natures, and the allegories assigned to them. . . . He

inquired whether I had some evidence from the writings of the Saints and commentators for assigning such allegories. I answered that actually there was no authority there except that which came from divine Grace. The good man replied, "I do not marvel that, for surely these are in the same spirit." [13]

Gerald mentioned that he had repeated some things without verification, but that he had learned these from truthful, distinguished men where he could. Such practice was that of St. Augustine in his *City of God.*[14] This realistic approach was new to most of his contemporaries. He says that when his work had been duly corrected "he did not wish to hide his light under a bushel but wished it to burn on a candelabrum where the English clergy thrived and excelled in learning." This candelabrum was Oxford. Since there were three divisions or distinctions his recitation lasted three days. On the first day the paupers of the whole town were invited to the hospice and heard it, the next day all the doctors of the various faculties and their better students. "Indeed this is a rich and noble thing because there are repeated here the *authentic* and *ancient* times of the poets. Neither the present day nor Antiquity had ever contemplated such a thing being done in England." [15] Note this appreciation of his novelty, in making exhaustive and original observations not attempted by others in his time. Likewise in the *Descriptio Kambriae* (Second Preface) he remarks: "Driven by a thirst for knowledge I have carried my investigations into the mysteries of Nature further than most of my contemporaries. . . . Accurate reading in such detail can be done only with much difficulty" (vi, 163).

So much did Gerald value his scientific research in these two topographic works that he sent them both to the Papal chancellor by the hand of a clerk designated as J., who brought also "two ounces of gold with which to ornament them." [16] Gerald gave away copies of these two books whenever he could.

It is of interest to review Gerald's earlier formal education in an effort to know why he was more original in observation than others who had similar schooling. He claimed to have had twenty years of formal study.[17] He began his formal education at St. Paul's Benedictine Abbey in Gloucester. Despite his predilection for churches rather than castles while playing as a child in the wet sand, he was slow in catching on to letters and required special tutoring supervised by his uncle the Bishop of St. David's.[18] We may assume that he did not go to Gloucester at a very young age. For major instruction, which then followed, he "crossed over three times into France, and made three stays [*status*] of several years each at Paris following the liberal arts. . . ." [19] "I want you to know this also, that when I had submitted for almost five years to the six arts and the trivium, especially for practice, but also because of praise received over some time, I then held classes myself in the schools, publicly." [20] This was because, "having equalled his masters he taught the trivium excellently, and was praised especially for the art of Rhetoric." [21] It is the intention of this present writer to make a detailed study, at some time, of the Paris masters whom Gerald knew. For this we must try to know the exact dates of his residences there. Gerald mentioned that "when he was applying himself vigorously to liberal studies in his youthful years" he was present on the night that Prince Philip was born (August, 1165).[22] Putting the five-year period mentioned and the year 1165 in focus we can infer that Gerald was making his first studies of the trivium in Paris in 1164–69. It was with money paid from tithes given by his brother Philip, by William Fitz Hay, and by Odo de Kerreu that he maintained himself there.[23] As his brothers and uncles were heavily engaged in the invasion of Ireland in 1169 we assume that in that year Gerald returned home. By his own admission he soon was persuaded to teach, and we believe that he returned to Paris in 1170 for that purpose, remaining until 1172 when he was again summoned home.[24] This would explain his first two journeys across the Channel, *one of nearly five years*, the other of several years. In 1176–79 he was once more in Paris, immersed in canon law and theology.[25] This was the third journey. We postulate that he was now studying with William de Montibus[26] and possibly with Stephen of Tournay at Sainte-Geneviève. At this time Paris was the center of an unusual burst of energy in theology and speculative inquiry. Peter Comestor, Robert Courçon, Stephen Langton, and Peter the Chanter were all great influences. Once more Gerald, after tasting the pleasure of some more brilliant teaching on his own, this time in canon law, was obliged to return home, for lack of money as well as for political reasons.[27] As archdeacon of Brecon, and as court cleric of Henry II for the next seven years, he was kept very busy; but he needed exercise of an intellectual kind, and this he states. At an early age Gerald had composed a *Mundi Cosmographia* which, in his catalogue of titles, he cites just before the *Topographia Hibernica*.[28] It seems, therefore, that for many years he had been thinking along the lines of natural philosophy. He says of his final schooling in Paris:

> . . . I performed for some time publicly in the schools. And then on the more mature advice of masters, with devout and avid enthusiasm, for three years and more, I began to polish the threshold of Theology. I established foundations of arts and letters through the grace of God, and Canon Law as well as Theological disciplines. Having gone forth from the schools and gymnasium I returned home and, recognizing that "the mind if it is idle is lost," in order not to become torpid through sloth, I [later] began the treatise of the Topography of Ireland with its secrets and mysteries, and with other kingdoms throughout the world, very diverse and still more strange, — *a task not attempted by any one else* [italics mine].[29]

Thus he changed to scientific observation after 1179. Much later he turned to Wales, and he intended to do the same for England.[30] He says specifically at that time that other authorities had treated the wonders to be found in the East, and that he wanted to do the same for the West.

In accord with contemporary terminology Gerald does not call his geographical treatises science. He refers to them as literature; but he mentions that critics have accused him of ill using his time.[31] He adds that fine histories of other lands have already been written: "I have thought it therefore more worthy to apply myself with industry to the arrangement of the history of my native land, which has been until now almost completely overlooked. . . . From such small beginning . . . one may come to treat matters of greater importance." In his later preface to Archbishop Stephen Langton (after 1213) he remarks that "some leading men . . . show so much contempt for literature that they immediately shut up in their cupboards fine works which have been presented to them and thus condemn them to eternal obscurity." He begs Archbishop Stephen to make *his* book public.[32]

It was after the dedication of the *Itinerarium Kambriae* in 1191 that Gerald began his *Descriptio Kambriae*. (When the *Itinerarium Kambriae* had its first preface in 1191 it was not dedicated specifically to anyone; but in 1197 it was dedicated to Bishop Hugh of Lincoln.) The years 1191 to 1194, when Gerald was working on the *Descriptio*, were most troublesome years politically. Richard, before leaving England, had attached Gerald to the justiciar William of Longchamp.

This William was a real Norman, no Englishman. He was unpleasantly deformed. Gerald turned vehemently against him; along with many others he associated himself with the incompetent Geoffrey, Archbishop of York — and thus with John. Even the incomparable Hugh of Lincoln went along with this. England was then in great confusion, and Gerald occupied his leisure hours with the *Descriptio*. Events passed. King Richard was taken prisoner in 1192; there was the collection for his ransom in 1193; William of Coutances, a moderate, wielded the real power in England. John was in France much of this time; he was in some disgrace and had little authority. Finally Richard returned, landing at Sandwich on March 13, 1194. In that year Gerald published his newly finished *Descriptio* and dedicated it to Richard's new Archbishop of Canterbury, Hubert Fitz Walter. Complete evidence is lacking, but it is probable that Gerald was living in Lincolnshire during the time of composition, and that, most probably, meant Chesterton.

Hubert Fitz Walter had been consecrated Archbishop of Canterbury in May, 1193, and soon was named justiciar by King Richard. King Richard spent only six months of his ten-year reign in England, so this justiciar was most important. In 1198 Hubert wrote to the Pope and gave his opinion of Gerald. This was expressed in the heat of anger; but it cannot be rejected as a general opinion which Hubert had of Gerald.

> A certain archdeacon of St. David's, Gerald by name, Wales by nation, who is either related by blood or by other associations with many magnates in Wales, has got himself elected Bishop by three canons. God knows, before whom I stand, and from whom no secrets are hid, that if I thought him suitable and called to such high dignity, by proper canonical election, I would consent to his confirmation and consecration, if he should care to ask it from me or any one else.[33]

It was unfortunate in 1194 that Gerald felt obliged to ask Archbishop Hubert to receive the first dedication of his *Descriptio*, for patronage reasons.[34] After 1196 he rededicated the work to Bishop Hugh of Lincoln, probably without changes. (Hugh had just permitted him to hold Chesterton.) After 1213 he wrote a second preface and a new dedication for Stephen Langton. It is worth noting that the *Itinerarium* and the *Topographia* suffered many additions and subtractions in the twenty years from 1194 to 1223, but that the *Expugnatio Hibernica* and the *Descriptio Kambriae* had very few.

Gerald was between forty-five and forty-eight years old when he composed the *Descriptio Kambriae*. This was an age of full maturity in the late twelfth century. The reader will bear in mind that Gerald was somewhat of a late-bloomer in his more literary writings. It has been established by actual count of mentions within the text of his works that the title to which he refers the most is Cicero's *De Officiis*, and the next in frequency is Seneca's *Quaestiones*.[35] It is likely that the *Quaestiones* had considerable influence on his scientific thought. It is probable that Robert Grosseteste served as Gerald's clerk in legal matters in 1195–96. It is not impossible that he could have been associated with him earlier, although it is likely that Grosseteste was at Cambridge studying medicine when the *Descriptio* was composed.[36] A witty man who was most certainly a prime companion for Gerald at this time was Walter Map (1140?–1210?).[37] He was a famous conversationalist and an individual of many talents. He was an itinerant judge, a charge which he must have practiced rather sporadically, and he had close participation of some kind with Anglo-Norman literature. He was, to be sure, an Archdeacon — first at Lincoln and then at Oxford after 1196. He had a living at Westbury-on-Severn, which he used as a summer home. He was a theologian, since he was designated to oppose the followers of Peter Waldo at the Lateran Council in 1179. On his way to Rome he stopped to visit with Count Henry I of Champagne, when he most certainly must have made the personal acquaintance of Chrétien de Troyes. In the *Ipomedon* of Hue de Rotelande these verses occur: "Do not put all the blame on me. I am not the only one who knows the art of lying. Walter Map has had his share in this sort of thing." It would seem that Walter was a bright young man who never really grew up. There were two classes of society that he hated beyond all measure: the Jews and the Cistercian monks. The Cistercians had an abbey at Flaxley, two miles from Westbury, and neighbors are not always friendly (*Opera*, IV, 219). Why Walter despised the Jews we do not know.

Gerald wrote a letter to Walter Map in which he took him to task. This is No. 24 in Gerald's *Symbolum Electorum* collection, written not long after 1196, and hence is almost contemporary with Gerald's *Descriptio Kambriae* (*Opera*, I, 271–89). Gerald reminds his friend Walter of the superiority of theology, and says that Walter has a fine foundation of learning, but that he continues to be sterile. He should leave the poets and his false idols, and devote himself to God. Note that Walter also had shifted to the Oxford region in 1196.

It is our plan, at present, to go rapidly through the text of the *Descriptio Kambriae*, remarking upon the validity of Gerald's comments when possible and indicating some possible sources. This work is in two parts. The first, which is our real subject of observation, has eighteen chapters in which there is discussion of the people and the topography of Wales. This is followed by an antithesis. There the faults and sins of the Welsh people are tabulated, and Gerald makes Machiavellian suggestions of ways to conquer them. (Antitheses such as this are a medieval commonplace.)

In his first preface Gerald begins,

> Of all the British writers only Gildas on occasions when this material has caused me to consult him, seems to be worthy of imitating. He commits to writing those things which he saw and knew, and deplores the destruction of his people, rather than giving descriptions. He has woven a true history not an ornate one. Therefore Gerald is following Gildas. Would that it were possible to follow Gildas in life and *mores*, following his knowledge more than his eloquence, his soul rather than his writing, his zeal more than his pen, his life more than his words.[38]

This acknowledgment by Gerald is somewhat misleading. Gildas did *not* supply him with information on the manner and customs of the Welsh people. It is for the second part of his *Descriptio*, where the sins of the Welsh are emphasized, that Gerald really uses Gildas.[39] This is because the *De Excidio et Conquestu Britanniae* (540) of Gildas was a "homily on the misfortunes of the Britons as due to their sins. . . . A large part of [the] work consists of a mere cento of passages from the Scriptures . . . which Gildas applies to his own fellow-countrymen."[40]

In Chapter One Gerald begins with mention of a corrupt expression, *Wallia*, which is in use for Cambria. This he explains further in his Chapter Seven, and the explanation there is a good one. The Anglo-Saxons used *Wealh* to designate their Celtic slaves. (Julius Caesar used a Latin cognate *Volcae*.) The area of Wales was called Walas in Anglo-Saxon. Gerald had none of our modern nicety of detail, but he recognized in the name *Wallia* an Anglo-Saxon word for "foreigner."

In the defining of the area of Wales, which he gives, Gerald conforms quite well to the territory which lay within Offa's Dike. Eskewin is near the exit of the present-day Severn tunnel. On a modern map, from Eskewin to Caer Gyby in Anglesea is about 145 miles. If this was an eight days' journey, as Gerald notes, that would indicate that some eighteen miles were covered in a day, whereas a normal day's travel in the Middle Ages can be figured at thirty-five miles. Of course, this terrain in Gerald's time was wild and rugged. The distance from Porth Mawr (near St. David's) to Walford (Herts) is about 105 miles. Gerald says that this was covered in four days. We cannot be absolutely sure of our identification of Williforde with Walford in Herefordshire, but this is likely. (For the name *Corinaeus* for Cornwall see Geoffrey of Monmouth's *Historia Rerum Britanniae* [ed. Edmond Faral], Chapter Eighteen, pp. 86–87.)

Chapters Two and Three, which treat of the genealogy of the princes of Wales, are tantalizing for what they do *not* tell. Gerald traces briefly the princes of South Wales as descended from Cadell, a son of Rhodri the Great. Howel Dda, he says, was a son of Cadell. According to the Welsh *Annals* this Rhodri died in 754, and Cadell the king of Powys died in 808.[41] Gerald notes that Welsh narrators have the histories of all these princes written in Welsh, "in libris eorum antiquis et authenticis, sed tamen Kambrice scriptam; eadem memoriter tenent, a Rotherico magno usque ad B.M. et inde usque ad Silvium, Ascanium, et Eneam; et ab Enea usque ad Adam generationem linealiter prodeunt."[43] Gerald purposely omits all this material because it would seem trifling to many, rather than "historica."[43] Our interpretation of Gerald's reticence is different: though aware of these early Welsh genealogies, he probably could not understand Welsh well enough to make use of them. He undoubtedly read the Welsh *Annals*, which are in Latin; but these give only the names and dates which he mentions. Gerald could have used Wace's *Brut*, and its predecessor the *Historia Regum Britanniae* of Geoffrey of Monmouth, but Gerald did not think well enough of the veracity of these accounts. There is, for instance, his charming tale in the *Itinerarium Kambriae* where he brands Geoffrey as a notorious liar (*Opera*, VI, 57–58). We agree that *B.M.* (found in all the MSS.) stands for Belin Mawr (Belin the Great). Wace devotes much space (vv. 2313–3240) to this Belin, the son of Dumwallo. He is the Billing of Billingsgate in London. He was credited with the founding of Kaer-Usc or Caerlion (vv. 3205–3218). He is mentioned as king of all Britain. The *Annals* record that he died in 627.

Apropos of Chapter Four Professor Josiah Cox Russell has estimated that at the time of Domesday (1086) there were some 100,000 people in Wales, compared with 1,100,000 in England. By 1340 there were 200,000 in Wales.[44] The cantreds of Wales are estimated and studied by J. E. Lloyd in his *History of Wales from the Earliest Times to the Edwardian Conquest* (London, 1939), Chapter Eight, and after him by Russell. Russell remarks that there were fifty cantreds in Wales in the earlier Middle Ages (each of these having some 400 villages rather than 100).[45] Gerald states that there were fifty-four cantreds: twenty-nine in South Wales, twelve in North Wales, and six in Powys. Gerald expatiates on the *paupercula cathedra Lanelvensis, cui et Powisia subest.*[46] This very tiny cathedral, St. Asaph's, the smallest in Wales and England, was destroyed by Owen Glendower in 1402.

J. K. Wright remarks on the Welsh geography in the *Descriptio*, having very much in mind what Gerald himself says in his Chapter Five:

> Certainly among the works of our mediaeval period there is none that vies with the *Descriptio Kambriae* either in richness and correctness of detail or in vividness of presentation. . . . His knowledge of the Welsh rivers (Severn, Wye, Usk, Dee), the mountains in which they take their source, and their courses seaward was far more accurate than his knowledge of the streams of Ireland.[47]

For Gerald's remarks on strange fish one might read our article which treats those fish mentioned by him in the *Itinerarium*.[48]

Gerald has the honor of being the first man in western Europe to understand the concept of a sound law: initial *s-* becomes *h-*.[49] In our opinion this is most important evidence of his power of analysis, which was certainly superior to that of most of his contemporaries. His observations in Chapter Six on the relationship of Welsh, Cornish, and Breton is additional proof of his fine judgment in matters of language. Today one should not attempt a precise opinion on the superiority of northern Welsh to southern Welsh, but Gerald's reasons for making his own decision are good. What he says about English and the superior variety employed by Bede, Rhabanus, and King Alfred is also remarkable. His explanation of the etymology of *Wallia* has already been discussed.

The material in Chapters Eight through Eleven cannot be examined critically by moderns with any profit. We could elaborate on these matters from our reading in the *Mabinogi* and elsewhere, but Gerald will remain the better authority. Be it noted that cleaning of the teeth is emphasized also by Guillaume de Lorris in his *Roman de la Rose* (v. 2166): "Lave tes mains, tes denz escure," so that the practice could have been quite widespread (but not with Gerald and his acquaintances, since he remarks upon it as unusual). The term *brychan* in modern Welsh means "spots, specks, tartan, and plaid"; so *brachan* (*Opera*, VI, 184), defined as "cloth hard and rough which the region manufactures," can be fully understood by us.

In Chapter Twelve Welsh musicianship is stressed, and with this no one today is disposed to quarrel. In Chapter Thirteen the statement on the Scots and northern English, who sing in two parts, and on the Welsh, who sing in as many parts as there are individuals participating, is very commonly quoted.[50] We are ready to admit that Gerald was a competent language observer, but are not entirely sure of his qualities as a musician. It is possible that some information of this kind could have come to him from Adam of Saint-Victor, whom he most certainly knew in his Paris days. Adam was a Breton, and a distinguished musician.

It is at this point that we have said we would end our commentary. The remainder of the *Descriptio* is distasteful to the Welsh, mediaeval and modern, even though it was most certainly inspired by Gildas. The spirit of *Sic et Non*, which was introduced so brilliantly by Abelard early in the twelfth century, could be carried to great lengths. We find some of this in the *De arte honeste amandi* of Andreas Capellanus. Perhaps we are to assume that, following the method of Abelard, the author sought to correct the faults of the Welsh by letting them see how easily their vices could lead to their complete undoing. Of course Gerald considered himself betrayed by the chapter at St. David's, and he was living at this time outside of Wales, in the Diocese of Lincoln (which included the Oxford area at that period). These contrary remarks may indicate bitter musings by this man whose *amour propre* had been wounded to the breaking point.

NOTES

1. Of very great value is the life by Sir Maurice Powicke in the *Bulletin of the John Rylands Library*, XII (1928). Harold E. Butler in *The Autobiography of Giraldus Cambrensis* (London, 1937) repeats little more than what Gerald says himself in his *De rebus a se gestis* and in the *De jure et statu Menevensis Ecclesiae*.
2. We have, of course, made constant use of the *Giraldi Cambrensis Opera* (Rolls Series, 8 vols.) for text and observations on the MSS., etc. We will cite this reference briefly as *Opera*, with volume and page added. Gerald's catalogue is in *Opera*, I, 409–19.
3. *Opera*, I, 394.

4. J. C. Davies, "The *Kambriae mappa* of Giraldus Cambrensis," in *Journal of the Historical Society of the Church in Wales*, II (1950).
5. *Opera*, I, 414–15.
6. *Ibid.*, I, 422.
7. J. K. Wright, *Geographical Lore of the Time of the Crusades* (New York: American Geographical Society, 1925), pp. 254, 342. See Konrad Miller, *Mappaemundi die ältesten Weltkarten* (Stuttgart, 1895–98), III, Fig. 23, for the best of these maps of Britain.
8. C. H. Williams in *Journal of the Historical Society of the Church*, I (1947), 6–14. This was the principal address delivered by Professor Williams on the celebration of Gerald's eight hundredth birthday at Manorbier in 1946.
9. *Opera*, VI, 20; V, xlix.
10. *Ibid.*, I, 79.
11. *Ibid.*, I, 65.
12. *Ibid.*, V, li.
13. *Ibid.*, I, 409–10. V, 47–57, is the section on birds.
14. *Ibid.*, I, 425.
15. *Ibid.*, I, 72–73; VI, 163.
16. *Ibid.*, I, 308.
17. *Ibid.*, III, 336.
18. *Ibid.*, I, 22; = IV, 107.
19. *Ibid.*, I, 23: "tresque status annorum plurium Parisius in liberalibus disciplinis faciendo."
20. *Ibid.*, I, 410; "cum per lustra fere sex artibus indulserim."
21. *Ibid.*
22. *Ibid.*, II, 292.
23. *Ibid.*, I, 28.
24. *Ibid.*, I, 23: "trivium ibidem egregio docuit, et praecipuam in arte rhetorica laudem obtinuit." In 1170–72 he was 25–26 years old.
25. *Ibid.*, I, 45.
26. See H. Mackinnon in *Essays in Mediaeval History Presented to Bertie Wilkinson* (Toronto, 1969), 32 ff.
27. *Opera*, I, 46–49.
28. *Ibid.*, I, 414; III, 333.
29. *Ibid.*, I, 410.
30. *Ibid.*, VI, 156, 158.
31. *Ibid.*, VI, 156, 162.
32. *Ibid.*, VI, 8.
33. *Ibid.*, I, 120; III, 13, 165.
34. *Ibid.*, VI, xxii, xxxix.
35. Unpublished dissertation by Edward E. Best, in the library of the University of North Carolina at Chapel Hill: "Classical Latin Prose Writers Quoted by Giraldus Cambrensis" (1957).
36. J. C. Russell, in *Harvard Theological Review*, XLVIII (1955), 200–202.
37. A. Boutemy, *Gautier Map, Conteur Anglais* (Collection Lebègue, n.d.), pp. 23 ff. On the interchange of verses over the gift of a staff, see *Opera*, I, 362–63.
38. *Opera*, VI, 158.

39. *Ibid.*, VI, 207–8.
40. J. D. Bruce, *The Evolution of Arthurian Romance*, I (Baltimore, 1922), 5–6.
41. *Annales Britanniae* (Rolls Series, 1857).
42. We translate: "in their old and authentic books, written in Welsh; they retain this same material in memory, from Rodri the great to B. M. and then down to Silvius, Ascanius, and Eneas; from Eneas to Adam's generation they proceed lineally" (*Opera*, VI, 167–68).
43. *Trutanica*: "trifling."
44. J. C. Russell, *British Medieval Population* (Albuquerque, N. M., 1948), pp. 54, 319.
45. *Ibid.*, p. 335.
46. It will be recalled that Gerald had despised Adam dou Petit Pont, when he was Bishop of Saint Asaph. *Opera*, I, 32, 39.
47. Wright, *op. cit.*, p. 340.
48. *Modern Language Forum*, XXVII (1942), 101–10.
49. C. C. Coulter and F. P. Magoun, Jr., "Giraldus Cambrensis and Indo-Germanic Philology," in *Speculum*, I (1926), 104–9.
50. Gustave Reese, *Music in the Middle Ages* (New York, 1940), pp. 387 ff., 392, 407.

The Planctus *of Oedipus*

TEXT AND COMMENT

Paul Maurice Clogan

LONG AFTER SOPHOCLES' DRAMATIC TRILOGY and centuries before Sigmund Freud's analysis of potent psychological forces in man's life, the parricidal and incestuous story of Oedipus exerted a strange fascination over the medieval mind. In the history of the transmission of the myth of Thebes from antiquity into the Middle Ages, the ancient story of the sons of Oedipus and of the royal house of Thebes underwent several transformations as the myth developed and evolved, first becoming legend and later romance. Of these transformations, perhaps the most conspicuous and difficult to account for is the addition and use of the infamous story of Oedipus: the unfortunate birth in Thebes, parental abandonment in Corinth, murder of Laius his father, victory over the Sphinx, incestuous marriage to Jocasta his mother, and tragic and ironic recognition of his crime.

The myth of Thebes was known in the Middle Ages in both classical and vernacular narratives. The *Thebaid* of Statius brought together and treated very freely the various legends based upon ancient Greek accounts of the Seven Against Thebes and synthesized the history and the myth of Thebes in the form of an epic.[1] Yet the narrative of the *Thebaid* begins with the exile of Polynices, Oedipus' son, and ends with Creon's death at the hands of Theseus. The full story of Oedipus is not narrated; there is only the famous invocation to Tisiphone, the cruel goddess of torment, in which Oedipus curses his sons and describes briefly his *angst* as a "living death" (I, 46 ff.). Moreover, the Old French *Roman de Thèbes*, which freely adapted the myth from epic to romance and to the taste and interest of a twelfth-century aristocratic audience, added several new episodes including the story of Oedipus and placed it as a prologue at the beginning of the narrative of the siege of Thebes.[2] The direct and immediate source of this more than 500-line addition to the myth of Thebes remains unknown. To account for it and other extensive variations, Leopold Constans, who

The research for this study was made possible by a generous grant from the American Philosophical Society.

233

studied the manuscript and textual traditions of the *Roman de Thèbes*, conjectured the existence of a medieval Latin prose treatise on the legend of Thebes.[3]

The *planctus* of Oedipus, edited here for the first time, offers further proof of the popularity and use of the story of Oedipus in the learned language of the Middle Ages. For apart from the classical and vernacular narratives, the myth of Oedipus influenced a great many tales of incest between mother and son, including the legend of Judas in the *Legenda Aurea* and the innocent incest in the legend of St. Gregory In addition, the myth of Oedipus and that of Laius, Polynices, Adrastus, and the Seven Against Thebes were collected and recorded by Hyginus in his *Fabulae* and later by Mythographus Secundus.[4] The text of the *planctus* is preserved in at least four manuscripts,[5] one of which dates from the twelfth and three from the thirteenth century. Two of the manuscripts contain the text of the *Thebaid* of Statius, and in one of these (Laurenziana Edil. 197) the *planctus* of Oedipus is accompanied by eight medieval Latin love lyrics.

Diri patris infaustra pignora
Ante ortus dampnati tempora
Quia nostra sic iacent corpora
Mea dolent introrsus pectora.

Fessus luctu confectus senio   5
Gressus *tu*mens labente venio
Quam sinistro natus sim genio
Nullo capi potest ingenio.

Cur flu*x*erunt a viro semina
Ex quibus me concepit femina?   10
Infernalis me regni numina
Produxerunt in vite lumina.

Si me numquam vidisset oculus
Hic in pace vixisset populus
Si clausisset hec membra tumulus   15
Hic malorum non esset cumulus

O in quanto dolore senui
Hanc animam plus iusto tenui
Viri fortes et nimis strenui
Quam *ne*fanda vos nocte genui.   20

Ab antiqua rerum congerie
Cum pugnarent rudes materie
Fuit moles huius miserie
Ordinata fatorum serie

Cum infelix me pater genuit   25
Tesiphone non illud tenuit
Alimenta dum mater prebuit
Ferrum mihi parare debuit.

Incestavi matris cubilia
Vibrans ferrum per patris ilia;   30
Quis hominum inter tot milia
Perpetravuit umquam similia?

Turpis fama Tebani germinis
Mundi sonat diffusa terminis
Quadrifidi terrarum liminis   35
Tangit metas vox nostri criminis.

Me infami rerum luxuria
Infernalis sedavit furia
Si deorum me odit curia
Confiteor non est iniuria.   40

Me oderunt revera superi
Patentibus hoc signis comperi
Umbram sontem istius miseri
Aborrebunt *eti*am inferi.

Scelus meum dat fame pabula   45
De me sonat per orbem fabula
In patenti locatum specula
Referetur crimen per secula.

Solatio leventur ceteri
Consolator me solum preteri   50
Necesse me luctu deteri
O utinam nil possem fieri.

Nomen meum transcendit Gargara
Me Rodope, me *na*rrant Ismara
De me Sirtis miratur barbara   55
Scelus meum aborrent Tartara.

O quam male servastis filii
Constituta*s* vices exilii
Caro nitans ad instar Lilii
Quid de vobis sumam consilii?   60

Si pudore carerent aspera
Minus esset sors nostra misera
Sed pudenda Tebarum scelera
Mare clamat tellus et sidera.

Quod dolore nondum deficio   65
Ex innato procedit vicio

Gravi demum pressus exicio
Mortis horam iam sicio.

Cordis mei vulnus aperui
Quando mihi oculos erui   70
Supplicium passus quod merui
Me*um* regnum iure deserui.

Parentele oblitus celebris
In cisterne me clausi latebris
Instar agens nenie funebris   75
In merore vexi ac tenebris.

Ibi digne indulgens domui
Meum in vos virus evomui
Ut gladium linguam exacui
Imprecansque vobis non tacui.   80

Quod patebat vox detestabilis
Ira complet deorum stabilis
Cruciatus est ineffabilis
Quem patimur gens miserabilis.

The style of the *planctus* belongs to a type of poetry that was very much in vogue in medieval France and England. It emerged as a distinct genre in the early Middle Ages displacing the formal satire of the ancients and was usually impersonal, conceptual, and often allegorical, sometimes taking the form of a diatribe, lamentation, homily, or fable.[6] The genre was influenced by the *De Planctu Naturae* of Alanus de Insulis in which Nature was elaborately described and depicted as lamenting the sins and shortcomings of mankind. The literary term *planctus* was given as title to various complaints of the Soul and of the Flesh, of Christ and of the Virgin, to certain religious lyrics, and to lamentations on particular catastrophes. Indeed, the *planctus* became one of the familiar forms of medieval love poetry which, from the time of antiquity, often developed the theme of the sorrow or grievance of the unaccepted or rejected lover, who lamented the unresponsiveness of his mistress and who naturally found the "complaint" a suitable form of expression of his sentiment. The *planctus* of Oedipus, however, is directed against the gods, and especially Tisiphone, who by their decrees doomed him from the very beginning. The poem takes the form of a monologue in rhyming quatrains in which Oedipus bemoans his unhappy lot, regrets the sorry state of his kingdom and world, and through the complaint attempts to relieve his anguish. Accordingly, the *planctus* can be divided into three sets of seven stanzas of rhyming quatrains: lines 1–28 explain the melancholic mood and set forth the causes and effects of the crime; lines 29–56 analyze the act of incest and its social and cosmic implications; and lines 57–84 examine the personal tragedy and attempt to relieve the anguish.

In the first set of stanzas, lines 1–28, a solemn tone and the tragic character of the narrator are established by allusion to striking details of the myth. Lines 1–8 identify and establish Oedipus' alienation from father and kingdom and the anguish this has caused him. Even before birth, he was damned by the Delphic Oracle of Apollo that warned Laius he should beware of death at his son's hands. When Oedipus was born, his "horrible father" snatched him from the nurse's arms, pierced his feet with a nail (hence the proper name Oedipus, "swollen foot"), and abandoned him on Mount Cithaeron. In the iconography of the birth and finding of Oedipus, he is frequently represented as hanging from a tree by his pierced feet and discovered by shepherds. His birth was like those of other legendary or semilegendary child princes, such as Moses, Romulus, and Cyrus, who were either exposed on a mountain or delivered to the waves in an ark. Existence for Oedipus has been an ironic fulfillment of his fate that was ordained in a series of decrees from the beginning of time (21–24). Now at the end of life, wearied by lamentation and weakened by old age (5–6), he remains embittered, and his only recourse is to voice a complaint against his parents and especially the Furies who were responsible for his tragedy. The cruel Tisiphone allowed Laius to beget him, and Jocasta nourished him with food instead of iron (25–29).

The *planctus* becomes specific in the second set of stanzas, lines 29–56, as the crime and its social and cosmic implications are examined. The act of incest is described in strong, vivid language (29–33) that suggests both the force of fate and the ugly nature of incest. Oedipus agonizes over the social taboo, for his wicked deed taints the fame of a Theban offspring, the voice of his crime will be heard throughout the world, and his name will become legend as his story is referred through history (33–36). His crime is so great that the gods will hate him and even the dead will abhor his shadow (37–44). Yet this punishment is not cathartic or purgative; for while others can be consoled in punishment, he is only weakened unto death by lamentation (49–52). Finally, the cosmic tragedy of his crime overwhelms Oedipus as his name echoes on the mountain tops of Gargara, Rhodope, Ismara, and in the infernal regions of Tartara (53–56).

In the last part of the poem, lines 57–84, the theme of the *planctus* turns from the cosmic back to the personal tragedy of the crime, and an attempt is made to relieve the anguish. The evil of the infamous deed continues to exist in the hostility of his children, who have cursed their father, divided his kingdom, and driven him into exile (57–64). But it was in exile and blindness that Oedipus discovered a new self-knowledge that enabled him to identify his eyes with his crime:

> Cordis mei vulnus aperui
> Quando mihi oculos erui. [67–70]

For according to one ancient account of the myth, when Oedipus recognized his tragic mistake, he dug out his eyes with Jocasta's infamous brooch of Thebes that was originally fashioned by Vulcan for Harmonia against her wedding day and had always brought suffering to all who possessed it. The act of self-blinding symbolizes castration, for living in exile and darkness, Oedipus was able to a degree to exculpate the crime and regain his dignity (73–80). At the end of the *planctus*, the pessimistic tone of the lament is somewhat lightened by this new awareness, and Oedipus finds new strength to continue to voice his complaint.

As a result, the *planctus* is a moving and poetic expression of the medieval attempt to narrate in the form of a complaint the tragic and ironic story of Oedipus and to represent the introspective and anguished state of his mind. The poet's intention is to describe Oedipus' concern with fate, chance, and the forces of the cosmos, both conscious and unconscious, that condition his relationships with his parents and fellow men. Its presence in at least four manuscripts of different origin supports the contention that the story enjoyed an independent and popular existence apart from the classical and vernacular narratives of the myth. The edited text of the *planctus* ought to provide a sound basis for further understanding and appreciation of the medieval awareness of perhaps the most important myth of Western civilization.

NOTES

1. On the classical myth of Thebes, see P. Kohlmann, ed., *Achilleis et Thebais* (Leipzig: B. T., 1884) and H. W. Garrod, ed., *Thebais et Achilleis* (Oxford: O. C. T., 1906). For the best collections of facts on the theory of Oedipus, see especially Carl Roberts, *Oedipus*, 2 vols. (Berlin, 1915); L. W. Daly in Pauly-Wissowa, *Real-Enzyklopädie*, XVII (1937), 2104ff.; *ibid.*, *Suppl.*, VII (1940), 769ff.; Domenico Comparetti, *Edipo e la Mitologia Comparata* (Pisa, 1867): H. J. Rose, *Modern Methods in Classical Myth* (St. Andrews,

1930), 24ff., who argues that "Oedipus is a real person, about whom fabulous details had gathered, following on the whole the line of well-known folk tales"; Marie Delcourt, *Oedipe ou la légende du conquérant* (Paris, 1944), pp. 11ff. on the exposition legend; and K. Niebler, *Die Oedipussage in der Attischen Tragödie* (Diss. Heidelberg, 1961). For the artistic iconography of the myth of Oedipus, see G. Cressedi, *Enciclopedia dell'Arte Antica, Classica e Orientale*, III (Dan-Herc, 1960), 217–19.

2. See Leopold Constans, ed., *Le Roman de Thèbes*, 2 vols., in "Société Anciens Textes Français" (Paris, 1890), especially I, 1–27.

3. See Constans, II, cxix–cxxi; and Edmond Faral, *Recherches sur les sources latines des contes et romans courtois* (Paris, 1913), p. 400.

4. See *Hygini Fabulae*, ed. M. Schmidt (Iena, 1872), sect. LXVI *Laius*, and LXVII *Oedipus*; and *Scriptores Rerum Mythicarum Latini Tres*, ed. G. H. Bode (Cellis, 1834; reprinted Georg Olms Hildesheim, 1968), Mythogr. II, 230.

5. See (1) Cambridge, Trinity College, MS. 822 (R. 9. 21. 394) (saec. xii), fol. 222b–23; (cf. M. R. James, *The Western Manuscripts in the Library of Trinity College, Cambridge: A Descriptive Catalogue*, II [Cambridge, 1901], 263–64); (2) Cambridge, St. John's College, MS. 87 (D.12) (saec. xiii), fol. 50v; (cf. M. R. James, *A Descriptive Catalogue of the Manuscripts in the Library of St. John's College, Cambridge* [Cambridge, 1913], p. 116); (3) Firenze, Biblioteca Medicea Laurenziana, Edil. MS. 197 (saec. xiii), fol. 130r–31v; this important manuscript was written in France and also contains the text of the *Thebaid* of Statius and the eight medieval Latin love lyrics, similar to the famous collection in the *Carmina Burana*; (cf. H. Walther, *Initia Carminum ac Versuum Medii Aevi Posterioris Latinorum/ Alphabetisches Verzeichnis der Versanfänge mittellateinischer Dichtungen* [1959], 4511; and W. Meyer, *Studi lett. e ling. dedic. a Pio Rajna* [Milano, 1911], p. 149); and (4) Berlin, MS. (saec. xiii), fol. 113; (cf. M. Édélestand du Méril, *Poésies popul. lat. inédites du Moyen Âge* [Paris, 1854], pp. 310–13. For the basic text I use Trinity College MS. 822 emended by Berlin MS. 34.

6. For an interesting and stimulating survey of a much neglected topic, see John Peter, *Complaint and Satire in Early English Literature* (Oxford, 1956), pp. 1–39.

Verses on the Life of Robert Grosseteste

Richard W. Hunt

THE WORK OF S. HARRISON THOMSON gave a new impetus to the study of Robert Grosseteste, and by a happy chance I am able to contribute to this volume in his honour some verses on Grosseteste which came to light in a manuscript recently acquired by the Bodleian Library, Oxford. The manuscript is a Psalter written and illuminated in England in the late thirteenth century.[1] It is work of good, but not of the highest, quality and shows signs of much use over a considerable period of time. The miniatures are badly rubbed.

The origin and history of the book are not known. On the last leaf (fol. 171) is an inscription of the fifteenth century, which has been almost scraped off. With the help of the ultraviolet lamp it is possible to read: *Iste liber pertinet* [   ] *domus sive hospitalis* [   ] *london* [   ] *comodavit* [   ] *in nativitate S. Kenelmi anno domini millesimo quadringentesimo qu* [   ]. The name (or names) of sixteenth- or seventeenth-century owners have been obliterated (fol. 170[v], 171). There is no name of any later owner, but inside the front cover in a sloping, spidery hand is *Inspexi*. On the spine is the number *63*. The binding is mediaeval, pink skin (much faded) over boards, probably executed *c.* 1400.[2] It has been clumsily rebacked with a piece of parchment. The manuscript was put into Sotheby's Sale on 6 July 1964 by Major Charles Fellowes, where it was lot 231. It was bought by Messrs. B. Quaritch for the Bodleian Library, where it has been referenced MS. Lat. liturg. d. 41.

Prefixed to the Psalter is a gathering of four leaves, of which the first leaf is pasted down to the front board. On the third and fourth (now fol. 2 and 3) are the verses here printed. They are written in a bookhand of university type in two columns of 42–44 lines. The hand is contemporary with the text of the Psalter, that is, late thirteenth or early fourteenth century. The heading *Frater Hubertus de vita beati Roberti quondam Lincolniensis episcopi* is written in a charter hand of the same date.

Before commenting on the verses I will give a summary from which I have stripped the flowers of thirteenth-century Latin poetical rhetoric. The divisions are those indicated in the manuscript.

(1–10) Lincoln and Britain weep for the death of Bishop Robert. Let the holy troop of friars mourn the death of their parent.

(11–16) I will praise him even though my merits are not equal to the task. Lest I seem ungrateful, I will offer my mite.

(17–24) He was the light of the Church. Suffolk rejoices in such a man. England rejoiced in such a patron. He was a wise counsellor of his country. Lincoln exulted in him as bishop, and flourished.

(25–34) Cruel death, why did you carry him off? The world needed him.

(35–42) He was the strength of the Church, and defender of its liberty.

(43–58) He was fearless in standing up to the enemies of the Church, and in reproving wrongdoers. He did not fear the King himself.

(59–62) The life of this just man was pleasing to the just, but evil men disapproved of him.

(63–80) Robert outshone all the clergy. There was such grace in his tongue. True in judgment, discreet in understanding, eloquent in speech, farseeing in counsel, mighty in knowledge, he was a paragon of the virtues.

(81–88) He was a good shepherd, and did not entrust boys with the care of his sheep.

(89–98) He never wasted a moment. He was always engaged in prayer, or contemplation, or meditation, or reading, or teaching, or in doing something useful. He was assiduous in sacred studies, and at the same time the liberal arts had a claim on his time. He had around him boys of good birth whose manners he formed. He taught them Greek and Latin. This was his pleasure and recreation when he was at leisure.

(99–104) His household was a model, and he chose his officials with great care for their character.

(105–10) He was a great dispenser of hospitality, and generous in giving.

(111–16) He was a father and patron to the poor, needy, and sick.

(117–18) He taught the young to feed the poor.

(119–22) Wherever he went, he succoured the sick, and fed them from his own table.

(123–38) Both orders of Friars, Dominican and Franciscan, lament him. He was their father and protector. He loved to have Friars about him, and he used them to lighten his burden. He could not live without Friars. To whom will they now turn?

(139–48) Now that the shepherd is dead, the flock is not safe. Evils are gaining ground.

(149–66) Who will now rise up to keep our enemies in check? O may someone succeed him who will care for the honour of Christ, and who will be zealous to put in order the house of the Lord, one who is not to be turned from the path of virtue, and can sow the good seed.

(167–78) His comportment among the people was admirable. There was no levity in his actions, speech, or gesture. There was great edification in his look. Everyone regarded him as a pattern. In church no one was more devout. Who can tell of his devotion at the altar? Raised above himself, he often seemed oblivious of himself. He was always grave in church, agreeable in hall, and happy in his chamber.

(179–86) He was wholly set on heavenly things. The word of the Lord was always on his lips. He delighted always to speak of Christ and to magnify him.

(187–92) Now that he has laid aside the veil of flesh, he rests a victor after the strife, and tastes the joys he thirsted after.

To come across a new document headed "On the life of the blessed Robert, once bishop of Lincoln," and to find in it no biographical information, except that Grosseteste was born in Suffolk, was at first a disappointment. The writer might, for example, so easily have settled for us the question whether Grosseteste studied in Paris. Further reading helped to remove this feeling, which did less than justice to the intentions of the author of the verses. What we are given is a picture of Grosseteste the man of God, the bishop, and the scholar seen by a contemporary. This is something which is not supplied by any other source.[3]

We do not know who Hubert was, but the title "frater" indicates that he was a friar, a member of one of the two orders, Dominican and Franciscan, which Grosseteste did so much to foster. We tend to associate Grosseteste with the Franciscans, but Hubert puts both orders on an equality:

> Verbum qui domini [i.e., the Dominicans] dispensant atque Minores
> Patrem deplangunt occubuisse suum.   [123–24][4]

From the knowledge which he shows of the mode of Grosseteste's life, and from his statement that gratitude must outweigh his feeling of insufficiency (15–16), we may conjecture that he was one of the friars whom Grosseteste attached to his service. That he was writing within a short time of Grosseteste's death is evident from the whole tenour of the verses.

Hubert was schooled in the precepts of verse writing inculcated by the writers of the *Artes versificatoriae*. For his apostrophe to cruel death he has borrowed a phrase from Geoffrey of Vinsauf,[5] and there are some close parallels to Matthew of Vendôme. Writing in this tradition he could hardly avoid stock comparisons with biblical figures (33–34), or with the great men of the past:

> Hic ratione Plato, stellis Tholomeus,[6] Ulixes
> Eloquio, Nestor mente, rigore Cato.   [67–68]

It is not easy to distinguish between conventional ornaments and the real Grosseteste. But there are many genuine touches. That Grosseteste was a lover of the liberty of the Church who did not suffer it to be treated like a serf is known from his writings and from the testimony of others, but it is worth having the impression of a contemporary, even if partial, to the part he played:

> Incumbebat ei pondus totale, columpna
> Forcior et melior stabat in ede dei.   [41–42]

In the next section, where we are told of his zeal against the enemies of the Church, it is the genuine Grosseteste whom neither the King's majesty nor the loss of possessions terrified (45–46). Again his refusal to give benefices with cure of souls to boys (83) is based on a well-known incident in his life.[7] His patronage of the two orders of Friars has already been mentioned. The passage devoted to them rings true, in spite of the piling up of verbs:

> Ut fetus teneros mater, sic fovit, amavit,
> Protexit, pavit, appreciavit eos.
> Vivere nescivit sine fratribus intus et extra,
> Semper habebat eos, semper adhesit eis.   [131–34]

I would specially call attention to two passages. The first is the description of his intellectual activities. The pedestrian verse of the couplet underlines the ceaseless activity of Grosseteste:

> Orans, contemplans, meditansve legensve docensve
> Aut aliquid faciens utile semper erat.   [91–92]

The conclusion of this section is interesting. Grosseteste, we are told, used to bring up boys of good birth:

> Litterulis Grecis[8] hos imbuit atque Latinis,
> Hic iocus, hec requies quando vacabat erat.   [97–98]

We should like to know more about these *pueri*. Finally Hubert has attempted in a dozen lines (167–68) to portray the effect of Grosseteste's personality, the impression he made on the man in the street, his seriousness, his great devotion in church. As though to lighten the effect, Hubert ends the section:

> Mestus in ecclesia, iocundus in aula,
> In camera gaudens, et velut agnus erat.   [177–78]

At the end of the verses, after a line left blank, is the first verse of a hymn to Grosseteste, which was perhaps written in anticipation of the canonization which was never secured.[9]

In the edition which follows I have retained the spelling of the manuscript, with its slight inconsistencies.[10] The beginning of each section is marked in the manuscript by a paragraph sign, which I have represented by leaving a space.

NOTES

1. The Psalter is followed by the Canticles, the *Quicumque*, the Litany of Saints (including SS. Alban, Elphege, Thomas Becket, Ethelbert, Oswald, Kenelm), and the Office of the Dead with music. There is no Kalendar at the beginning.
2. I owe this information to Mr. Graham Pollard, who observed that it was not the original binding.
3. Closest is the Lanercost Chronicle, ed. J. Stevenson (The Maitland and Bannatyne Clubs), Edinburgh, 1839, which presumably depends on the chronicle of a Franciscan, Richard of Durham, composed between 1280 and 1287; see A. G. Little, *Franciscan papers, lists, and documents*. Manchester, 1943, p. 48.
4. Compare the entry in the *Annales* of the Dominican, Nicholas Trivet (ed. T. Hog), London, 1845, p. 243: "Hic fratres ordinis tam Predicatorum quam

Minorum sincera caritate amplectens eos habuit continue in comitiva sua."
The Lanercost Chronicle, depending on a Franciscan source (see above,
n. 3), only mentions the Franciscans. Was Hubert perhaps a Dominican?

5. It is from the lament for King Richard I, which circulated separately, as
well as being incorporated in the *Poetria nova.*

6. The word "stellis" presumably stands for astronomy. It is the one interesting
touch in the catalogue.

7. See Ep. 17, ed. Luard (Rolls Series), 1861, pp. 63–65, and J. H. Srawley in
*Robert Grosseteste. Essays in commemoration of the seventh centenary of
his death,* ed. D. A. Callus. Oxford, 1955 (repr. 1969), p. 159.

8. Roger Bacon's encomium of his knowledge has been endorsed by modern
scholars; see Callus in *Robert Grosseteste,* pp. 36–43. It was further illustrated by Miss R. Barbour's discovery of the copy he had made of Ps. Dionysius Areopagita in Greek, for which see *Bodleian Library Record* vi (1958),
401–16, with plates.

9. For the attempts at securing canonization see E. Kemp in *Robert Grosseteste,* pp. 243–46.

10. But in l. 151 I have jibbed at "wlpes."

FRATER HUBERTUS DE VITA BEATI ROBERTI QUONDAM LINCOLNIENSIS EPISCOPI

Vergit ad occasum patrie sol, lucifer orbem
    Deserit, expallet sole cadente solum.
Solis in occasu Lincolnia plange; sepulto
    Lumine sub tenebris obtenebrata dole.
5   Sancta cohors fratrum doleat de morte parentis,
    Mortem deplorent opilionis oves.
Tanto patrono viduata Britannia plange,
    Plange tibi solis occubuisse iubar.
Mortis caligo lucem subtraxit, obumbrat
10   Eclipsis solem morte, Roberte, tua.

Pontificis sacri depromere gestio laudes,
    Set fateor minor est vox mea laude sua.
Plus sua promeruit bonitas quam voce referre
    Sufficiam, superat laus sua scire meum.
15   Ne tamen ingratus videar, mea minima templo
    Cum muliere volo paupere parva dare.

Sicut sol mundum radians illuminat, iste
    Sic fuit ecclesie lux, decor atque decus.
Se genuisse virum talem Suthfolcia gaudet,
20   Gaudet quod tanta predita prole fuit.
Anglia gaudebat tanto dotata patrono,
    Sanus enim patrie consiliator erat.
Exultabat eo Lincolnia presule, presul
    Dum fuit, urbs viguit, floruit urbis honos.

16 *Mk. xii. 41.*

25   Mors fera, mors nequam, mors impia cur rapuisti
             Talem de mundo? Mundus egebat eo,
          Mundus egebat eo, quia mundus, iustus, honestus,
             Prudens, magnanimus atque disertus erat.
          Non eguit mundo, set mundus eo, quia mundi
30   Hic lampas, mundi mundificator erat.
          Quis nunc inventus illi similis probitate,
             Sensu, doctrina, religione, fide?
          Hunc probitas confert Iosue, sensus Salomoni,
             Iob pietas, Paulo dogma, fidesque Petro.

35   Ecclesie robur, Robertus robore firmo
             Templum suffulsit, quo bene stante stetit.
          Ecclesie rector, ac libertatis amator
             Ecclesiam servam non tulit esse suam.
          Set nunc de medio sublato presule, templi
40   Ceperunt omnes iam titubare bases.
          Incumbebat ei pondus totale, columpna
             Forcior et melior stabat in ede dei.

          Accinctus zeli gladio desevit in hostes
             Ecclesie, spernit dampna, minasque necem.
45   Regia maiestas non terruit hunc, neque rerum
             Dampna; minis, dampnis pretulit ipse deum.
          Pro grege sustinuit hic dura, luposque lupercus
             Strenuus arcebat ne raperentur oves.
          Dure corripuit reprobos, sua crimina nulli
50   Palpavit, fauctor noluit esse malis.
          Ense cicatrices secuit, pars mortua vivam
             Ne traheret, medicus quippe peritus erat.
          In mites mitis, in sevos sevus, in equos
             Equus, et in nocuos extitit ille nocens.
55   Nunc leo, nunc agnus, reprobis leo, mitibus agnus,
             Agnus erat gaudens, set leo sepe dolens,
          Scilicet eiusdem est, quamvis pugnare videtur,
             Supplicibus mitem, sontibus esse trucem.

          Vita viri iusti iustis placuit, set iniquis
60   Displicuit; laus est displicuisse malis.
          Iusti laudabant iustum, reprobi reprobabant,
             Noctua nam noctem laudat, alauda diem.

          Sicut sol lunam vincit splendore, Robertus
             Sic toti clero prenituisse datur.
65   Hic fuit in clero cleri flos, clerus in illo
             Obstupuit, lingue gracia tanta fuit.

26 *Galfridus de Vino Salvo, Poetria nova 422: Mundus egebat eo.*
48 *Strenus* cod.

Hic ratione Plato, stellis Tholomeus, Ulixes
    Eloquio, Nestor mente, rigore Cato.
Floribus ut variis estas depingitur, iste
70   Moribus eximiis sic redimitus erat:
Iudicio verax, discretus mente, disertus
    Verbo, consilio providus, arte potens,
Mundicie thalamus, viciis infestus, amicus
    Virtutum, iuris regula, plebis amor,
75 Vexillum fidei, legis tutela, sophie
    Fons, prelatorum gemma, lucerna gregis.
Invide, quid cernis in eo quod carpere possis?
    Cogeris invitus facta probare viri.
Ad se laudandum probitas sua provocat hostes,
80 Tot dotes nequam lingua negare nequid.

Pavit oves rebus, exemplo, voce, carere
    Effectu verbum noluit ipse dei.
Non ovium curam pueris concessit, adultos,
    Discretos, mundos pascere iussit oves.
85 Rexit, direxit, instruxit, quippe talentum
    Acceptum studuit multiplicare deo.
In sermone velud fax ardens, alter Elyas,
    Alter Eliseus orbe superstes erat.

Noluit hic umquam torpere per ocia, nulla
90 Preteriit frustra temporis hora sui.
Orans, contemplans, meditansve legensve docensve,
    Aut aliquid faciens utile semper erat.
In sacris studiis fuit assiduus, simul artes
    Ingenue tempus detinuere suum.
95 Ingenuos pueros secum vir sanctus alebat,
    Quos informabat moribus ipse sacris.
Litterulis Grecis hos imbuit atque Latinis,
    Hic iocus, hec requies quando vocabat erat.

Eius sancta domus, bene morigerata, quieta
100 Extitit, ac omni rusticitate carens.
Cavit enim ne quis viciosus, ne quis adulter,
    Ne quis mendosus esset in ede sua.
Vir sanctus sanctos querebat habere ministros,
    Mundos, compositos, pacificosque pios.

105 Hospiciale decus viguit vivente Roberto,
    Eius enim nulli ianua clausa fuit.

67–68 Matt Vindocinen, *Ars versif.* ed. Faral, *p. 52, ll. 3–4: Ulixes eloquio;*
    p. 125, l. 62: Nestor mente, rigore Cato.

Notis, ignotis communis erat sua mensa,
    Mensa satis dives potibus atque cibis.
Noluit in terris thesauros condere, large
110   Dispersit, largus munera larga dabat.
Pauperibus patrem se prebuit atque patronum,
    Menbra dei secum semper habebat edens.
Procumbens lavit devote plebis egene
    Sepe pedes, iungens oscula flensque super.
115 Subveniens miseris, egris, nudis et egenis,
    In menbris studuit semper amare capud.

Edocuit pueros propria de lance cibare,
    Christi membra monens ad pietatis opus.

Per villas adiit egros ubicumque iacebant,
120   Large denarios distribuendo suos.   .
Egrotos propria de mensa pascere iussit,
    Quos didicit variis decubuisse locis.

Verbum qui domini dispensant atque Minores
    Patrem deplangunt occubuisse suum.
125 Hic pater et tutor fuit ordinis huius et huius
    Ordo gratus ei semper uterque fuit.
Illi complacuit fratrum presencia, fratrum
    Adventus, fratrum copia, sermo frequens.
Consortes oneris fratres, decrevit habendos,
130   Ut levius posset ferre laboris onus.
Ut fetus teneros mater, sic fovit, amavit,
    Protexit, pavit, appreciavit eos.
Vivere nescivit sine fratribus intus et extra,
    Semper habebat eos, semper adhesit eis.
135 Quis modo tutor erit pupillis fratribus, ad quem
    Confugient, a quo subvenietur eis?
Presidium fratrum iacet ecce iacente Roberto,
    Auxilium languet eloquiumque tacet.

Defuncto pastore suo grex non bene tutus
140   Extat, dum non est qui tueatur eum.
Iam lupus insidians querit quem devoret et iam
    Nititur heu miserum dilaniare gregem.
Pullulat impietas pietate iacente, malorum
    Crescit amor, crescit absque timore nephas.
145 Vepribus horrescit tellus inarata, labruscas
    Invisas vitis non bene culta facit.
Inter triticeas segetes zizania surgunt,
    Nequicie semen hostis ubique serit.

	Fugit in exilium Pallas dea virginitatis,
150	Et Venus et Veneris filia regna tenent.
	Quis nunc hastutas vulpes de vite repellit?
	Quis nunc latrat oves dilacerante lupo?
	Quis nunc insurgit surgentibus hostibus, aut quis
	Non latet ad belli fata vocante tuba?
155	Quis nunc intrepidus manet ad discrimina, quis nunc
	Cornua non retrahit ense minante necem?
	Tytirus heu noster obiit qui cornibus hostes
	Terrebat, necdum par reperitur ei.
	O si succedat Christi qui zelat honorem,
160	Qui studeat domini rectificare domum,
	Qui prece, qui precio, qui vi, qui munere flecti
	Nesciat, inceptum dissipet omne nephas,
	Agrum mundificet, tollat zizania, spinas
	Evellat, semen spargat ubique bonum,
165	Vepribus abscisis virtutes inserat, agrum
	Irriget, ut melius pululet orta seges.

	In populo mire semper se gessit, in actu,
	Dictu vel gestu nil levitatis erat.
	Eius in aspectu fuit edificacio magna,
170	Pro speculo populus totus habebat eum.
	Nullus in ecclesia devocior extitit illo,
	Orans, flens, tundens pectora semper erat.
	Qualis in altari fuerat quis dicere possit?
	Ploratus, gemitus quis numerare queat?
175	Extra se raptus, supra se mente levatus,
	Sepe videbatur nescius esse sui.
	Mestus in ecclesia, iocundus semper in aula,
	In camera gaudens et velut agnus erat.

	Nil sapiebat humi sua conversacio, celum
180	Intendens, sola carne colebat humum.
	Terram despiciens celum sitiebat, ab imo
	Se tollens abiit totus in astra poli.
	Descivit penitus mundi contagia, sermo
	Divinus sonuit semper in ore suo.
185	De te, Christe, loqui, te magnificare iuvabat
	Semper, nescivit nescius esse dei.

	Sed iam deposito carnis velamine, celum
	Ingressus, meritis premia digna metit.
	Post palmam victor requiescit, quodque sitivit

150 supra v. *filia* scr. *scil. Dione quasi duos nectens in amore.*
179 *Cf. Matt. Vind. Ars, p. 121, l. 9: Nil sapit humanum sua Conversatio.*

190   Iam gustat plene, quodque cupivit habet.
      Commutantur ei fixis fluitantia, risu
        Lamentum, celo terra, quiete labor.

     *   *   *

        O Roberte presulum
           Decus et flos cleri,
        Sanctitatis speculum
           Et amator veri,
        Causam piam exulum
           Dignare tueri,
        Reis placans oculum
           Iudicis severi.

191 *Cf. ibid., p. 122, l. 39: Commutane studet fixis flitantia, certis Vana, polo terras, hospitiumque domo.*